International Relations Theory

The third edition of this innovative textbook introduces students to the main theories in international relations. It explains and analyzes each theory, allowing students to understand and critically engage with the myths and assumptions behind them. Each theory is illustrated using the example of a popular film.

Key features of this textbook include:

- discussion of all the main theories: realism and neo-realism, idealism and neo-idealism, liberalism, constructivism, postmodernism, gender, globalization and environmentalism
- a new chapter on environmentalism, climate change and Al Gore's *An Inconvenient Truth* including use of the film *WALL-E*
- innovative use of narratives from films with which students will be familiar: *Lord of the Flies, Independence Day, Wag the Dog, Fatal Attraction, The Truman Show, East is East, Memento* and *WALL-E*
- an accessible and exciting writing style which is well illustrated with film stills in each chapter, boxed key concepts and guides to further reading.

This breakthrough textbook has been designed to unravel the complexities of international relations theory in a way that gives students a clearer idea of how the theories work, and of the myths associated with them.

Cynthia Weber is Professor of International Relations at the University of Lancaster. She is author of several books and numerous articles in the field of International Relations.

D1392652

International Relations Theory

A critical introduction

Third edition

Cynthia Weber

Routledge
Taylor & Francis Group

LONDON AND NEW YORK

First published 2001
by Routledge
Second edition published 2005 by Routledge
Third edition published 2010 by Routledge
2 Park Square, Milton Park, Abingdon, Oxon, OX14 4RN

Simultaneously published in the USA and Canada
by Routledge
270 Madison Avenue, New York, NY 10016

Routledge is an imprint of the Taylor & Francis Group, an informa business

Typeset in Century Old Style and Futura
by Keystroke, Tettenhall, Wolverhampton
Printed and bound in Great Britain by
TJ International, Padstow

British Library Cataloguing in Publication Data
A catalogue record for this book is available from the British Library

Library of Congress Cataloging in Publication Data
Weber, Cynthia.
International relations theory: a critical introduction/Cynthia Weber.—3rd ed.
p. cm.
Includes bibliographical references and index.
1. International relations—Philosophy. I. Title.
JZ1305.W43 2009
327.101—dc22   2009002262

ISBN 10: 0–415–77819–0 (hbk)
ISBN 10: 0–415–77842–5 (pbk)
ISBN 10: 0–203–87414–5 (ebk)
ISBN 13: 978–0–415–77819–0 (hbk)
ISBN 13: 978–0–415–77842–8 (pbk)
ISBN 13: 978–0–203–87414–1 (ebk)

For Lyn and Charles Weber

and

for Bob DiClerico

Learning depends upon freeing the message from the constraints of the situation at hand.

Roland Barthes

Contents

CONTENTS

Plates

Figures

Tables

Boxes

Preface to the third edition

As the orangish-red map on the cover of this volume suggests, the earth—and debates about the earth—have been heating up in recent times. Concerns about global warming are recontextualizing IR Theory and being recontextualized within IR Theory. They recontextualize IR Theory by changing the scale of IR concerns from clashes or cooperation among sovereign nation-states or (more recently) "civilizations" to clashes and cooperation between humans and the earth, "culture" and "nature" on a planetary scale. As such, concerns about global warming are reconstituted within IR Theory as genuine security risks to all states and all of civilization. And we are told that we have a moral imperative to tackle this planetary emergency if we want our children and our planet to survive.

This third edition includes a new chapter devoted to the newly dominant myth about global warming, "human-made climate change is an inconvenient truth." Popularized by Nobel Peace Prize recipient and former US Vice President Al Gore, Jr., this myth is interesting not just because of what it says but also because of how Gore says it. In particular, among the most interesting things about Gore's myth is that it was visual before it was textual. First a slideshow, then a film, and only later an accompanying book and supportive website, *An Inconvenient Truth* crystallizes Gore's ideas into a succinct soundbite supported by stunning imagery presented in the "high tech" format of documentary. It is therefore unsurprising that it takes an even more visually spectacular film to get us to think about what must go without saying in order for Gore's myth to appear to be true. What might be surprising, though, is that this film comes from a company renowned for producing animated fiction films (like *Toy Story* and *The Incredibles*) that are accessible to children but edgy enough for adults. The company is Pixar Studios, and the film is their 2008 production *WALL-E*. Reading Gore's myth through *WALL-E*, this new chapter explores not the truth or falsity of human-made climate change but its convenience or inconvenience, for whom, and at what cost to the environment and to Gore's claim to be an environmentalist.

In writing this new edition, I owe all my usual intellectual debts. Richard Ashley and François Debrix bear mentioning again, as they kindly read and commented on this new chapter. So, too, did a diverse group of individuals situated at the intersections of IR Theory and critical environmental studies—Simon Dalby, Tim Luke, Matthew Patterson, and Mark Lacy. Thanks to all of them, and thanks also to three anonymous reviewers. I also want to thank the editorial team at Routledge – including Craig Fowlie, Nicola Parkin, Emma Hart and Eleanor Rivers – who all made this a better book. In particular, I want to thank my editor Craig Fowlie, who has worked with me on these last two editions. Craig not only grasped the promise of a new chapter on Gore's myth about global climate change; he also exercised extreme patience in waiting for me to find the right film through which to analyze it. Finally, my thanks go to Anne-Marie Fortier, for her support throughout.

The authors and publishers would like to thank the following for granting permission to reproduce material in this work.

Dialogue quoted from the following films are transcrips made by the author:

- *Memento*: Courtesy of the Ronald Grant Film Archive © Newmarket Capital Group
- *East is East*: Courtesy of the Ronald Grant Film Archive © FilmFour
- *Fatal Attraction*: Courtesy of the Ronald Grant Film Archive © Paramount Pictures
- *Independence Day*: Courtesy of the Ronald Grant Film Archive © Centropolis Entertainment
- *Wag the Dog*: Courtesy of the Ronald Grant Film Archive © New Line Cinema
- *The Truman Show*: Courtesy of the Ronald Grant Film Archive © Paramount Pictures
- *Lord of the Flies* Plates 2.3 and 2.4: Courtesy of Lord of the Flies co, Source: Ronald Grant Film Archive
- *Lord of the Flies* Plates 2.1, 2.2 and 2.5 : Courtesy of Lord of the Flies co, Source: BFI
- *WALL-E*: Courtesy of the Ronald Grant Film Archive © Walt Disney/Pixar Animation.

Every effort has been made to contact copyright holders for their permission to reprint material in this book. The publishers would be grateful to hear from any copyright holder who is not here acknowledged and will undertake to rectify any errors or omissions in future editions of this book.

Preface to the second edition

Since the first edition of this textbook went to press in 2000, the worlds of international relations theory and international politics have faced considerable challenges. In 2000, Michael Hardt and Antonio Negri published a book called *Empire* that spoke to the precise moment of international life we were all then living—how to make sense of resistance (especially anti-globalization movements) in an era of globalization. They offered us a new myth for a new millennium— "Empire is the new world order." And, in so doing, they temporarily revived the tradition of neo-Marxism, a tradition that in the view of many observers of international politics had lost its ideological relevance in the post-Cold War world.

Hardt and Negri's myth captured the imagination of many until September 11, 2001, the day of the terrorist attacks in New York City, Washington, DC, and Pennsylvania. Almost immediately, a new mythmaker and a new myth grabbed international attention. Back in 1993, Samuel Huntington had argued that the new world order would be defined by clashes not primarily among sovereign nation-states but among what he called civilizations. As President George W. Bush declared war on terror, it was Huntington's myth "There is a clash of civilizations" that framed international debate, for it seemed to have predicted the so-called clash between the civilizations of "Western Christianity" and "Eastern Islam." One of the interesting features of Huntington's myth is that its intellectual roots are not primarily in traditional security studies but in the often forgotten debates of modernization and development theory. It is only by returning to Huntington's contributions to these debates that the fullness of his clash of civilizations myth and its implications for international politics can be appreciated.

What we've seen in this new millennium so far, then, is the emergence of two powerful new myths based upon two theoretical traditions that had pretty much been written off by the majority of IR theorists—neo-Marxism and modernization and development theory. This is a noteworthy development, especially when considered in light of Francis Fukuyama's claims that with the perfection of the ideals of liberalism, we are at the end of history. New ideologies have not captured international attention in the same way that *new combinations* of ideologies have. Hardt and Negri, for example, combine neo-Marxism with postmodernism to construct their myth "Empire is the new world order" while Huntington combines modernization and development theory with more traditional securities studies to argue "There is a clash of civilizations." This does not mean that no new ideologies are emerging or will emerge. Rather, it does mean that as new myths make their way into the international arena, we had better pay close attention to their ideological roots, however *passé* we might have thought they were.

This is precisely what this second edition does. It brings us up to date with IR myths by contextualizing these myths in relation to their theoretical traditions in order to understand what makes these myths appear to describe just the way things are at precise historical moments. But, of course, this book does more than merely explain and understand IR myths. It also critically analyzes them. It asks of each myth "what must go without saying in order for this myth to appear to be true?" And, as before, it investigates this question by turning to popular films as alternative worlds that both illustrate and deconstruct these IR myths. So, for example, the myth "Empire is the new world order" is reconsidered through the 2000 film *Memento*, and the myth "There is a clash of civilizations" is re-read through the 2000 film *East is East*. As in the previous edition, reexamining IR myths through popular films not only allows us to rethink the IR myths themselves. It also enables us to think more deeply about the relationship between IR theory and popular culture.

In writing this revised edition, I owe all the intellectual debts I owed in the first edition and more. Annette Davison, Jenny Edkins, Tracey Golstein, Mark Lacy, Patricia Molloy, Adam Morton, Sasha Roseneil, Craig Warkentin, Jutta Weldes, and my students at Leeds University have all provided helpful comments, advice, and/or support. François Debrix has again proved to be an exceptionally perceptive reader, critic, colleague, and friend. And the anonymous reviewers provided helpful comments. What I also realized as I read through the first edition and worked on this second edition is that my training in IR theory—the things I take for granted as known—was exceptional. At Arizona State University, certainly Richard Ashley but also Pat McGowan, Karen Rasler, and Steve Walker and, beyond ASU, Michael Shapiro and Rob Walker provided me with much of my introduction to IR theory, although each of them would of course write their own introduction differently. I thank them all. A sabbatical supported by the University of Leeds and a visiting Professorship at the New School for Social Research gave me the time and space to rethink and rewrite this book. Thanks to Duncan McCargo at Leeds and David Plotke at the New School for arranging this institutional support, as well as for being individually supportive. Finally, thanks to the staff and editors at Routledge for letting me continue this story in a second edition.

Preface to the first edition

After a sabbatical from Purdue University a few years ago, I couldn't wait to get back into the classroom. I had missed my interactions with students and had a renewed appreciation for the practice of teaching. But I had a number of problems. Like many teachers, I had intellectually outgrown my well-worn way of introducing international politics and international relations (IR) theory to students, but I never had the time to do more than tinker with examples or simulation exercises in an attempt to remedy this. Also, as at many other universities, the introductory course I taught in international relations was a prerequisite for later courses. As such, it was expected to familiarize students with key themes from long-standing IR traditions like realism, idealism, historical materialism and their neos, and introduce them to new perspectives like constructivism, postmodernism, gender, and globalization. This could be done by opting for an approach that narrated the historical development of IR traditions and debates or, alternatively, for a more topical approach to the subject and the field. Beyond these two standard options, there were no others.

My experiments in the classroom with these teaching techniques left me feeling both fulfilled and disappointed. I was pretty good at narrating the traditions of IR theory, situating them historically, and bringing them into lively conversation with one another. This allowed me to explore some exciting topics in the field as well, which students seemed to enjoy. All this was fulfilling. But I was disappointed with how students interacted with IR theory. Despite my best critical intentions, students would find a particular aspect of IR theory with which they could identify, attach themselves to it as "the way things are," and evaluate every other IR theory they would hear in relation to it. Most often, this theory was realism. Occasionally, it was idealism. And in some cases, it was historical materialism or gender. It wasn't that I cared which theory students attached themselves to. I didn't prefer them to believe one theory over another. My aim was to get them to critically rethink *all* the theories. And I failed miserably.

Why did I fail? If a theory is presented to students as if it narrates just the way things are in international politics and if this way of making sense of the world taps into students' own preconceptions about the world, then it is extremely difficult to get students to think critically about the theory. So I had to do better. But how? How could I both stick to the brief of what an introduction to international relations or international relations theory is generally supposed to be while at the same time presenting the IR theories and topics in ways that allow for their genuine critical reconsideration?

IR Theory: A Critical Introduction is my answer to this question. Its approach is both traditional and non-traditional. It is traditional because it is organized around the major traditions of international relations theory—realism, idealism, historical materialism, constructivism, gender, and globalization. It is non-traditional because it reexamines these IR traditions by asking the critical question, "What makes the stories these IR traditions tell about international politics *appear* to be true?" What, for example, makes realism's story about sovereign nation-states locked into a battle for survival or idealism's story about the possibilities of international cooperation so compelling? In this book I suggest that what makes these IR stories appear to be true are the IR myths upon which they are based.

IR myths are *apparent truths*, usually expressed as slogans, that IR traditions rely upon in order to appear to be true. The "truth" or the "falsity" of an IR myth is beside the point. Examining how an IR myth functions to make an IR tradition appear to be true is the point. So, for example, the IR myth "international anarchy is the permissive cause of war" is the *apparent truth* upon which realism and, these days, neorealism, depend. Similarly, "there is an international society" is the IR myth that makes the stories told by idealism and neoidealism appear to be true.

None of this should come as a surprise to IR theorists. We know that different IR traditions rely upon very different IR myths in order to appear to be true. So how do we make sense of these contradictory ways of seeing the world for our students? The usual strategy is to "test" the validity of the IR myths against the "facts" of international politics to determine which IR myth (and therefore which IR tradition) offers the most accurate description of international politics. Proving that an IR myth, tradition or theory is wrong so that it can be replaced by another one which is "true" is usually what we mean by doing "critical IR theory."

But what if we push our analysis just a bit further? What if we unpack not just IR traditions but the IR myths upon which they are based? What if we ask of IR myths (as we do of IR traditions), "What makes the story they tell about international politics appear to be true?" What makes international anarchy *appear* to be the permissive cause of war, or why does there *appear* to be an international society?

If we pursue these questions, then we not only push our analysis of IR traditions further. We push what it means to do "critical IR theory." Why is this the case? Because the alternative way of doing critical IR theory proposed in this book allows us to examine not only how one "truth" replaces another "truth" but also how "truths" get constructed. This is beyond the scope of most traditional critical IR theory which concerns itself only with evaluating which "truth" appears to be most "true." By declaring one theory "true" and another one "false," traditional critical IR theory cannot then go back and examine what makes the "true" theory *appear* to be true. For example, realism critiques idealism by "proving" its IR myth "international anarchy is the permissive cause of war" is "more true" than idealism's myth "there is an international society." But, in so doing, realism cannot ask what makes its IR myth about international anarchy *appear* to be true. And, without critically analyzing its own IR myth, realism ultimately proves nothing.

Asserting the "truth" of one IR myth over another in no way guarantees the "truth" of an IR myth, no matter how much empirical evidence is amassed to support the "truth" of the myth. This is the case because the "truth" of an IR myth depends as much upon *how* empirical evidence is organized into a coherent story about international politics as it does on the evidence alone. This is a central problem with how critical theory is usually practiced in the discipline of international relations.

International Relations Theory takes this problem seriously. How it takes it seriously is by shifting its analytical emphasis away from looking for "empirical evidence" to support the "truth" of an IR myth toward an investigation of the *organization* of "the facts" that make an IR story about international politics *appear* to be true. Doing critical IR theory in this way means that we have to suspend our usual preoccupation with getting to the "real truth" about an IR myth, tradition, or theory and ask instead, "What makes a particular story about international politics *appear to be true*?" Or, to put it somewhat differently, "How does the 'truth' function in a particular IR myth?"

It is not accidental that *IR Theory* as my answer to how to teach international relations theory better should focus on stories and how they are told. If the world is made up of "facts" and stories that organize those "facts," then there is no more important skill to pass on to students than to make them better readers and writers of stories, better interpreters of not just "the facts" but of the organization of "the facts." With this in mind, *International Relations Theory* does not try to be a comprehensive textbook crammed with every "fact" about international life or even international theory. By focusing on the major IR traditions of realism, idealism, historical materialism, constructivism, postmodernism, gender, and globalization, it attempts to help students to read and write their world better by arming them with the ability critically to ask, "How does the 'truth' get told?"

Hopefully, all this takes me far along the critical road to teaching IR theory. But it leaves me with one more major problem. How do I get students interested in doing alternative critical IR theory? What could possibly motivate and engage students who are so often bored with reading and writing and who are likely to find IR theory incomprehensible at first?

Good teaching means starting to where your students are and bringing them to where you want them to be, rather than always expecting them to know how to come to where you are. Over the years, I have found that students enjoy engaging with visual media. Students are into television and film. And, what's more, they tend to be excellent readers and writers of visual media. To get students to be better readers and writers of IR theory, the place to start is to get them to apply what they already know about reading and writing visual media to international politics.

How do I do this? By teaching them IR theory through popular films that they know about and like. That's why this book uses *Lord of the Flies* to teach students about how the anarchy myth works in realism and neorealism, *Independence Day* to teach them about how the international society myth functions in idealism and neoidealism, *Wag the Dog* to introduce them to the debates around social constructivism and postmodernism, *Fatal Attraction* to make them aware of the political stakes of thinking about gender as a variable, *The Truman Show* to reconsider the myth that history is over and how this myth supports neoliberal stories about "globalization," *Memento* to shed light on how neoMarxism reorders history as the history of Empire and resistances to Empire, and *East is East* to explore the lingering influence of modernization and development theory on contemporary security studies.

As this brief synopsis illustrates, I use popular films as vehicles through which students can rethink IR theory and IR myths. The films are used not only to illustrate a particular IR myth but to show students something more besides, and this something more is how the IR myth functions. Put differently, popular films not only illustrate IR myths and the IR traditions they support. Popular films provide students with answers to the question, "How does an IR myth *appear* to be true?" In so doing, popular films point to how politics, power, and ideology are culturally constructed and how the culture of IR theory might be politically reconstructed.

Again, this should not surprise IR theorists, especially those who are attentive to the current debates concerning IR theory and popular culture. For my starting point is to think about IR theory as a site of cultural practice, and this book is a critical reconsideration of what must go without saying in order for the traditional cultural practices of IR theory to function.

International Relations Theory is written with undergraduate students in English-speaking universities in mind. It can be used on its own to structure an introductory course on international relations or IR theory, or it can be used to supplement either historical/theoretical or topical presentations of IR. Each myth is accompanied by "Suggestions for further thinking." These suggestions make the book adaptable to lecture- or seminar-style teaching and extend and upgrade the material from the undergraduate level to the postgraduate level.

This book was also written with my colleagues in mind. I hope it will offer them insights about innovative ways of teaching as well as about the disciplinary culture of IR theory.

I have many people to thank for their intellectual generosity toward me and this project. The sage advice of Jim Rosenau, who encouraged me as I prepared for my first teaching post to combine my teaching and my research by being theoretically imaginative in the classroom, and of Cynthia Enloe, whose challenge to us all to write accessibly and for a general readership, oriented me as I undertook this project. At Purdue University, I benefited enormously from conversations with colleagues, including Bob Bartlett, Pat Boling, Berenice Carroll, Ann Clark, Rosie Clawson, Mark Tilton, Keith Shimko, Michael Weinstein, Linda White, and Lee Wilson. While I may not have discussed this project directly with some of these colleagues, they contributed to the project nonetheless by providing a supportive intellectual environment and a place for me to experiment with my teaching. Graduate students in my "IR Myths Course," especially Julie Webber, Deems Morrione, and Maartin Rothman, and undergraduate students in "Alternative IR" provided invaluable insights to this project.

Moving to the United Kingdom in 1999 meant that I gained a number of new critical eyes on the project. At the University of Leeds, Kevin Theakston granted me a timely sabbatical which allowed me to finish the book. Other colleagues in the

Institute of Politics and International Studies, especially Hugh Dyer, Jason Ralph, and Rhiannon Vickers, and in the Institute for Communication Studies, especially Jayne Rodgers, were particularly supportive. My students in my undergraduate course "Popular Culture and International Relations" at the University of Leeds acted as my final sounding board for the manuscript before its publication. They saved me from many a misstep.

The invitation from Bob Eccleshall of the School of Politics at The Queen's University of Belfast to spend my sabbatical in the School allowed me to finish the manuscript there and to receive helpful feedback on the project from students and colleagues at Queen's, especially Alan Finlayson. I also benefited from presenting some of this material at the University of Kent London Centre for International Relations, where I particularly would like to thank Vivienne Jabri and Jef Huysmans for their detailed comments.

Yale Furguson and Barry Jones provided me with my first forum in which to experiment with the mixing of film and international theory on the New Frontiers panel at the 1998 ECPR meetings in Vienna. Taking a chance on this unusual form, Walter Carlsnaes published the resulting paper as "IR: the Resurrection OR New Frontiers of Incorporation" in the *European Journal of International Relations* 5(4): 435–50 (1999), which forms the basis for arguments presented in Chapters 4 and 5.

My editor at Routledge, Mark Kavanagh, offered support and advice throughout. His belief in and enthusiasm for this project was much appreciated. Like Mark's advice, the thoughtful reviews of this manuscript by Roxanne Doty and by two anonymous referees made this a better text.

François Debrix read the entire manuscript, commenting on it as I produced it. He is a wonderful reader and writer of stories, and I thank him for his intellectual generosity. If it hadn't been for Marysia Zalewski, who encouraged me to tell my stories about IR theory using film and who forced me to consider the bigger intellectual and political picture at every turn, this book could not have been written. Nor could this book have been written without the intellectual guidance of John MacLean, Richard Ashley, Thais Morgan, and Diane Rubenstein, each of whom introduced me to a different mode of critical thinking. I thank them all.

This book is dedicated to my folks, Lyn and Charles Weber, whose support and encouragement especially over these past few years has been invaluable. This book is also dedicated to Bob DiClerico, a professor at West Virginia University where I studied as an undergraduate, who instilled in me an enthusiasm for teaching thanks to his great skill as a teacher. It is his example of excellence that guides my teaching to this day.

Chapter 1

Introduction

Culture, ideology, and the myth function in IR theory

International politics is a huge field. It explores everything from wars to revolutions to global gender inequalities to demands for international human rights to international trade. To try to make sense of international politics, we often turn to IR theory. IR theory makes organizing generalizations about international politics. IR theory is a collection of stories about the world of international politics. And in telling stories about international politics, IR theory doesn't just present what is going on in the world out there. IR theory also imposes its own vision of what the world out there looks like.

We use IR theory to make sense of the world of international politics. But how do we make sense of IR theory? Of course, we can learn all the stories IR theory tells us about the world. We call these stories IR traditions and name them neorealism, neoidealism, historical materialism, constructivism, gender, globalization, neo-Marxism, modernization and development theory, and environmentalism. But just learning the stories IR theory tells doesn't tell us much about IR theory itself. It doesn't tell us, for example, how IR theory works. What makes the stories IR theory tells about international politics so compelling? What makes the stories IR theory tells about the world of international politics *appear to be true*?

My answer is that IR theory—a collection of stories about international politics—relies upon IR myths in order to appear to be true. What is an IR myth? An IR myth is an *apparent truth*, usually expressed in slogan form, that an IR theory relies upon in order to *appear to be true*. IR myths, in other words, are the building blocks of IR theory, of the stories IR theory tells about the world of international politics. They are that part of the story that is so familiar to us that we take it for granted. And our taking IR myths for granted is necessary for IR theories to appear to be true.

For example, think of the slogans "international anarchy is the permissive cause of war" and "there is an international society." Such slogans are IR myths. Realists rely upon the knowledge that "international anarchy is the permissive cause of war" to explain why sovereign nation-states inevitably find themselves in conflict with one another and why balance of power politics is the key to managing such conflict. Idealists, in contrast, rely upon the knowledge that "there is an international society" in order for them to be able to tell their stories about progress among sovereign nation-states on a global scale to the point that conflict among them might be transcended. If we questioned these IR myths, then the stories told by IR traditions like realism and idealism would not necessarily appear to be true.

Why do I refer to these building blocks of IR theory as IR myths? Is it because I believe that IR myths—like myths generally—are false? Absolutely not! IR myths may be true, and they may be false. The truth or falsity of an IR myth is not important for understanding how IR myths function as the building blocks of IR theory. So why call the building blocks of IR stories IR myths? I call them IR myths because of the "mythologizing function" or "myth function" they perform. It is the myth function of these building blocks of IR theory that makes the stories told by IR theory appear to be true.

What is the myth function in IR theory? How do IR myths make an IR theory appear to be true? And why is it important for us to study the process by which IR myths make IR theories appear to be true?

These are the questions I address in this chapter. I do so by considering IR theory's relationship to three concepts—culture, ideology, and the myth function in IR theory.

Culture

Raymond Williams, a pioneer in the field of cultural studies and cultural theory, noted of the term culture that it is "one of the two or three most complicated words in the English language" (Williams, 1983: 87). Williams has a point. Culture is one of those terms that everyone seems to understand but no one seems to be able adequately to define.

Often, when we think of culture, we think of traditional arrangements within particular states or societies. For example, we may say that there is something called US culture or UK culture. But this way of thinking about culture suggests that there is something stable, identifiable, and generalizable that we can point to as a culture. When we unpack a term like "US culture", we find so many contradictions, incompatibilities, and complexities within it that the term itself seems to mean little. For example, how can we meaningfully make sense of the militia movement, the religious right, rugged individualism, and anti-capitalism not to mention regional, rural, class, race, sexuality, and age "sub-cultures" collected under the one term "US culture?" Not very easily.

For this reason, theorists who think about what culture is have tried to come up with less static and more open definitions of culture. These definitions focus on how culture is related to meaning rather than trying to pin culture to a particular place at a particular time, like the contemporary US (see Box 1.1). According to Stuart Hall, this is because "culture . . . is not so much a set of *things*—novels and paintings or TV programmes and comics—as a process, a set of *practices*," what others have called "signifying practices" (Hall, 1997: 2; Storey, 1997: 2). For Hall, "culture is concerned with the production and the exchange of meanings—the 'giving and taking of meaning'—between members of a society or group" (1997: 2). Or, as John Hartley defines it, culture is "The social production and reproduction of sense, meaning, and consciousness" (in O'Sullivan et al., 1994: 68). Culture has to do with how we make sense of the world and how we produce, reproduce, and circulate that sense.

Box 1.1 What is culture?

"Culture is concerned with the production and exchange of meanings—the 'giving and taking of meaning'—between members of a society or group" (Stuart Hall, 1997)

"The social production and reproduction of sense, meaning, and consciousness" (John Hartley, in O'Sullivan et al., 1994)

"an ensemble of stories we tell about ourselves" (Clifford Geertz, 1975)

We circulate our sense about the world in many ways, and one of the ways we do this is through stories. This is why another cultural theorist, Clifford Geertz, described culture as "an ensemble of stories we tell about ourselves" (Geertz, 1975: 448). For Geertz, these stories are not always conscious. They can be composed of beliefs we consciously hold as well as of habits we unconsciously perform. Cultural stories are composed of both sense (consciousness) and common sense (unconsciousness). Common sense is what we know but don't think about, what Roland Barthes described as "what-goes-without-saying" (Barthes, 1972: 11).

Studying culture understood as "sense making," "signifying practices," or "an ensemble of stories, beliefs, and habits" means we have to pay attention to how meanings are made. We must think about how meaning making relies upon what is said and what goes without saying. And we must recognize that cultures aren't just "there," fully formed for us to study. Indeed, it may be impossible for us to identify "cultures" as objects of study at all. Studying culture means looking at how what we objectify as "culture" is made. And part of what makes culture and helps to distinguish some "cultures" from other "cultures" are cultural practices that produce, organize, and circulate meanings through stories told about the world.

IR theory can be studied as a site of cultural practice. IR theory is "an ensemble of stories" told about the world it studies, which is the world of international politics. Studying IR theory as a site of cultural practice means being attentive to how IR theory makes sense of the world of international politics. We have to ask of IR theory: How do the stories it tells about the world of international politics become sense and common sense? And why do we take for granted the sense IR theory makes of our lives in relation to international politics?

My answer to these questions is that IR theory relies upon IR myths in order to transform its culturally produced stories about the world into common sense about the world that we take for granted. But before we explore this process in detail, let me introduce another important concept that plays a part in this process. This concept is ideology.

Ideology

Unlike the term culture, ideology is a term for which formal definitions confidently abound (see Box 1.2). The most common way ideology is defined is as "a fairly coherent and comprehensive set of ideas that explains and evaluates social conditions, helps people understand their place in society, and provides a program for social and political action" (Ball and Dagger, 1995: 9). It is a ready-made set of meanings and interpretations that can help us to make sense of our world and tell us how to act in relation to our world.

This way of defining ideology assumes that all ideologies are consciously held. And many are. Examples of "conscious ideologies" are liberalism, conservatism, socialism, feminism, ecologism, and even vegetarianism. Conscious ideologies are easily identifiable. We know what they are, and we can subscribe to them or reject them.

While conscious ideologies like liberalism and conservatism are powerful because they can politically mobilize people and "raise consciousness" about political

---

Box 1.2 What is ideology?

Conscious ideology: "a fairly coherent and comprehensive set of ideas that explains
and evaluates social conditions, helps people understand their place in society,
and provides a program for social and political action" (Ball and Dagger,
1995)

Unconscious ideology: ideology that is not formally named and that is therefore
difficult to identify. It is the common sense foundation of our worldviews that
is beyond debate.

---

situations, another type of ideologies—"unconscious ideologies"—are arguably even
more politically powerful. Unlike neatly packaged, easily identifiable, named
ideologies, unconscious ideologies lack proper names. This makes us less likely to
be able to identify them as ideologies. This is why they are also called "anonymous
ideologies" (Barthes, 1972).

An example of an unconscious ideology is "boys will be boys." It would be
difficult to attribute this ideology to anyone in particular both because no one person
or one ideological tradition claims it as their own and because it appears to those
who hold it to be "just the way things are" or the way things ought to be. In this
sense, unconscious ideologies are "profoundly unconscious" (Althusser, 1969). We
use them to help us make sense of our worlds, very often without realizing it. And
because we don't realize we hold unconscious ideologies or use them to make sense
of our worlds, we very rarely interrogate them. We very rarely ask difficult questions
about them that might upset them as common sense (see Box 1.3).

If conscious ideologies are those ideologies packaged as programs for political action that we debate in the political arena, unconscious ideologies are the
foundations of our ideological and political thinking that we place beyond debate.
Unconscious ideologies, in other words, "go without saying." We don't like to
have our unconscious ideologies—our common sense—articulated, much less
questioned. When they are, our way of making sense of the world is potentially
threatened.

Box 1.3 Examples of conscious and unconscious ideologies

Conscious ideologies	*Unconscious ideologies*
Liberalism	Boys will be boys
Conservatism	America has a classless society
Socialism	English people are white
Feminism	Everyone I know is straight

How is ideology related to culture? If culture is a site of meaning production, ideology is a site where meanings that are culturally produced are transformed into just the way things are or the way things ought to be. Some of this is done explicitly. For example, if you declare your allegiance to a particular named conscious ideology like conservatism, you are declaring that conservatism really truly describes how the world is and how it ought to be. You are consciously transforming your cultural views about the world into *the* view of the world as it naturally is.

But a lot of the transformation from the cultural to the ideological goes without saying because it employs anonymous, unconscious ideologies. In this respect, unconscious ideologies are akin to cultural habits. We enact them all the time without thinking about them. And, in the case of unconscious ideologies, these unconscious habits in our thinking transform what is cultural or produced into what appears to be natural or just the way things are (Barthes, 1972).

It is this process of transforming meanings from cultural to natural that I want to explore in relation to IR theory and IR myths. And it is this process that is explained though the myth function in IR theory.

The myth function in IR theory

IR theory is a site of cultural practice in which conscious and unconscious ideologies are circulated through stories that *appear* to be true. The stories we recognize and hold consciously we call IR traditions (like realism and idealism). The stories we don't recognize as ideologies because we don't have names for them and hold unconsciously I call IR myths (like "international anarchy is the permissive cause of war" and "there is an international society") (see Box 1.4).

While we debate the "truth" of IR stories organized into IR tradition, we rarely reflect on what makes these stories seem to make so much sense. In other words, we rarely consider how unconscious ideologies or IR myths function in these stories called IR traditions. Rather, we generally accept IR myths as forthright expressions of how the world works, and we allow these IR myths to function as the building blocks of IR traditions that narrate complicated explanations of how the world is and how it ought to be (see Box 1.5).

If IR theory narrates a particular view of the world from the perspective of various IR traditions, an IR myth is what helps make a particular view of the world *appear* to be true. The *myth function* in IR theory is the transformation of what is particular, cultural, and ideological (like a story told by an IR tradition) into what

---

Box 1.4 What is an IR myth?

An IR myth is an *apparent truth*, usually expressed as a slogan, that an IR theory or tradition (like realism or idealism) relies upon in order to appear to be true.

Examples: "international anarchy is the permissive cause of war"; and "there is an international society."

Box 1.5 What is the myth function in IR theory?

The *myth function* in IR theory is the transformation of what is particular, cultural, and ideological (like a story told by an IR tradition) into what *appears* to be universal, natural, and purely empirical.

Cultural interpretation → Myth function → "Natural fact"

---

appears to be universal, natural, and purely empirical. It is naturalizing meanings—making them into common sense—that are the products of cultural practices (Barthes, 1972). Put another way, the myth function in IR theory is making a "fact" out of an interpretation.

Why describe this process as the myth function in IR theory? Because this process of making what is cultural and disputed into what is natural and therefore goes without saying is the work or the function IR myths perform in IR theory.

Analyzing how these transformations from cultural meanings into naturalized facts occur in our everyday encounters with IR theory is the purpose of this book. And by undertaking this analysis, we are not only examining the intersections of IR theory and everyday cultural practices, we are also analyzing the intersections of IR theory and political power. Why is this the case?

Transforming the cultural into the natural is a highly political practice that depends upon all sorts of complex configurations of power. Precisely how power works to mythologize something cultural into something natural varies from context to context. But in a general sense, *power works through myths by appearing to take the political out of the ideological*. This is because something that appears to be natural and unalterable also appears to be apolitical. Yet these sorts of "natural facts" are arguably the most intensely political stories of all, not just because of what they say (what the specific myth is) but because of what they do (they remove themselves and the tradition they support from political debate). This is why Barthes refers to myths as "depoliticized speech" (Barthes, 1972).

"Re-politicizing" IR theory and IR myths requires us to suspend our interest in the "truth" of IR theory (whether or not a specific theoretical interpretation is really right or wrong) so we can refocus our attention on how cultural configurations of power and ideology make a theory or story *appear* to be true.

Why myths?

Why focus our attention on IR myths? Why disrupt our sacred IR stories by proclaiming them to be composed of myths? And why consider the myth function in IR theory? Is the point to rid IR theory of culture and ideology? Certainly not! Cultural practices will always mediate our encounters with the so-called "facts" of international politics. And ideologies will always force us to consider questions of truth.

Asking questions about what makes IR theories function *as if they were true* is not the same thing as asking us to abandon our beloved myths. Nor does it amount to exposing IR myths as false because the truth or falsity of an IR myth can never be validated or invalidated. That's part of what makes it so powerful. By asking questions about the myth function in IR theory, we will not lose our precious IR myths. Rather, these IR myths bound up in IR theories will lose some of their *apparent truth*. They will return to the realms of interpretation, culture, and ideology and cease to make unopposed claims to a status as common sense, natural, or purely empirical. In other words, IR myths will return to the realm of the political where what they say and what they do can be analyzed and debated.

By disrupting the *apparent truth* of IR myths, opportunities arise for new theories of IR to be written. Yet these, too, will be myths. So why bother interrogating the myth function in IR theory if we will never escape it? The answer to this question is in the question itself. *Because we will never escape the myth function in IR theory, we had better interrogate it.* We had better prepare ourselves to be the best critical readers of IR myths we possibly can be. Otherwise, we will just be repeating cherished stories about IR without grasping what makes these stories *appear* to be true, without appreciating what makes them function. We will be circulating a particular way of making sense of the world without knowing how to make sense of that sense. That would make us look pretty naïve.

Plan of the book

In the following chapters, we will interrogate the myth function in IR theory by addressing three aspects of everyday IR myths.

1   What does the myth say?
    Before we can analyze critically how a myth works (its function), we must first be familiar with what the myth says (its content). We will do four things to help us understand the content of each myth:

    a   select a classic IR text that uses the myth
    b   situate the IR text in its particular IR tradition (like realism or idealism)
    c   summarize the text
    d   explore how the IR text makes use of the IR myth.

    For example, for the IR myth "international anarchy is the permissive cause of war," we will do the following four things: select Kenneth Waltz's texts *Man, the State, and War* and *Theory of International Politics*, situate them in relation to the IR traditions of realism and neorealism, summarize their main arguments, and explore how they use the IR myth "international anarchy is the permissive cause of war."

2   How does the myth function?
    If the myth function in IR theory is to succeed, it has to be invisible. We have to forget it is even taking place, that cultural meanings are being transformed into common sense. And, in all of the IR myths explored in this book, the myth function in IR theory is extremely successful. But this presents us with a

problem. How can we identify the myth function in IR theory? And how can we critically analyze the myth function in IR theory if IR theory does such a good job of explaining our world to us—to the point that we believe IR myths as true and the worlds they help to create are just the way things are?

One answer is to think about IR theory in relation to "other worlds." As critical readers of myths, we are more likely to recognize and be able to interrogate myths in worlds in which we do not live—other "cultures," other times, other locations. But where can we find "other worlds" that are both different enough to our own so that we can critically read the myths in them and similar enough to our own so that we can identify with them enough for them to make sense to us?

My answer is to look to popular films for these "other worlds." Popular films provide us with ready-made, somewhat delimited "other worlds." In the vast cinemascapes of popular culture, there is no shortage of worlds for us to view critically. Even if a film is set in our "culture," in our sovereign nation-state, and in our times, the world the film presents is not "our" world, for we do not occupy this cinemascape. Yet because the film tries to depict our world, we usually understand this "other world" and identify with it. This gap between occupying a cinematic world and identifying with it enables us to critically read "other worlds" and the myths in them.

Another reason for turning to popular films is because they are one of the narrative spaces of visual culture. They are a way in which stories get told in visual culture. Nicholas Mirzoeff argues that "visual culture used to be seen as a distraction from the serious business of text and history. It is now the locus of cultural and historical change" (1999: 31). If that is the case, we had better learn how to read visual culture and the transformative processes that occur within it.

Accessing visual culture through popular films allows us to consider the connections between IR theory and our everyday lives. Using popular films in this way helps us to get a sense of the everyday connections between "the popular" and "the political." We can see, for example, how IR myths become *everyday* IR myths—because they are circulated, received, and criticized in and through everyday, popular forms like films.

Drawing upon these ideas, we will interrogate the myth function in IR theory by doing three things:

a   select a film that illustrates the myth function in a particular IR myth;
b   summarize the film;
c   relate the film to the IR myth. Here we will ask two important questions:
   • How does the film make sense of the world (Dyer, 1985)?
   • What does the film say is typical and deviant in that world (Dyer, 1985)?

The popular films used to explore the myth function in IR theory are: *Lord of Flies*, *Independence Day*, *Wag the Dog*, *Fatal Attraction*, *The Truman Show*, *Memento*, *East is East*, and *WALL-E*. *Lord of the Flies* reconsiders the realist/neorealist myth "international anarchy is the permissive cause of war"; *Independence Day* looks at the idealist myth "there is an international society";

Wag the Dog offers insights into the constructivist myth "anarchy is what states make of it" and introduces us to the social constructivist/poststructuralist debate; *Fatal Attraction* illustrates and critiques the gender myth "gender is a variable" while exploring the gender/feminist debate; *The Truman Show* demonstrates how the neoliberal myth "it is the end of history" makes neoliberal theories of globalization function at the expense of historical materialist theories of globalization; *Memento* explores how the neoMarxist myth "Empire is the new world order" selectively remembers the neoMarxist/postmodernist debate; *East is East* questions the notion of "civilizations" upon which the myth "there is a clash of civilizations" depends; and *WALL-E* explores just how convenient or inconvenient combating human-made climate change is, for whom, and with what environmental (and environmentalist) consequences.

3   What does this critical analysis of the myth function in IR theory tell us about IR theory culturally, ideologically, and popularly?

This question will be considered in the conclusion by asking two questions that take us directly to the power politics of IR theory:

- How does IR theory make sense of the world?
- What does IR theory say is typical and deviant in that world?

These questions take us to the heart of how IR theory produces and circulates meanings about international politics. They also point to the relationships among the politics of IR theory, the politics of the popular, and the politics of storytelling.

Suggestions for further thinking

Topic 1 Mythology as methodology

Roland Barthes proposed semiology as a methodology for exploring the ideological function of myths in his book *Mythologies*. While his early work focused on exposing and putting right the "ideological abuse" hidden in myths (and especially in "bourgeois norms"), Barthes' later work explored more complex ways of thinking about how meanings are pluralized through reading and writing. Reading Barthes' early work on myths through his later writings, like *S/Z*, produces what Laura Kipnis calls a "postmodernized Barthes." It is a postmodernized Barthes who Craig Saper constructs and deploys in his book *Artificial Mythologies*. It is a similarly post-modernized Barthes who informs my reading of IR myths. For a sense of how to apply some of these ideas to reading films, James Monaco's chapter on signs and syntax is helpful.

Suggested reading

Roland Barthes (1972) "Myth Today," in *Mythologies*, trans. Annette Lavers. New York: The Noonday Press.

Roland Barthes (1974) *S/Z: An Essay*, trans Richard Miller. New York: Hill and Wang, pp. 3–16.

James Monaco (2000) "The Language of Film: Signs and Syntax," in *How to Read a Film*. Oxford: Oxford University Press, pp. 152–225.

Craig Saper (1997) "Introduction" to *Artificial Mythologies*. See also the "Preface" by Laura Kipnis. Minneapolis: University of Minnesota Press.

Topic 2 Culture, form, and IR theory

The conversation about "cultures" is an old one in international politics, especially in those variants of international studies that tend toward what might be called "area studies"—studies of particular regions of the world. Some very rigid ways of thinking about culture continue to be circulated in IR theory, especially in the wake of the end of the Cold War, as the work of Samuel Huntington illustrates (see Chapter 8).

Another strain of discussions involves critical ways of thinking about culture, cultural forms, and their relationships to IR theory. Some of these have been ushered into the field of international studies thanks to critical ways of thinking about identity politics. Yosef Lapid and Friedrich Krotochwil, for example, challenge IR theorists to change their conceputalizations of IR theory by "adding" a critical conception of culture to their work. Another position, expressed by Roland Bleiker, is less concerned with revising the content of IR theory through the inclusion of critical considerations of culture than it is with thinking about how different cultural forms, like poetry, offer us ways not to "add" culture or cultural forms to IR theory but to move beyond the tired debates that traditional expressions of IR theory require. Following the lead of Michael Shapiro's work that takes IR debates about culture beyond the nation-state and into cinematic states, François Debrix and Cynthia Weber carry the discussion of culture to transnational spaces while Jutta Weldes takes it out of this world altogether.

Suggested readings

Roland Bleiker (1997) "Forget IR Theory," *Alternatives* 22(1): 57–85.

François Debrix and Cynthia Weber (eds) (2003) *Rituals of Mediation: International Politics and Social Meanings*. Minneapolis: University of Minnesota Press.

Yosef Lapid and Friedrich Kratochwil (eds) (1996) *The Return of Culture and Identity in IR Theory*. Boulder, CO: Lynne Rienner.

Michael Shapiro (1997) *Violent Cartographies: Mapping Cultures of War*. Minneapolis: University of Minnesota Press.

Michael Shapiro (1999) *Cinematic Political Thought: Narrating Race, Nation and Gender*. New York: New York University Press.

Jutta Weldes (1999) "Going Cultural: *Star Trek*, State Action, and Popular Culture," *Millennium* 28(1): 117–34.

Jutta Weldes (ed.) (2003) *To Seek Out New Worlds: Exploring Links Between Science Fiction and World Politics*. London: Palgrave Macmillan.

Chapter 2

Realism

Is international anarchy the permissive cause of war?

The claim that international politics is anarchical is almost universally embraced by IR theorists and practitioners (for an alternative view, see Chapter 7). This is in part because the myth of international anarchy seems so straightforwardly to describe what we know about international politics. First, the anarchy myth assumes that international politics is composed of sovereign nation-states and that these sovereign nation-states are beholden to no higher power. That is what it means to be sovereign—for a state to have absolute authority over its territory and people and to have independence internationally. In international theory, all states in international politics are assumed to be sovereign, even though there are debates about degrees and/or kinds of sovereignty (Jackson, 1990). And while some IR theorists consider sovereignty itself to be a myth (Bierstieker and Weber, 1996), most regard it as the primary fact of international political life.

The second "fact" of international political life—and the second assumption of the anarchy myth—is that there is no world government. This is why sovereign nation-states are beholden to no higher power. There just is no higher power than that of a sovereign nation-state. Because there is no higher power that a state *must* obey, states are said to have international independence. This is so even if a state joins an international organization like the United Nations or NATO. This does not impinge upon a state's sovereignty or international independence because state membership in these organizations is voluntary. So a state can quit an organization if it wants to.

Combining the absence of world government with state sovereignty, many IR theorists conclude that international politics is anarchical. But this conclusion only makes sense if one more assumption is made. This third assumption has to do with the meaning of anarchy. In political theory, "anarchy" denotes a lack of order. We usually describe states experiencing civil wars as anarchical, for example. But in international theory, "anarchy" denotes a *lack of an orderer*—someone or something who/which self-consciously imposes order in a top-down way onto sovereign nation-states. So in international theory anarchy prevails even if there is order (like power balancing among sovereign nation-states or one hegemonic state being able to call most of the shots like the US does). These sorts of "order" are still considered to be anarchical because there is no world government (see Box 2.1).

There are countless versions of the anarchy myth, each with a very different way of describing and mythologizing the "realities" of international anarchy. Yet of all of these anarchy myths, the one that is the most well known and the most widely accepted is Kenneth Waltz's myth "international anarchy is the permissive cause of war," a myth that dates back to 1954.

Box 2.1 Three assumptions of the international anarchy myth

1 International politics is composed of sovereign nation-states
2 There is no world government which means there is no international orderer
3 The absence of a world government or orderer by definition means that international politics is anarchical

---

Why is Waltz's myth "international anarchy is the permissive cause of war" so influential? And why has it endured nearly half a century? One reason is that Waltz's myth does more than make anarchy the context in which sovereign nation-states carry out their day-to-day politics. In Waltz's anarchy myth, international anarchy becomes the answer to the question that spawned IR theory as an academic discipline after World War I. That question is "Why do wars occur?" By causally linking international anarchy to war, Waltz did more to popularize the anarchy myth than any other IR theorist before him or since.

Another reason has to do with the historical timing of Waltz's myth. As a US academic writing during the Cold War, Waltz seemed to explain the constant disposition to go to war that existed between the US and the Soviet blocs. With no world government, cold war could (and often did) become hot war at any time. US policymakers had to plan accordingly by (they believed) increasing US defenses. And so Waltz's myth persisted as accepted theoretical and diplomatic wisdom in the US until (at least) the end of the Cold War.

Yet another reason is that Waltz's anarchy myth has been theorized from the perspectives of both realism and new- or neorealism (see Table 2.1). Both realism and neorealism accept the three fundamental assumptions that make the anarchy myth function—first, that the world is composed of sovereign nation-states; second, that there is no world government which means there is no international orderer; and third, that the absence of world government or an international orderer by definition means that international politics is anarchical. From these three elements, realists and neorealists both predict that sovereign nation-states in a system of international anarchy will behave conflictually. While individual wars may be stopped from time to time, war itself cannot be transcended. But why?

Table 2.1 Realism vs. neorealism

	Realism	neorealism
Interest of states	Survival	Survival
How to achieve survival	Increase power because world government unachievable	Increase power because world government unachievable
Human nature	Man is flawed and therefore prone to conflict. This explains why cooperation is never guaranteed and world government is unachievable	Man may or may not be flawed. Human nature is not essential to an explanation of conflict
Anarchy	The environment in which sovereign nation-states act	Describes the social relations among sovereign nation-states that causally explain why wars occur

Realists and neorealists agree that the overriding goal of states in this environment of international anarchy is to survive. This is their overriding interest. And the only way that states can reasonably ensure their survival is to increase their power. Power protects states because states with less power might fear those with more power and therefore be less likely to attack them.

Additionally, realists and neorealists agree that there is no way out of international anarchy. It is *un*realistic to think that a world government could be formed because states would never be secure enough—and therefore trusting enough—to give up their power to a world government.

With all this in common, what do realists and neorealists disagree about? One thing they disagree about is the issue of human nature. Realists like Hans Morgenthau, for example, argue that the nature of man (and he meant the gender exclusive term "man"; see Tickner, 1992: Chapter 2) is fundamentally flawed. In Morgenthau's account, man may not be purely evil, but he is certainly tainted by original sin. And that means that pessimism about how man and groups of men (organized into sovereign nation-states) will behave is the only realistic way to approach international politics. At its root, then, international politics will remain anarchical and conflictual because of the nature of man.

Neorealists, of whom Kenneth Waltz was the first, disagree. They argue that instead of looking to "natural" causes of conflict, we need to look to "social" ones instead. Following Jean-Jacques Rousseau, Waltz argues that the organization of social relations rather than the nature of man is what determines whether or not we have war. Why? Because good men behave badly in bad social organizations, and bad men can be stopped from behaving badly if they are in good social organizations. States go to war, then, because they are in a bad social organization. And Waltz calls that bad social organization international anarchy. "International anarchy is the permissive cause of war." So, realists and neorealists differ on how they conceptualize international anarchy. For realists, it is just the environment in which sovereign nation-states act. For neorealists, international anarchy describes the social relations among sovereign nation-states that causally explain why wars occur.

In this chapter, I will consider the myth "international anarchy is the permissive cause of war" and the specific uses Kenneth Waltz makes of this myth. I will do so by examining what have become two of the most famous books about IR theory, both authored by Waltz. In the first, *Man, the State, and War* (first published in 1954), Waltz makes his famous argument that "international anarchy is the permissive cause of war." In the second, *Theory of International Politics* (1979), Waltz extends international anarchy from a cause of war into a systemic ordering principle of the international system, a move which gives birth to the tradition of neorealism. I will summarize the arguments Waltz makes in each of these books, relate his arguments to the myth "international anarchy is the permissive cause of war," and reconsider the myth function of Waltz's arguments about international anarchy through the film *Lord of the Flies*.

Lord of the Flies tells a story about moving from one type of order (hierarchy) into another (anarchy), suggesting that anarchy is what allows conflict to occur. As such, it illustrates the arguments Waltz makes in his two books. Yet *Lord of the Flies* also offers insights into what makes Waltz's anarchy myth function by showing us how fear is both a crucial and an externalized component of Waltz's anarchy myth

(Ashley, 1989). Without fear, Waltz's arguments fail to be persuasive. What would international politics be like if fear functioned differently than it does in Waltz's myth? What would this mean for IR theory? These are the sorts of questions a functional analysis of Waltz's work allows us to consider.

What does the myth say?

Why do wars occur? This is the question Kenneth Waltz asked himself in the early 1950s. Waltz's question is as old as war itself, possibly because "to explain how peace can be more readily achieved requires an understanding of the causes of war" (Waltz, 1959: 2). By the time Waltz posed this question, many answers to it already existed. These answers fell into three categories (or as IR theorists came to define them, were found at the three "levels of analysis" or in the "three images"). These three categories/levels/images are: the individual, the state, and the state system. In *Man, the State, and War*, Waltz argued that the major causes of war are to be found at each of these levels of analysis, with none of them alone being sufficient to explain why wars do or do not occur.

How did Waltz come to this conclusion? Waltz began by looking at the first category/level/image—man. For Waltz, as for so many other IR theorists, the term "man" denotes the individual level and particularly an interest in human nature, forgetting of course that not all individuals are men. The first image explanation of war goes like this:

> the locus of the important causes of war is found in the nature and behavior of man. War results from selfishness, from misdirected aggressive impulses, from stupidity. . . . If these are the primary causes of war, then the elimination of war must come through uplifting and enlightening men or securing their psychic-social readjustment.
>
> (Waltz, 1959: 16)

This is the "men behaving badly" explanation of war. Man behaves badly because he is bad by nature. He acts unreasonably or he prioritizes selfish goals over communitarian goals, and this is why conflicts and wars occur. This is the sort of "natural man" realist IR scholars invoke to explain the recurrence and repetition of wars. But, as idealist IR theorists point out, men do not always behave badly (see Chapter 3). Some men seem to be good by nature—they act reasonably to pursue the common good. There is a fundamental goodness to man, and if that fundamental goodness could be universalized—if all men could access their fundamental goodness—then all men could behave well. Conflicts and wars could be averted altogether.

In reviewing these pessimistic and optimistic descriptions of the nature of man, Waltz noted a couple of problems. First, he suggested that the "causal importance of human nature" is generally exaggerated by all human nature theorists. Can we really say that human nature *alone* causes war? Not for Waltz, for how can pessimists explain why wars don't occur all the time and how can optimists explain why they occur some of the time? Human nature explanations of war don't seem to account for variations in the presence or absence of war. And, anyway, don't good men as well as bad men sometimes make war? Waltz concludes that human nature is too complex to be so directly and causally linked to war as the sole explanation for why wars occur (Waltz, 1959: 40).

Second, this insufficiency of human nature to explain the presence or absence of war means that we must look to social and political institutions to supplement our understanding of why wars occur. For example, if human nature cannot be changed—whether it is always good or bad—then we cannot decrease the occurrence of war by trying to change it. All we can do is look to social and political institutions that do change and try to change them to decrease the likelihood of war. Conversely, if human nature can be changed, then we still need to look to social and political institutions because human nature would be changed through interactions with these institutions. All this leads Waltz to conclude that human nature itself is never sufficient to explain the presence or absence of war. It must be supplemented by an analysis of social and political institutions. This leads Waltz to investigate second level/image explanations of the causes of war.

At the second level of analysis, Waltz asks whether the occurrence of wars can be explained by the internal organization of states and societies. Just as first image theorists argue that there are good and bad men, second image theorists argue that there are good and bad states, either because of their formal governmental arrangements (democratic vs. autocratic, for example; see Chapter 3) or their less formal social arrangements (who owns the means of production; see Chapter 6). Like first image analyses, second image theories claim that bad actors (this time states) make war, and good actors preserve the peace. But, as before, these sorts of explanations raise critical questions for Waltz. For example, if bad states make war, what will change bad states to good states (Waltz, 1959: 114)? Not surprisingly, there is no agreement among second image theorists on just what to do. Some suggest good states would be democratic, others say they should be monarchical, others still say socialist (Waltz, 1959: 120). And, Waltz suggests, even if second image theorists could agree on what a good state was, there is still no guarantee that a world of "good states" would be a peaceful world. Like "good men," "good states" sometimes make war.

Once again, Waltz concludes that this level of analysis is incomplete. This state level needs to be supplemented by the international level, for, as Waltz puts it, "the international political environment has much to do with the ways in which states behave" (Waltz, 1959: 122–3). And this leads Waltz to consider the third level of analysis or third image in his quest to understand why wars occur.

Waltz summarizes the third image as follows: "With many sovereign states, with no system of law enforceable among them, with each state judging its grievances and ambitions according to the dictates of its own reason or desire— conflict, sometimes leading to war, is bound to occur" (Waltz, 1959: 159). It is worth quoting a somewhat lengthy passage by Waltz in which he details the linkages between anarchy, state actions, and conflict.

> In anarchy there is no automatic harmony. . . . A state will use force to attain its goals if, after assessing the prospects for success, it values those goals more than it values the pleasures of peace. Because each state is the final judge of

its own cause, any state may at any time use force to implement its policies. Because any state may at any time use force, all states must constantly be ready either to counter force with force or to pay the cost of weakness. The requirements of state action are, in this view, imposed by the circumstances in which all states exist.

(Waltz, 1959: 160)

In a situation of international anarchy as Waltz describes it, no "supreme authority" like an international government can stop states from forcefully pursuing their own interests. Waltz concludes that "war occurs because there is nothing to prevent it" (Waltz, 1959: 188). This is why Waltz describes international anarchy as "a permissive or underlying cause of war" (Waltz, 1959: 232).

As a permissive cause of war, international anarchy is also the limit on states' abilities to cooperate with one another. Because there is no one to enforce co-operation, states will act in their own self-interests rather than in the interests of the state system. Waltz elaborates this point with reference to the parable of the stag hunt, told by Jean-Jacques Rousseau.

Assume that five men who have acquired a rudimentary ability to speak and to understand each other happen to come together at a time when all of them suffer from hunger. The hunger of each will be satisfied by the fifth part of stag, so they "agree" to co-operate in a project to trap one. But also the hunger of any one of them will be satisfied by a hare, so, as a hare comes within reach, one of them grabs it. The defector obtains the means of satisfying his hunger but in doing so permits the stag to escape. His immediate interest prevails over consideration for his fellows.

(Waltz, 1959: 167–8)

So, for Waltz, international anarchy explains both why wars ultimately may occur and why there are limits on cooperation among states in the international system. Without a leader to punish a hunter who defected from the stag hunt or an international government to punish a rogue state, cooperation can never be guaranteed and conflict is always a serious possibility.

Yet even though Waltz argues that only international anarchy has the power to explain why wars *may* occur, he stresses that individual and state-level factors still need to be considered when we think about why specific wars *do* occur. For Waltz, the first and second images constitute the immediate causes of war. If individuals and states do not pursue war-like policies or do not pursue selfish interests that could not also be understood as in the general interest of all states, then even though the third image of international anarchy permits the occurrence of war, there would be no war (Waltz, 1959: 238).

Another way to put it is like this: if individuals and states have nothing to *fear* from one another, then they have no cause to fight wars with one another. Something in addition to international anarchy is always required to explain why we move from a situation in which wars *may* occur to a situation in which wars *do* occur. Overall, then, in *Man, the State, and War*, Waltz argues that all three images need to be considered together to determine whether or not wars will occur (see Table 2.2).

Table 2.2 Causes of war for Waltz

Location	Description	Type of cause
First image	Nature of man	Immediate
Second image	International organization of states and societies	Immediate
Third image	International anarchy	Permissive

And because Waltz locates the immediate causes of war in either individual men or states understood as collective men, realists are able to embrace his myth "international anarchy is the permissive cause of war".

Theory of International Politics might be described as a book in which Waltz both builds upon and forgets much of what he wrote in *Man, the State, and War*. What Waltz builds upon is the weight which he gives to international anarchy in explaining international conflict. What he forgets is to include first and second image explanations in his analysis of why wars occur. In this later book, then, there are no serious discussions of individuals or of the internal arrangements of states and society. Sovereign nation-states are Waltz's principle actors, but instead of the complexity they had in *Man, the State, and War*, Waltz now discusses them as (at worst) billiard balls that knock one another around or (at best) firms that freely compete with one another in the international system (Waltz, 1979: 91).

To be fair to Waltz, *Theory of International Politics* is not meant to have the wide sweep of *Man, the State, and War*. Waltz claims that this later book is concerned only with elaborating the working of the international level. But, this later book is in some ways not just an extension of the earlier book. This is because instead of arguing that an understanding of the international requires an understanding of individual and state-level factors as he did in *Man, the State, and War*, Waltz elevates his third image of international anarchy into a principle that at times seems to be downright determinist. International anarchy has much more explanatory purchase in *Theory of International Politics* than it did in *Man, the State, and War*. International anarchy seems to dictate how states in the state system must behave, rather than suggest (as it did in his earlier book) how they *might* behave. This is because in *Theory of International Politics*, international anarchy becomes the structural ordering principle of international politics, from which all state behaviors seem to flow. As a result, *Theory of International Politics* marks a clear break between realism and neorealism.

Without getting into too much dry detail, Waltz's argument in *Theory of International Politics* (summarized in Table 2.3) is this: The behavior of actors in a system depends upon how they are organized. The two major forms of organization that matter for politics are hierarchy and anarchy. Hierarchy describes how politics is organized within states—with a clear center that has a monopoly on the legitimate uses of power and a distribution of labor among various branches of government. Anarchy describes how politics is organized globally, between states

Table 2.3 Waltzian neorealism

	Structure		
	Ordering principle	Formal differentiation	Distribution of power
Domestic	• Hierarchy • Centered	• Heterogeneous • Dissimilar	Monopoly
Global	• Anarchy • Decentered	Heterogeneous	Oligopoly
	Consequences		
	Political processes	Relationships	Goals
Domestic	Specialization	High interdependence	Maximize welfare
Global	• Imitation • Balancing	Low interdependence	Maximize security

in the international system—with no clear center of power, significant power held by at least two states (or poles as they are called in IR theory), and each state functioning like every other state in international politics because there is no division of labor to speak of among states.

Waltz argues that these different structures of hierarchy and anarchy—these different ways of organizing political power—result in different consequences for actors. Again, actors will behave differently depending upon how they are organized. So, for example, within a domestic, hierarchical organization, political processes can be specialized because there are different branches and levels of government, these various government sectors are all highly interdependent upon one another, and their overriding goal is to maximize the welfare of the citizens of their states. In contrast, within a global, anarchical organization, states cannot be specialized because there is just one state doing all the tasks. Therefore, rather than specializing, states in the state system imitate one another's behaviors. They attempt to be as independent of other states as they can be, and they strive to maximize the international security of their state (Waltz, 1979: Chapter 5).

What this means for the everyday practices of states is that domestically, states strive to make life as good as they can for their citizens. Quality of life issues prevail domestically, and, importantly, they can prevail because security issues are mostly solved within states. Certainly, crimes and sometimes rebellions occur, but there is a general agreement within a state as to where authority resides and therefore who can exercise power. With security issues muted within states, states can focus on welfare issues.

In contrast, Waltz argues, security issues are never solved within the state system. Because there is no orderer—because international anarchy prevails—there is never anything or anyone to prevent conflicts from occurring. States are forced to look out for their own interests. The overriding interest of a state is to survive—to carry on being a state. And, Waltz argues, in a situation of structural anarchy, the best chance states have for surviving is to maximize their power. Sure, states could all give up their power to some world government and transform international anarchy into international hierarchy. Then states could cease to worry about security issues and focus on issues of international welfare. But, Waltz (who is often called a structural-, new-, or neo-realist) agrees with other realists that this is a utopian pipe dream. It isn't going to happen. And, even if it did, then we'd be discussing what happens in hierarchical structures, whereas the point of Waltz's *Theory of International Politics* is to elaborate what happens in anarchical structures.

In international anarchy, because all states recognize that it is in their overriding self-interest to maximize their power, that's what Waltz says they do. To do anything else is crazy because a state without enough power is a vulnerable state. And, anyway, it is too scary for states not to try to maximize their power. This is what Waltz calls the "security dilemma." He argues that when one state sees another state trying to increase its power to increase its security, it gets scared, feels threatened, and recognizes that it too must increase its power. But, of course, that scares the other states, and basically there is this mad spiral in which all states are trying to have more power than all other states. According to Waltz, this competition for power among states is not always as dangerous as it at first sounds. It doesn't have to lead to war, so long as no state has significantly more power than another state or coalition of states, so long as states in combination are in a stable "balance of power" arrangement.

But power does not always balance out like this. Waltz argues that power is most likely to balance out in this way when there are only two poles—when there is a bipolar system. When there are more than two poles, things get trickier. Balances are harder to strike. Risks increase. Wars are more likely to occur. International anarchy remains the permissive cause of war (Waltz, 1979: Chapter 6).

Overall, Waltz's two books mythologize international anarchy as the permissive cause of war. The first book explicitly links anarchy to war, while the second book explains state behavior—whether conflictual or merely competitive—from the first principle of international anarchy. And both books reserve a place for fear as what either explains the immediate causes of war (men or states behaving badly) or the seemingly inevitable behaviors of states locked into a competition for power in international anarchy.

The film *Lord of the Flies* cleverly plays with these themes of good and bad individuals, good and bad "states," and differing forms of organization (hierarchy vs. anarchy). As such, it nicely illustrates many of the points Waltz makes in his two books. But, most importantly for our purposes, *Lord of the Flies* invites us to reconsider the use Waltz makes of fear in his analyses of international anarchy. In *Man, the State, and War*, states may fear one another because of the bad behavior of either ruling individuals or rogue states. Fear, in other words, is located in the first or second image. But by the time we get to *Theory of International Politics*, fear seems to be located in the third image—in international anarchy itself because it is anarchy that makes states behave as they do (to maximize their power) and it is consequently this behavior that leads other states to fear them.

Lord of the Flies explores all of these locations of fear, while suggesting one more. Maybe fear is not something fixed in one or more levels of analysis. Maybe fear is not a consequence of state behavior in a system of structural anarchy. Instead, maybe fear is something that is actually missing in a situation of international anarchy, and because it is missing it must be invented and skillfully deployed. Put differently, maybe fear is the final supplement or addition to Waltz's myth that "international anarchy is the permissive cause of war," a supplement not necessarily found in any of his three images (Ashley, 1989).

Lord of the Flies

The film *Lord of the Flies* is based on William Golding's novel of the same name which was published in 1954, the same year Waltz's *Man, the State, and War* was published. The 1963 British version of the film, directed by Peter Brook, was re-released in the British Classics video series in 1999. An American version of the film, directed by Harry Hook, was released in 1994. The American film version makes several critical deviations from Golding's novel that present obstacles to rethinking Waltz's anarchy myth through it (see "Note on the US film *Lord of the Flies*" at the end of this chapter). In contrast, the British version follows Golding's novel more closely and, it must be said, is simply a more powerful presentation of the story. It is for these reasons that I will focus my attention on the British 1963 version of the film.

Lord of the Flies is set during World War II when the United Kingdom was being bombed by Germany. Because of the heavy bombing many English cities experienced, a mass exodus of British children was organized—some to the British countryside and others out of the UK altogether. Such is the plight of the British schoolboys (aged about 5 to 12) whom we encounter in the film. They are presumably being flown from war-torn Britain to Australia when their plane crashes on a remote, uninhabited Pacific island. No adults survive the crash.

The opening photomontage and soundtrack depict the boys' transition from life in England to life on the island. In it are seen and heard the sights and sounds of English school life—boys in a class photo, at their desks, in the dining hall, in chapel, playing cricket, and teachers organizing their activities and watching over them. Then, abruptly, the pace in which images and sounds are introduced quickens, and we see and hear missile launches, war planes, and bombing raids violently inserted into the montage. Finally, we see photos of the boys' planned evacuation, their plane caught in a storm, a map of the Pacific, and the plane crashing near an island. The photomontage ends, and the action begins.

This opening starkly introduces the two worlds of *Lord of the Flies*—the lost world of hierarchy from which the boys have just exited and the island world of anarchy they have just entered. Hierarchy is marked by rules, reason, law and order, all of which are ensured (at least from the boys' point of view) by the presence of grown-ups. Anarchy is unmarked as the film opens. The film is the story of how the boys behave in a situation of anarchy, in a world without adults (see Table 2.4).

How *Lord of the Flies* makes sense of the world is by exploring what happens to boys when they move from one world (the world of school/home/nation-state)

Table 2.4 How does *Lord of the Flies* represent hierarchy and anarchy?

Hierarchy	Anarchy
Characterized by rules, reason, law and order, all of which are guaranteed by the presence of adults	Characterized by the absence of guarantees to order or reason because of the absence of adults

Table 2.5 What is typical and what is deviant in the two worlds of *Lord of the Flies*?

	Familiar world	Island world
Typical	Hierarchy	Anarchy
Deviant	Anarchy	Hierarchy

into another world (the lost island world). What these two worlds represent is a reversal of what the boys are accustomed to as typical and deviant. In the familiar world of school/home/nation-state, what is typical is hierarchy and what is deviant in that world is anarchy. But in the lost island world the boys now find themselves inhabiting, anarchy is typical and hierarchy is deviant (see Table 2.5). How will the boys cope in this deviant, new world of anarchy?

Not surprisingly, the boys' first coping strategy is an attempt to create hierarchy within anarchy. There may be no grown-ups on the island, but that does not mean there has to be an absence of civilized order. As one of the boys puts it, "We've got to have rules and obey them. After all, we're not savages. We're English, and the English are best at everything. So we've got to do the right things." The boys are not only all English. They are all English schoolboys. This means that even though the boys are from different schools (indicated by their different uniforms), they have an implicit if not explicit knowledge of social codes that can be mobilized to create and sustain organizing hierarchies. And this is precisely what the boys draw upon to establish their new order.

The boys elect Ralph as their leader. Ralph is the boy who was responsible for bringing all the stranded boys on the island together by blowing into a conch shell as one would blow on a trumpet. The conch becomes the symbol of rules and rights. Whoever holds the conch at assembly has the right to speak and be heard. Jack, the leader of a group of choirboys from one school, is the only boy who could really challenge Ralph's leadership. Ralph wisely gives Jack control over his choir, and Jack (who seems to be the only boy on the island in possession of a knife) decides that they will be hunters. Piggy, the voice of reason from the old world, is responsible for taking names and minding the little ones. These jobs suit Piggy for, as his name implies, he is physically unfit for much else.

Life goes on rather blissfully for some time. Images of happy boys working together to build shelters, playing games and gathering fruit fill the screen. Jack's boys amuse themselves by exploring the island and trying to kill wild boar. However

Plate 2.1 Ralph blows the conch shell to call the stranded schoolboys to assembly.
Courtesy of Lord of the Flies co, Source: BFI.

they spend their time, all the boys agree that they have one overriding goal in common—to be rescued. They decide to build a fire on the mountain top which they will keep going so that a plane or a ship might see them. Jack volunteers his hunters for this job. The rules seem to be well in place, and everyone seems to be working within them for the common good.

All proceeds well until one day a plane flies overhead, and Ralph and the other boys on the beach realize that the fire has gone out. Jack's hunters are euphoric because they have killed their first wild boar. But because of their increased attention to their "need for meat," they have neglected to uphold their part of the bargain—keeping the fire alight. Jack's boys have shifted their priorities. The film represents this change both visually and musically. Visually, Jack appears increasingly warrior-like as the film proceeds—first with his knife, then his spear, and finally with his painted face. Musically, the peaceful, civilized music Jack's choir sang as they first appeared gives way over the course of the film to a drummed, war-like rendition of their Latin song. In many scenes, a chant about hunting and killing unites Jack's choir/hunters, and not their original song.

It is not surprising that goals would diverge and agreements would be abandoned in the absence of an orderer. As Waltz would remind us, in a situation of structural anarchy, there is nothing or no one to enforce the rules or common goals. Yet, at this stage anyway, there is an orderer, and that orderer is Ralph. He was

Plate 2.2 Jack's choirboys.
Courtesy of Lord of the Flies co, Source: BFI.

elected chief by the other boys. But his interests and those of Jack begin to conflict. Jack is interested in hunting, a skill that will help the boys survive on the island. This is his immediate reality and his immediate aim. In contrast, Ralph is more interested in the longer-term possibiliy of rescue because he does not believe that the boys can survive indefinitely on the island.

As the film proceeds, this conflict of interests is exacerbated until the hierarchy of Ralph as elected chief breaks down because Jack directly challenges him. The challenge begins when Ralph tries to protect Piggy's right to speak because Piggy is holding the conch.

Jack interrupts Piggy: Shut up you fat slug.
Ralph: Jack, let him speak. He's got the conch!
Jack: And you shut up you. Who are you anyway just sitting there telling people what to do? You can't hunt, you can't sing.
Ralph: I'm chief. I was chosen.
Jack: Why should choosing make any difference, telling people what to do?
Ralph: The rules, you're breaking the rules.
Jack: Who cares!
Ralph: Because the rules are the only thing we got.
Jack: Bullocks to the rules.

In this scene, Ralph is right. Indeed, he is too right for his own good. The rules are all the boys have of the hierarchy they attempt to create in this world without grown-ups. But because they don't have any grown-ups—because they don't have anyone whose authority is unchallenged because of their structural position—there is no way to enforce the rules. As Jack proves in this scene, the rules mean nothing without the power of enforcement.

It isn't long after this that the hierarchy which the boys have clung to unravels altogether. Jack leaves the group, going off on his own. He is eventually joined by Roger (a hunter) and then the rest of the hunters. Increasingly, the boys break up into two distinct societies on the island—those organized around the principle of rescue who work at keeping the fire going and those organized around the principle of survival who spend their time hunting wild boar. As time goes on, almost all of the boys join Jack's "tribe." He gives them food. He offers them protection.

And things get even worse from this point. Not only are the boys divided over what goals to prioritize, but they end up in deadly conflict with one another. It seems to begin by humiliating Ralph and Piggy, underscoring their weakness by feeding them bananas when they have asked to share the meat of a kill. Then Jack and his boys steal Piggy's glasses, thereby taking control over the ability to make fire and leaving Ralph and Piggy nothing immediate to offer the boys, apart from the fading

Plate 2.3 Piggy and Ralph.
Courtesy of Lord of the Flies co, Source: Ronald Grant Film Archive.

possibility of rescue. When Ralph and Piggy go to Jack's end of the island in an attempt to get Piggy's glasses back, Jack and his tribe treat them badly by taunting them and threatening them. And then Roger intentionally pushes a rock over the cliff, killing Piggy (the voice of hierarchical reason) who is holding the conch (the symbol of rules and order). Ralph runs away, only to be eventually hunted down by Jack and his tribe.

Jack's tribe smoke Ralph out of the forest by setting it on fire. Ralph scrambles through the forest, pursued by Jack's boys, as the hunting chants of Jack's tribe grow louder and louder in Ralph's head. Eventually, Ralph makes his way to the beach. He falls at the feet of a British naval officer, who has come to investigate the island because of the massive fire. The soundtrack falls silent, as Ralph and the boys pursuing him try to comprehend their situation. The camera focuses on the naval officer and his crew. The soundtrack plays again, this time a trumpet arrangement of the original choir music so sweetly sung by Jack's boys earlier. Anarchy gives way to hierarchy. Order is restored. The stunned boys prepare to reenter the world of enforceable hierarchy that they left so long ago.

Lord of the Flies seems to make a pretty good case for Waltz's myth that "international anarchy is the permissive cause of war" and that, in a world of structural anarchy, the necessary pursuit of survival in this self-help world may well lead to conflict. Whether one goes with Waltz's thesis in *Man, the State, and War*, that an immediate cause of war like human nature (a first image problem) or bad social organization (a second image problem) is needed to supplement international anarchy or his thesis in *Theory of International Politics*, that the structure of anarchy is enough to explain why competition among actors will occur, thereby leading to the possibility of either balancing or war, *Lord of the Flies* seems to support Waltz's myth that "international anarchy is the permissive cause of war."

The film takes us through five moves that support Waltz's myth. First, there is the loss of hierarchy (no adults). Second, there is the attempt to reimpose hierarchy with rules and elections. Third, hierarchy fails because there is no one to enforce the rules. Fourth, conflict breaks out among the boys, resulting in a war between the two groups and the intentional killing of Piggy. Finally, anarchy ends with the reintroduction of adult authority. Even though this is where the film ends, we know that the behavior the boys exhibited on the island will not match their behavior in the world of adults. The music, if nothing else, confirms this.

As compelling a case as this may be for Waltz's thesis, there is a crucial move missing from the above list—a move that puts Waltz's thesis about anarchy into doubt. For, as this missing move demonstrates, it is not just the lack of hierarchy that leads to conflict or that makes it possible. What is missing from this list and what is clearly illustrated in the film is the supplemental function of fear in Waltz's anarchy myth. Without fear, the move from hierarchy to anarchy is not *necessarily* the move from the ability to prevent war to the inability to prevent war (see Box 2.2).

As *Lord of the Flies* tells the story of the boys' departure from hierarchy and their making sense of their lives in anarchy—marking anarchy first by cooperation and then by conflict—it also tells a parallel story about the boys' increasing fear. Certainly, there is the fear of being on an uninhabited island in the aftermath of a plane crash without any adults. But in addition to this rational fear, the film introduces more and more irrational fear. Initially, this fear is something held by the

---

Box 2.2 Where does fear figure in Waltz's myth as enacted in *Lord of the Flies*?

Loss of hierarchy
(symbolized by lack of adults)

Reestablishment of hierarchy with rules and election
(symbolized by the conch shell)

Fear becomes widespread among boys
(symbolized by their belief in the beast)
This is what goes without saying in Waltz's myth

Hierarchy fails
(symbolized by Jack leaving the group and starting a rival group)

Conflict occurs
(Jack's and Ralph's groups fight/Piggy is killed)

Anarchy ends
(symbolized by the rescue of the boys and the reintroduction of adults)

---

little boys. One of them asks early on what the bigger boys are going to do about the "snake-thing."

Ralph: The snake-thing?
Piggy [into whose ear the little boy is speaking for Piggy to speak for him at the assembly]:   Now he says it was a beastie.
Ralph: Beastie? [He and the other boys laugh]
Piggy: A snake-thing, ever so big. He saw it.
Ralph: When?
Piggy: When he was hiding in the jungle in the dark. He says, "When the rain stopped, it turned into one of them things like ropes in the trees and hung in the branches." He says, "Will it come back tonight?""

The boys look scared.

Ralph: But there isn't a beastie. I tell you, there isn't a beast.
Jack: Ralph's right, of course. There isn't a snake-thing. But if there was, we'd hunt and kill it.

In this scene, the beast is introduced by a little boy, and its existence is denied by both Ralph and Jack. But there is a critical difference between how Ralph and Jack deal with the existence of a beast. Ralph sticks firmly to the argument that there is no beast. Jack, in contrast, seems to agree with Ralph, yet he leaves open the possibility that there is a beast by saying that "if there was, we'd hunt and kill it." Something that does not exist does not need to be hunted and killed.

It is Jack, not a little boy, who next brings up the beast. He does so when he defends his hunters for their neglect of the fire when the plane passed overhead. He tells the boys at assembly:

Jack: We're hunters. And if there is a beast, it is my hunters who will protect you from it.

Jack leans down to a little boy, Percival, for whom Jack then speaks.

Jack: He says the beast comes out of the sea.

The boys look scared.

Another boy: My daddy said they hadn't found all the animals in the sea. My daddy said there are animals—what do you call them—that make ink and are hundreds of feet long and eat whales whole.
Someone else shouts: A squid can't come out of the water.
Another boy: Maybe he means it's some kind of ghost.
Another boy: Maybe that's what the beast is—some kind of ghost.
Piggy: I don't believe in no ghosts, ever.
Jack: Who cares what you believe, fatty. [Laughter]
Simon: Maybe there is a beast . . . What I mean is, maybe it's only us.
Someone: Nuts.
Ralph: We should have left this 'til daylight. We're tired. We'll have a vote—on ghosts I mean. And then we'll go back to the shelters. Who thinks there may be ghosts?

Almost all the boys raise their hands.

While Jack is increasingly using the beast as a way to shift the boys' priorities from being rescued on the island to surviving on the island, the fear of the beast has spread from just the little boys to almost all of the boys. And, as Jack realizes, encouraging the boys' belief in and fear of the beast is a good way to challenge Ralph's authority. It is *after* this meeting that Jack says bullocks to the rules, that the hierarchy the boys created on this anarchical island turns competitive rather than cooperative.

Soon after this meeting, the twins Sam and Eric think they see the beast on a mountain top. They saw something swaying in the breeze. They say as they ran down the mountain, the beast followed them and nearly caught them.

Jack: We'll hunt it.

Jack, Ralph, and a group of bigger boys go to hunt the beast. The hunt lasts until after dark, when the boys arrive on the mountain top and see "the beast." They run down the mountain screaming. The "truth" of the beast has now been established. It is only *after* the beast seems to move from fiction to fact that Jack gets fed up with Ralph's rules about fires and rescue and leaves the group, to eventually be joined by his hunters and most of the other boys.

One day, after Jack's tribe has killed another wild boar, Jack cuts off the boar's head and leaves it as a gift for the beast. As Jack and his tribe celebrate their kill late into the night, Simon (who said before that the beast could be us) climbs up the mountain and comes face to face with the beast, without fear. He discovers that "the beast" is a dead paratrooper hanging from a tree. This is why he appears to move. And his parachute is swaying in the breeze. This is what Sam and Eric saw. Simon descends the mountain in the dark. Jack's tribe is celebrating wildly, chanting "kill the beast, cut his throat, spill his blood." They see something move in the brush. Someone says, "It's the beast," and the boys kill it. Of course, it is Simon.

Simon must die because he is the one who has the knowledge that there is no beast, and without a beast, it would be harder for Jack to make his claim to leadership against Ralph. For survival seems extremely urgent when there is a threat. Ralph is no threat. Piggy is no threat. The few little boys they look after are no threat. But the beast is a "real" threat. The beast is what is necessary to make a threat to survival seem real. And even killing Simon, whom Jack claims was the beast in disguise, is not enough to kill the beast. Jack makes this clear as his tribe prepares for another hunt.

Jack: Tomorrow I'll hunt again. Then we'll leave another head for the beast. Some of you will stay and defend the gate. The beast may try to come in. Remember how he crawled. He came disguised. The beast may try and come, even though we gave him the head of our kill. So watch, and be careful.
Boy: But didn't we . . . Didn't we . . .
Jack: No, how could we kill it?
Another boy: He told us. The beast was disguised.

The beast—or the fear it represents—can never be killed because it is a necessary fear. It is necessary for Waltz's anarchy myth to function.

The function of fear in Waltz's anarchy myth

Lord of the Flies not only illustrates the seeming truth of Waltz's anarchy myth—"international anarchy is the permissive cause of war"—but it also shows us what makes Waltz's myth function. As the film illustrates, anarchy alone is insufficient to cause or even allow for conflict. Anarchy requires fear to differentiate the behavior of those acting within it from their behavior within hierarchy. The absence of adults symbolizes the move from hierarchy to anarchy in the film. But hierarchy persists in the absence of adults *until fear is introduced*. Without fear, there is nothing in the film or in Waltz's myth that suggests that anarchy would be conflictual rather than cooperative.

As the film illustrates, fear can be found in any of Waltz's three images. The way Golding's novel is often read is as a testimony to the evilness of human nature that comes out in extreme situations. Man is by nature evil. The rules are all we've got. We had better cling to the rules to avoid behaving like beasts in a state of nature. This is one way to interpret Simon's declaration that the beast may only be us. One can make the case that Jack, especially, is lured to some initial savage state of man.

Plate 2.4 Jack's choir transformed into painted-faced hunters.
Courtesy of Lord of the Files co, Source: Ronald Grant Film Archive.

It is his increasing irrationality and how seductively he presents this irrationality as rational on the island that is the immediate cause of conflict among the boys. Read in this way, fear is a first image problem.

But, of course, Golding's story is an allegory of what is happening among sovereign nation-states during World War II. States, too, are behaving badly. Germany is taking over Europe and bombing the United Kingdom. Because there is no world government to mediate the Allied/Axis dispute, World War II occurs. Jack's tribe can be read as a bad organization that spreads conflict rather than adhering to the initially agreed-upon goal of rescue through cooperative fire building. Because there is no adult to prevent disputes between Jack's wild survivalists and Ralph's rational rescue wannabes, Jack's tribe and Ralph's group come into conflict. This is a second image way of describing the location of fear. Either of these explanations follows from a reading of Waltz's *Man, the State, and War*.

In *Theory of International Politics*, Waltz no longer relies on his first and second images to supplement war. He suggests that anarchy itself is the location of fear. The structure of anarchy means states must compete for power in order to survive in this self-help system. The security dilemma is an attribute of international anarchy, according to Waltz. Because security questions can never be finally resolved in a situation of structural anarchy, competition is unavoidable and conflict is likely. So, on this third image reading of *Lord of the Flies*, the boys end up in deadly conflict with one another because fear is located in the insecurity of international anarchy itself.

While each of these locations of fear at first seems to make a lot of sense, none of them can be persuasively upheld when we remember that prior to the introduction of the beast—the representation in the film of fear—the boys got on well (see Box 2.2). They did not at all seem like boys behaving badly because they were evil by nature, so the film fails to make the case for fear being located in the first image. Nor do they organize themselves badly into competitive and increasingly conflictual groups before they believe in the beast and vote it into existence. So a second image explanation of fear is also discredited. It is only after most of the boys embrace the fear of the beast that conflict occurs within anarchy. Anarchy itself, then, is never the location of fear. Anarchy does not create the fear that Waltz theorizes in *Theory of International Politics*. Rather, *fear creates the effects that Waltz attributes to anarchy—prioritizing survival, self-help over cooperation, and either conflict or competitive balancing.* According to the film, then, the source of fear is not internal to any of the three images—individuals, internal social and political organizations, or anarchy. So where is fear located?

To think about this question, let's reexamine Simon's declaration that the beast may only be one of us. Simon is the one boy who knows the "truth" about the beast—that there is no beast, that the beast is but a dead paratrooper, and that the boys have

Plate 2.5 Jack transformed from head choirboy into tribal leader.
Courtesy of Lord of the Flies co, Source: BFI.

33

nothing to fear except (as the old saying goes) fear itself. Simon recognizes that the boys are afraid, and he recognizes that the boys are probably just scaring one another. The boys in various ways invent the beast—by land, then by sea, and then by air—as something to fear. But the fear isn't a fear of human nature or bad social and political organizations or international anarchy. The fear is the fear of fear itself. By inventing this fear among themselves and then deploying it against themselves, the boys bring about all the effects of international anarchy that Waltz predicts in his two books. But, crucially, before the boys embrace and deploy this fear, none of Waltz's predictions about international anarchy are actualized.

Fear, then, is the final supplement to Waltz's theory. It is not a first image problem. It is not a second image problem. And, it is not (as so many IR theorists have been persuaded to believe) a third image problem systematically built into the structure of international anarchy. *Fear is what is always missing from Waltz's theory.* But without adding fear, none of the competitive and potentially conflictual things Waltz predicts will occur in a system of structural anarchy do occur. Put differently, the ways in which Waltz deploys the myth "international anarchy is the permissive cause of war" make no sense without Waltz's theories being supplemented by fear, a fear that is *not* a necessary attribute of any of his three images (see Table 2.6).

Since this is the case, then it is important to look at how fear is characterized by Waltz. Waltz characterizes fear is as something that always divides people, states and societies, and worlds. Even if fear leads to balancing among states (something that could not be illustrated in the film because Ralph's group never had the power to compete with Jack's group), this balancing is never a cooperative endeavor. It is always the result of fear. But there is absolutely *nothing* in either of Waltz's books that ever makes the case for theorizing fear in this way. Fear simply is assumed to be divisive.

What if fear functioned differently? What if fear united people for good rather than divided them for evil (or even benign) competition? International anarchy would not look the same. Anarchy would mean something very different in IR theory.

Table 2.6 The locations of fear in *Lord of the Flies*

Location	Description	Illustration
First image	Human nature	Jack and his followers' increasing savagery
Second image	International organization of states and societies	Jack's bad tribe against Ralph's good tribe
Third image	International anarchy	Competitive, self-help system in which boys create security dilemma on island
None of Waltz's images	Irrationally generated by the boys themselves and externalized	The beast

Anarchy, however much it was supplemented by fear, would not be a permissive cause of war because war would not be the likely outcome of a fear that united people around a good cause.

It is this fear functioning for cooperative ends that we find in the neoidealist myth about international anarchy. This is the myth we will explore in our next chapter.

Suggestions for further thinking

Topic 1 Neorealism

Waltz's *Theory of International Politics* is widely regarded as the book which laid the theoretical foundation for the IR tradition of neorealism. There is an abundance of commentary on this subject. Some classic statements include Robert O. Keohane's 1986 edited volume *Neorealism and its Critics*. This book reproduces several chapters from *Theory of International Politics* and includes a wide array of criticisms of Waltz's work, from institutionalist to critical theory to postmodern perspectives. More recently, Barry Buzan, Charles Jones, and Richard Little collaborated on a book that is not so much a critique of Waltz's work as it is a critical extension of it. The authors make the case for a selective Waltzian neorealism, one that both drops some of Waltz's ideas and supplements Waltz's ideas with their own. What is missing from these traditional critiques of neorealism are any sustained gender analyses of Waltz's work. Christine Sylvester's book *Feminist Theory and International Relations in a Postmodern Era* and J. Ann Tickner's chapter in *Gender and International Relations* correct this oversight.

Suggested readings

Barry Buzan, Charles Jones, and Richard Little (1993) *The Logic of Anarchy: Neorealism to Structural Realism*. New York: Columbia University Press.

Robert O. Keohane (ed.) (1986) *Neorealism and its Critics*. New York: Columbia University Press.

Christine Sylvester (1994) *Feminist Theory and International Relations in a Postmodern Era*. Cambridge: Cambridge University Press, especially chapter 3.

J. Ann Tickner (1992) *Gender in International Relations: Feminist Perspectives on Achieving Global Security*. New York: Columbia University Press, especially chapter 2.

Topic 2 The uses of fear in IR Theory

Richard Ashley's 1989 engagement with Waltzian neorealism argues not only that "statecraft is mancraft" but that fear is a vital supplement to Waltz's theory of international anarchy. Many of the themes initially expressed by Ashley are picked up on and applied more generally by David Campbell in his work on international security.

Suggested reading

Richard K. Ashley (1989) "Living on Borderlines: Man, Poststructuralism, and War," in James Der Derian and Michael Shapiro (eds) *International/Intertextual Relations: Postmodern Readings of World Politics*. Lexington, MA: Lexington Books, pp. 259–321.

David Campbell (1999) *Writing Security*, 2nd edition. Minneapolis: University of Minnesota Press.

Note on the US film of *Lord of the Flies*

If you can't find the British version of *Lord of the Flies*, it is best to read William Golding's novel (which is worth reading anyway) rather than turning to the 1994 American version of the film directed by Harry Hook. The American version makes many critical deviations from Golding's book which change the motivations for the boys' actions on the island and (most importantly for our purposes) which change the function of fear. First, the boys in the American version are all from the same American military academy. They already know one another, they have a pre-established social hierarchy and rigid military hierarchy, and they bring values like the importance of conflict and survival to the island rather than developing them on the island because of their changed circumstances. Second, a wounded adult (Captain Benson) survives the plane crash. His presence and his possible recovery mean that hierarchy may be guaranteed by an adult. This doesn't happen because (bizarrely) Captain Benson rushes off in the middle of the night in a feverish state to take refuge in a cave. Some of the boys think he has died. But, as Simon discovers, it is Captain Benson who is "the monster." Finally and most importantly, fear is not the motivation for the breakdown of the boys' hierarchy and their entering into a savage anarchy. Jack leaves the group when Ralph criticizes him for letting the fire burn out. This is well before there is widespread fear of "the monster."

Idealism

Is there an international society?

If the myth "anarchy is the permissive cause of war" suggests that conflict is an inevitable aspect of international affairs so long as anarchy prevails, then the myth "there is an international society" offers some hope that the conflictual aspects of international anarchy—and possibly international anarchy itself—can be overcome. According to this myth, transforming international politics from conflictual to cooperative does not necessitate moving from anarchy to hierarchy—from an international system without an orderer to an international system with an orderer. Instead, all it requires is mediating or replacing anarchy with community. In other words, world government may not be the only way out of anarchy. International community—a formal or informal collective and cooperative set of social relationships among sovereign nation-states—may be an alternative to world government and an alternative to international anarchy.

This way of thinking about international community is most commonly associated with the IR tradition of idealism (a subset of the larger tradition of liberalism). Idealists believe that there is a basic goodness to people that can be corrupted by bad forms of organization. These bad types of organization are found at the level of the state and society. It is these bad forms of organization that divide people and lead to misunderstandings among them (see Table 3.1). If people could only be organized in ways that allow them to really, truly, and honestly communicate with one another, then they could see what they have in common and unite around common standards of goodness, truth, beauty, and justice. Or (somewhat less optimistically) they could at least put into place rules and laws to temper conflict and facilitate cooperation. Either way, good organizations can lead to good changes in people, all of whom are basically good—have a good moral core—even if they occasionally behave badly. And good forms of organization are possible not only domestically but internationally because even international social relations are marked much more by harmony (when there is pure communication) than by conflict.

Idealism is arguably the founding tradition of international relations theory (Walker, 1993). Even so, its influence over IR scholars and practitioners has waned over the years. Idealism is seen to have failed to "make the world safe for democracy" as President Woodrow Wilson claimed it could during World War I, even when its principles were institutionalized into international organizations like the League of Nations and later the United Nations. Realism won most of the important intellectual debates during World War II and the Cold War. And when its usefulness was threatening to fade away, Kenneth Waltz reinvented it as neorealism in his *Theory of International Politics*, thereby providing IR theorists with a seemingly timeless account of the behavior of actors in a situation of structural anarchy (see Chapter 2).

Table 3.1 Idealism

Actors	Nature of actors
Humans	All morally good
States and societies	Good—if organized through *pure* communication Bad—if organized through *impure* communication

However, as the Cold War thawed during the latter half of the 1980s and the Berlin Wall came down in 1989, Waltz's timeless truths about competition, conflict, and balancing in a system of structural anarchy no longer rang true. The East–West rivalry was over, arms control agreements seemed to proliferate faster than armaments, democracy spread internationally, and human rights and humanitarian intervention were given practical and not just rhetorical emphasis by many sovereign nation-states. These were not outcomes Waltz or any other realist or neorealist anarchy theorist would have predicted. Sure, if international anarchy had been replaced by international hierarchy—by a world government—then maybe these cooperative practices could be accounted for. But international anarchy as realists and neorealists defined it persisted in the aftermath of the Cold War, and neither realist nor neorealist scholars could satisfactorily explain the cooperative behavior they observed, especially in the realm of international security.

But while realist and neorealist scholars were stunned by some post-Cold War developments, neoidealist and (more broadly) neoliberal scholars were not. The basic international harmony of social and/or economic relations seemed to them to explain why we were suddenly experiencing a more cooperative international environment. One neoidealist scholar in particular—Charles Kegley—made the argument that the post-Cold War world looked very much like the world Woodrow Wilson envisioned decades before. Kegley first made this argument in his 1993 article "The Neoidealist Moment in International Studies?: Realist Myths and the New International Realities." He later clarified and crystallized it in his essay "The Neoliberal Challenge to Realist Theories of World Politics: An Introduction" (1995).

In this chapter I will explore how in both essays Kegley utilizes the myth "there is an international society" by "re-envisioning" Woodrow Wilson's classical idealist outlook for the post-Cold War era (Debrix, 1999). The myth that "there is an international society" presumably functions through a domestic analogy—by drawing a parallel between what happens within states in their domestic relations and what happens among states in their international relations. For Kegley, this means that social relations and proper societies do not stop at the borders of sovereign nation-states. If we can have social spaces within states, there is nothing preventing us from also have social spaces among states.

I will elaborate on Kegley's use of the myth "there is an international society" by summarizing what Kegley's essays say, relating it to the myth "there is an international society," and reconsidering the myth function of Kegley's arguments about post-Cold War international politics through the film *Independence Day*.

Set in a post-Cold War world, *Independence Day* comically and upliftingly tells the story of an alien invasion of the earth—an invasion which has the effect of uniting humanity against the common enemy of the alien invaders. It demonstrates that, even in the absence of an orderer—in an anarchical world—states can set aside their differences, unite for the greater good, and overcome international anarchy. As such, it illustrates many of the basic tenets of neoidealism that Kegley claims epitomize this post-Cold War world. Yet in telling this story, the film raises the question "Is there anything 'international' about Kegley's 'international society' or is it just an extension of one state's domestic society?" If the answer is that it is just an extension of one state's domestic society, then Kegley's supposed domestic analogy does not draw a parallel between a domestic and an international space. Rather than a domestic analogy, it is simply a domestication of international space. In other words, *Independence Day* suggests that the supposed post-Cold War "international society" may just be an enlarged domestic society. And if that is the case, then there is not necessarily an international society because there is nothing collective or collaborative about one state domesticating international space.

What does the myth say?

The most striking thing about Kegley's two essays is that they never make an argument for the myth "there is an international society." International society is simply assumed to exist. Its existence needs no defending. Arguments in defence of an international society simply go without saying. But if Kegley makes no argument for an international society and only mentions international society in passing in his essays, what makes his texts appropriate for illustrating this myth? The answer is that without assuming that an international society exists, the rest of Kegley's arguments make no sense. In other words, the existence of an international society is vital to Kegley's explanation of cooperation in a post-Cold War world.

Kegley's essays tell the story of post-Cold War cooperation not by focusing on the myth "there is an international society" but by focusing on the duelling traditions of realism and idealism. He acknowledges that during the Cold War, realist principles seemed to make sense. They explained things like "the lust for power, appetite for imperial expansion, struggle for hegemony, a superpower arms race, and obsession with national security" that marked "the conflict-ridden fifty-year system between 1939 and 1989" (Kegley, 1993: 133; 1995: 6). But then the Cold War ended. It was "the end of the world as we know it."

This led Kegley to wonder "whether it is time to revise, reconstruct, or, more boldly, reject orthodox realism" (Kegley, 1995: 3; 1993: 134). His answer is yes, for two reasons. One is that orthodox realism is at best incomplete because it cannot satisfactorily explain post-Cold War cooperation among states (Kegley, 1993: 134–5; 1995: 5–9; see Table 3.2). The other reason is that there is an existing tradition of

Table 3.2 What can realism explain and what can't realism explain?

Realism can explain	Realism cannot explain
Cold War conflictual activities among sovereign nation-states, e.g.:	Post-Cold War realities of cooperation among sovereign nation-states, e.g.:
"lust for power"	"march of democracy"
"appetite for imperial expansion"	"increase in liberal free trade agreements"
"struggle for hegemony"	"renewed role of the United Nations"
"superpower arms race"	"proliferation of arms control agreements"
"obsession with national security"	"international humanitarianism"

Source: Kegley, 1993, 1995

international theory that better explains this cooperation, and this is an idealism or liberalism that has its roots in the ideas of Woodrow Wilson.

Kegley argues the idealist worldview can be summed up in the following core principles:

1 Human nature is essentially "good" or altruistic, and people are therefore capable of mutual aid and collaboration.
2 The fundamental human concern for the welfare of others makes progress possible (that is, the Enlightenment's faith in the possibility of improving civilization was reaffirmed).
3 Bad human behavior is the product not of evil people but of evil institutions and structural arrangements that motivate people to act selfishly and to harm others—including making war.
4 War is not inevitable and its frequency can be reduced by eradicating the anarchical conditions that encourage it.
5 War and injustice are international problems that require collective or multilateral rather than national efforts to eliminate them.
6 International society must reorganize itself institutionally to eliminate the anarchy that makes problems such as war likely.

(Kegley, 1995: 4)

Read together, these six principles illustrate a movement in idealist theorizing from the individual level to the state level to the international level. They begin by focusing on theories of human nature, then try to account for human behavior not because of human nature but because of institutional and structural arrangements (how institutions and structures are organized), finally concluding that international society can be rearranged so that bad behavior (this time of states as well as of individuals) can be lessened if not eliminated. These are the very same three levels of analysis that Waltz identified in his book *Man, the State, and War.* But Waltz and someone like Kegley have very different ways of thinking about these three images. Most importantly for our purposes is how they think about the third image, the international level.

For Waltz, the international level is where anarchy is located. And because Waltz argues that anarchy is the permissive cause of war, then the international level is where war is located. In contrast, for Kegley, the international level is not where war is located. Violence and war are never finally located in any of the three images for Kegley. This is because war and conflict—bad behavior—can be eliminated if only political and social arrangements are better organized. In the place of anarchy at the international level, Kegley is keen to substitute "international society." If organized properly, international society can "eliminate the anarchy that makes problems such as war possible" (Kegley, 1995: 4). (See Table 3.3.)

This is precisely what Kegley implies is occurring in a post-Cold War era. He cites "the march of democracy" within states around the globe, increases in liberal free trade arrangements that assume trust and the benefit of all, strengthening of international law, the renewed role of international institutions like the United Nations to undertake collective security initiatives, the proliferation of arms control agreements, and international humanitarian responses to state human rights

Table 3.3 How do Waltz and Kegley differently characterize international politics?

Waltz	Kegley
International politics is anarchical, and anarchy is the permissive cause of war. Therefore, war and conflict are ultimately located at the international level and cannot be eliminated because anarchy cannot be eliminated.	International politics can be reorganized around international society rather than international anarchy, potentially eliminating problems like war and conflict without replacing international anarchy with international hierarchy (world government).

violations as evidence of the fulfillment of Wilson's specific idealist predictions about what international politics would look like (Kegley, 1993: 135–8; 1995: 10–14).

And so, to the six core principles that Woodrow Wilson embraced, Kegley offers a seventh, post-Cold War neoidealist principle:

> 7 This goal [of reorganizing international society so that it can eliminate the anarchy that makes problems such as war likely] is realistic because history suggests that global change and cooperation are not only possible but empirically pervasive.
>
> (Kegley, 1995: 4; my parentheses)

These post-Cold War developments are vitally important to Kegley. They seem to demonstrate empirically that neoidealism is a theory that describes things as they really are in the post-Cold War era, something idealism failed to do for its historical era. Even more importantly, they demonstrate that "the motives that animate the goals of state are not immutable. They *can* change" (Kegley, 1993: 135–7;1995: 11; italics in original). Conflict is not an inevitability in international life.

Kegley's point is not to dispute that the Cold War was a era marked by conflict and the disposition of the Eastern and Western blocs to go to war with one another. That happened. He accepts that. But, he argues, now that the Cold War is over, states are behaving cooperatively. That means they changed from being conflictual toward one another to being cooperative toward one another. And, given the history of superpower conflict during the Cold War, this change is a very big deal.

Why has the behavior of sovereign nation-states in a post-Cold War era become so cooperative? Before answering this question, let's just remind ourselves that the answer is *not* because the international system changed from being anarchical to hierarchical. The answer is *not* that during the Cold War there was no world government and in the post-Cold War era there is a world government. There is still no world government. Waltz believed that cooperation around security issues could occur if anarchy gave way to hierarchy. How does Kegley explain post-Cold War cooperation in the absence of hierarchy—in the absences of an orderer?

Part of Kegley's answer is that these changes from conflictual to cooperative behavior among states follow from a change in the international organization of states. The Cold War bipolar world system of two opposed blocs locked into a deadly battle with one another has given way to a new form of international organization, and this begins to explain why cooperation is occurring. It was the bad organization of international politics during the Cold War that kept idealist (and now neoidealist) principles of cooperation from being realized.

On this point, Kegley is not claiming that the end of the Cold War will mark the end of conflict altogether. He acknowledges, for example, that not all of Wilson's ideas make sense for the post Cold-War era. For example, Wilson did not think through all the implications and uses to which self-determination (letting people decide for themselves how and by whom they would be governed) might be put, and this has led to a lot of bloodshed within and among states in a post-Cold War era (Kegley, 1993: 137). But what it does mean is that—while it will never be a perfect state of affairs—with the end of the Cold War, states are now engaged in restoring "a place for morality in foreign policy" (Kegley, 1993: 138). They are pursuing collective, cooperative interests that all states have always had in common—like peace, justice, and a better way of life. These are interests about welfare within and among states rather than warfare among states. And these moral goals that lead to a better way of life for people and states are as much in states' individualistic national interests as they are in their collective interests (Kegley, 1993: 142). Because the world has been reorganized, they are realizable once again.

But for idealism and neoidealism, moral progress among sovereign nation-states does not result merely from the reorganizing of relations among sovereign nation-states. If the world changed from a bipolar system to a differently organized system, this in itself would not necessarily account for increased cooperation. For even realists and neorealists like Waltz acknowledge these changes within anarchy. Something else is at work in Kegley's argument, as it was in Wilson's, that makes cooperation possible. That "something else" is an international society. For a Neoidealist like Kegley, international society is the space in which moral progress occurs. But where does this international society come from? For any brand of idealist—including Kegley—it comes from drawing a domestic analogy. If there is society within states, then there can be (and in a post-Cold War world there is) society among states.

To understand the importance of this domestic analogy to the myth "there is an international society," let's explore two aspects of it. First, how does a domestic society serve as a space in which moral progress can occur? Second, how is this society "transferred" from the domestic or state level to the international level?

For a Neoidealist, the sovereign nation-state is not just a political space. It is also a social space. Indeed, government is the formal institutional expression of social relations within a state. If the state is organized in a good way, then it can organize its domestic social relations so that moral progress can occur within it. What is a good form of state organization for a Neoidealist, and how can this good form of state organization enable moral progress in its domestic society? For a Neoidealist, the best form of governmental organization is democracy.

Democracy is the best form of organization because it is the least restrictive on its people. It is the least repressive. It is the form of governance that most encourages freedom of expression among its people. Democracy is government by the people. So the voice of any democratic sovereign nation-state is really the collective voice of its people. This is important because, as all idealists believe, people are basically good. If they are free to express their goodness within their state, then

Figure 3.1 Democratically organized state and society

this goodness moves up from the individual level (good people) to the state level (good state). Furthermore, good people within a democratic state have a good influence on others within that state—those citizens who are behaving badly. Moral progress occurs within democratic sovereign nation-states, then, because this good form of political and social organization means that citizens behaving well "enlighten" citizens behaving badly. Selfishness diminishes, as does the motivation to do harm to one's fellow citizens, so long as people are free to express their internal goodness. And this purity of communication is something that the democratic state ensures (Figure 3.1).

Of course, not all sovereign nation-states are democratic. Some of them are organized autocratically—with state authority flowing from unenlightened governmental elites onto its repressed people. Neoidealists believe that it is these sorts of autocratic governments that cause conflict in international politics. They are the ones that don't work for the collective good because they don't really know what the collective good is, as they are unenlightened by their good people. They tell their citizens what to do rather than listening to them and representing their moral interests (Figure 3.2). If only these autocratic sovereign nation-states could be reorganized internally to become democratic, then the good people within them could enlighten their wayward leaders. This is why Woodrow Wilson wanted to "make the world safe for democracy."

Figure 3.2 Autocratically organized state and society

This answers the question "how does a domestic society serve as a space in which moral progress can occur?" What about the second question—"how is this society 'transferred' from the domestic or state level to the international level?"

Neoidealists offer two answers to this second question. The classic answer—Wilson's answer—is that by "making the world safe for democracy," democratic states will have an influence on autocratic states (either through benevolent enlightenment or though fighting just wars against bad governments to liberate their good people), transform them into democratic states, and we will end up with an international society of democratic states. If democracy is a form of governance that expresses the will of the people and if all states are democratic, then the individual "domestic societies" within states become one big collective "international society" among states (Figure 3.3).

Kegley accepts this answer and adds to it. He is excited about the international "march of democracy" in a post-Cold War era in part because democracies almost never wage war against each other (Kegley, 1995: 10). All this proves Wilson's point that democratic states develop international social relationships among themselves that are cooperative rather than conflictual.

In addition to this, though, Kegley stresses the influence of cross-border communication in connecting people within domestic spaces and lessening the separations among peoples. As Kegley puts it,

> People matter . . . public sentiment is captured instantaneously in our age of global communications knit together by cables, the airwaves, and the fax machine. The distinction between domestic and foreign affairs has broken down. . . . This also follows Wilson's belief that lowering barriers between countries would be a barrier to warfare.
>
> (Kegley, 1995: 11)

With all this communication among good people, domestic differences are giving way to common interests. Because the goodness of people is communicated, warfare

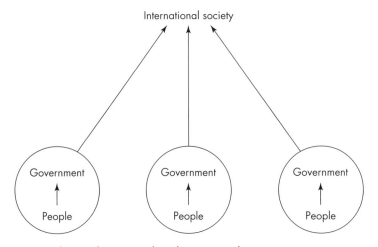

Figure 3.3 How does Wilson enact the "domestic analogy"?

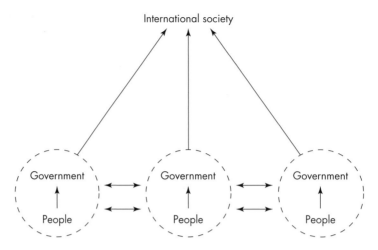

Figure 3.4 How does Kegley enact the "domestic analogy"?

(which is an outgrowth of an inability to communicate the goodness of people) is on the decline. In this international society—a society composed of states but also primarily of the people within states—moral progress is occurring, as people de-emphasize warfare and reemphasize welfare (Figure 3.4).

This is how Kegley transfers social relations that occur within states to social relations that occur among states. By analogy to domestic society, "there is an international society." It is this international society that, for Kegley, explains cooperation in the post-Cold War era. And it is Kegley's myth of post-Cold War international society that is explored in the film *Independence Day*.

Independence Day

The opening sequence of *Independence Day* sets the stage for an action/adventure story in which moral good triumphs over irredeemable evil. The camera's first image is of the US flag flying on the moon. From the flag, the camera takes us to a plaque left by US astronauts inscribed with the words "We came in peace for all mankind." The camera slowly zooms in on the word "peace." Then the moon trembles. A shadow passes over the moon. We follow the shadow to the edge of the moon until a shot of the earth appears in center frame. Entering our frame from the top is an alien spacecraft. It is this spacecraft that is casting this long shadow over the moon. Cut to white. Cut to an exterior of the Research for Extraterrestrial Intelligence Institute in New Mexico. Cut to interior shot. A young man is practicing his putting inside the listening station. Hi-tech equipment fills the room. The man hears a signal that we know and he suspects is being emitted by aliens. In the background, we hear R.E.M. singing "It's the end of the world as we know it, and I feel fine." This action takes place on July 2.

This opening sequence tells us a lot about the world of *Independence Day* and the struggles to come. The elements that the film will use to make sense of the world—humans vs. aliens, peace vs. conflict, and purity of communication vs. corrupted communication—are all evident in this sequence. *Independence Day* is not only a comically styled remake of an outer-space B movie, it is also the perfect script for telling Kegley's neoidealist tale of international cooperation in a post-Cold War era. And, most importantly for our purposes, the film offers us clues—even in this opening sequence—as to how to rethink functionally the myth "there is an international society."

On the heels of this opening sequence, *Independence Day* introduces us to an ensemble cast and their various interlinking storylines. The film gives us not one hero, but at least four (all of whom happen to be male) and possibly many more (including some women). The four central heroes are President Bill Whitmore, David, Steve, and Russell. President Whitmore is a veteran fighter pilot from the Gulf War. He is young. He is liberal. And he is moral. His morality is testified to by his wife who reminds the president that he is a bad liar. "Stick to the truth," she tells him. "That's what you're good at." President Whitmore represents the incorruptibility of communication. He cannot tell a lie—or, really, he cannot tell a lie and get away with it. It is President Whitmore who will take the lead in organizing the world's response to the alien invasion.

We find our next hero, David, playing chess with his aging father in New York's Central Park. David is a good son, and he was a good husband. Part of his story is that he has been divorced from the president's assistant, Connie, for four years but he still honors his commitment to their marriage. A sign of this is he still wears his wedding ring. David works as a computer troubleshooter for a satellite television company. He is also a committed environmentalist who, for example, rides a bike rather than drives a car and ensures that all his colleagues recycle their rubbish.

It is David who, in trying to restore uninterrupted service to his TV station's customers, discovers the alien signal hidden in the US satellites. At first, he is comforted to find that the signal is reducing itself and will disappear in seven hours. But when he sees the alien spacecraft—now broken up into pieces assembled over the world's major cities—he realizes that the signal he has found is an alien countdown to the destruction of humankind. He explains how the signal works in a conversation with his boss.

David: It's like chess. First you strategically position your pieces. Then when the timing's right you strike. See. They're positioning themselves all over the world using this one signal to synchronize their efforts. Then, in approximately six hours, the signal's gonna disappear and the countdown's gonna be over.
Boss: And then what?
David: Checkmate.

David goes to Washington, DC so that he can warn his ex-wife and the president. David is a morally good man who understands the technical workings of impure/alien communication. It becomes his task to disable this corrupted alien communication. He does so by planting a virus in the alien computer, thereby disabling the alien forcefields around the alien ships that have protected them from attack.

Plate 3.1 An alien spaceship over Manhattan.
Courtesy of the Ronald Grant Film Archive © Centropolis Entertainment.

It is our next hero Steve, a pilot in the US military who dreams of flying the spaceshuttle for NASA, who flies himself and David in an alien craft into the belly of the alien mothership where David plants his virus and thereby disables the alien defensive shields. Steve is our man of courage and adventure who actively unites goodness of purpose (the president's agenda) with technical know-how (David's plan to plant the virus).

While Steve (like President Whitmore) is our legitimate military hero, our final hero, Russell, is anything but legitimate. He is a drunken cropduster who fought in the "wrong war"—Vietnam. And he is a local laughing stock because he insists that 10 years earlier he was abducted by aliens. But Russell redeems himself when, fighting in the alien counteroffensive, he flies his plane with an undetachable live bomb into the body of the alien ship, destroying it. Russell, then, was always a good man who spoke the truth. He was just misunderstood. (See Table 3.4.)

As this plot and presentation of characters demonstrate, *Independence Day* makes sense of the world by closely following a neoidealist script. What is typical of this world is that it is inhabited by morally good humans who, when properly understood through good communication, are able to lead good moral, peaceful lives. The humans we are introduced to are all US citizens. Part of their ability to express their goodness, the film hints, is because they are organized in a moral way, in a democratic sovereign nation-state. So, like neoidealism, the film makes sense of the world by assuming that good people do good things in good organizations. This is also what is typical of the world (Box 3.1).

Table 3.4 The heroes in *Independence Day*

Hero	What makes him heroic
US President Bill Whitmore	This president cannot tell a lie and therefore symbolizes the incorruptibility of communication. As such, he is able to conceive of a morally just plan to beat the aliens and to mobilize a moral society through pure communication.
David, the computer troubleshooter for a satellite television company	He is a morally good man who understands the technical workings of impure/alien communication well enough to disable them. He does this by planting a virus in the alien computer.
Steve, the US military fighter pilot	A man of courage and adventure who actively unites goodness of purpose (the president's agenda) with technical know-how (David's plan to plant the virus) by flying an alien craft into the mothership.
Russell, the Vietnam veteran who is now a drunken cropduster and who claims to have been abducted by aliens years ago	Russell sacrifices himself for his children and the rest of humanity by carrying out a suicide mission that destroys an alien ship. He proves that he is a good man who was always speaking the truth but who was just misunderstood.

Box 3.1 What is typical in the world of *Independence Day*?

- Good people do good deeds in good organizations.
- Bad things follow from impaired communication.
- Human beings are morally progressive.

But then, just as in the aftermath of the Cold War, the world as we know it ends. In the historical Cold War script, evil (represented in the US view by the communist threat) is "defeated." But in this cinematic post-Cold War, post-communist script of *Independence Day*, a new evil is introduced. This new evil is the aliens.

The aliens are not initially treated as if they are evil. Because the moral goodness of human beings is assumed by neoidealism and by the characters in the film, it is not surprising that the film begins by extending this presumption of moral goodness to the aliens. Early on, the president addresses the nation, saying "The question of whether or not we are alone in the universe has been answered. Although it's understandable that many of us feel a sense of hesitation or even fear, we must attempt to reserve judgment." "To reserve judgment" here means to not assume the worst about the aliens but to assume the best about them until there is clear evidence to the contrary. Throughout, he resists the advice of the secretary of defense to attack the alien craft.

Steve echoes this sentiment when he tells his girlfriend Jasmine, "I really don't believe they (the aliens) flew over 90 billion light years to come down here and start a fight, to get rowdy." These views are widespread throughout the government and among the public. Keeping in mind that firing guns into the air can be a sign of celebration in Los Angeles, a local newscaster tells his audience "Once again the LAPD is asking Los Angelinos not to fire their guns at the visitor spacecraft. You may inadvertently trigger an inner-stellar war." And throughout the US at least, some groups of people gather to "party" with the aliens.

Because the aliens are assumed to be good by nature, the president authorizes an attempt to communicate with them—to express to the aliens that the earthlings mean them no harm. Communication itself is believed to be pure. Indeed, it is the president as we know who symbolizes the incorruptibility of communication. Not knowing how to communicate with the aliens, the government sends "Welcome Wagon"—a military plane with enormous light panels—up to greet the alien ship. The aliens fire on and destroy "Welcome Wagon," just as the president learns from David that the alien signal is a countdown to an alien attack. The president's bad decision to send up Welcome Wagon comes from having incomplete information. Communication was impaired, and bad things followed from that. The aliens proceed to destroy many major cities worldwide. The president and others (including David) flee on Air Force One. July 2 comes to an end.

Even in the face of all of this alien destruction of the earth, in the president's mind lingers the hope that the aliens' bad behavior is not attributable to the aliens being evil creatures. Yes, the president orders a counterattack against the aliens

Plate 3.2 The aliens destroy Washington, DC, and cities around the world.
Courtesy of the Ronald Grant Film Archive © Centropolis Entertainment.

on July 3, one that is justified even from a neoidealist point of view because it is defensive. Yet even when this counterattack with conventional weapons fails miserably, the president is still not persuaded by the secretary of defense to use nuclear weapons against the aliens. For while it is acceptable from a neoidealist perspective to defend one self in the face of aggression, it is not acceptable to attempt to annihilate a species that could be morally progressive. The president must know for sure whether the aliens are morally good or bad. He gets his answer when Steve brings a live alien to Area 51, where the president and his entourage have assembled.

An Area 51 scientist explains to the president that the aliens are very much like humans. Their bodies are frail like human bodies. But they lack vocal cords. They communicate through telepathy, through extrasensory perception. As a group of scientists are examining the live alien Steve has brought in, the alien "captures" one of them by first capturing his mind. He does this by looking into the scientist's eyes. He then manipulates the scientist's vocal cords to speak to the president and other onlookers.

Alien: Release me. Release me.
President: I know there is much we can learn from each another if we can negotiate a truce. We can find a way to co-exist. Can there be a peace between us?
Alien: Peace. No peace.
President: What is it you want us to do?
Alien: Die. Die.

Plate 3.3 The President with Area 51 scientists.
Courtesy of the Ronald Grant Film Archive © Centropolis Entertainment.

Then the alien links up telepathically with the president. Military personnel shoot the alien, wounding it enough for it to release the tormented president. The president speaks again.

President: I saw his thoughts. I saw what they're planning to do. They're like locusts. They're moving from planet to planet, their whole civilization. After they've consumed every natural resource, they move on. And we're next.

A soldier shoots and kills the alien.

President: Nuke 'em. Let's nuke the bastards.

The president's decision to "nuke the bastards" may seem like it veers from the neoidealist script into a more realist or neorealist one. Conflict marks the relationship between the humans and the aliens. The aliens want to annihilate the humans, and now the president wants to annihilate the aliens. Can this ever be justified in a neoidealist world?

   The answer is yes because the aliens are beyond the moral boundary of goodness and cannot be morally recuperated. It would not have been neoidealist for the president to just assume the aliens were bastards and to nuke them earlier, as the very realist secretary of defense advised him to do. But with all barriers to pure communication between the president and the alien removed through telepathy, the president knows for sure that the aliens are not morally progressive. They will not negotiate. They have done this before, to other species on other planets. The aliens are morally bad. They deserve to die. Defending the human species is a just cause. So is annihilating a morally unprogressive species. None of this contradicts the neoidealist principle that humans are morally good. For, as the president learns, there is nothing *morally* human about the aliens. And that is what matters to a neoidealist. The aliens, then, do not represent a departure from the neoidealist story. Rather, they represent what is deviant in a neoidealist world (Box 3.2).

   The nuclear option, of course, fails. The US military is unable to defeat the aliens. It is at this point that a new strategy is devised. And, of course, it is now July 4. First, David's idea to plant a virus in the alien computer—to corrupt corrupted communication—is embraced by the president. If successful, David's plan will mean that the defensive shields around the alien ships will be dismantled for about 30 seconds. If a counteroffensive were launched during that time, it would have a fair chance of success. Second, the president decides to coordinate such a counteroffensive worldwide. When the secretary of defense protests against this

---

Box 3.2 What is deviant in the world of *Independence Day*?

- Bad aliens do bad deeds *not* because they are badly organized but because their communication is impaired and because they are morally corrupt
- Alien communication is corrupted and corrupting
- Aliens are not morally progressive

Plate 3.4 Steve and David team up to fly an old alien ship into the alien mothership where they plant a virus that disables the ship's protective shields.
Courtesy of the Ronald Grant Film Archive © Centropolis Entertainment.

plan, the president fires him. The secretary of defense represents not only realism but also distorted and secretive human communication. For example, he kept Area 51 a secret from the president well after the aliens landed. His dismissal removes another barrier to a neoidealist success.

There is a problem, however. How can a worldwide counterattack be coordinated? Earthly satellites are ineffective forms of communication because alien ships interfere with them. And, even if they could be used, since the aliens have already used them against the earthlings, any message sent by satellite would surely be intercepted. The US military ends up spreading the word of its counterattack using the purest, most basic, and most universal of all military languages—Morse code.

Steve successfully flies the alien craft into the mothership. David successfully plants the virus in the mothership's computer, thereby disabling the alien defenses. Russell has his sacrificial and redemptive moment of glory when he penetrates the alien ship and blows it up. And, as word of this success is transmitted via Morse code around the world, earthly successes spread against the alien ships.

The message of *Independence Day*, then, is that international cooperation for a just cause leads to peace. Pure communication among humankind enables states to unite around such a just cause. And this just cause can be communicated, embraced, and implemented because "there is an international society." Or is there?

Fear and leadership in *Independence Day*

On this first reading, *Independence Day* seems to support all of the core principles of neoidealism, leading to a domestic analogy that draws a parallel between domestic society and international society. The film supports the idea that the defining characteristic of humans is that they are morally good. And, to illustrate this point, human kindness abounds in *Independence Day*. For example, when the aliens start destroying cities worldwide, there is no looting, extortion of services, or reckless living for the moment. Everyone seems to be focused on helping one another. As Jasmine roams the ruins of Los Angles, she rescues everyone she comes across, never asking for anything in return. Never mind that resources like food, water, and gasoline have become scarce commodities. The post-apocalyptic world of *Independence Day* is a space in which people are at their moral best and behave well.

In typical neoidealist fashion, this moral goodness is not confined to personal relationships among people. Good, cooperative behavior is observed at all levels of social interaction—the personal, the state, and the international. And, from a neoidealist standpoint, it is no surprise that the film's action begins to unfold in a democratic space—in the sovereign nation-state of the US. The implication here is that all this moral behavior on the part of US citizens is able to be expressed because these citizens have lived in a democratically organized state and society. Would this post-Cold War plot have been different if the action unfolded in the former Yugoslavia? We can only imagine that it would be. So much of the cooperative action

Plate 3.5 Jasmine and her son wander round Los Angeles in the aftermath of the alien invasion, rescuing survivors.
Courtesy of the Ronald Grant Film Archive © Centropolis Entertainment.

we see in the film is attributable to good people organized into good states and good societies.

It is not a stretch, then, in either the film's script or the script of neoidealism to invoke the domestic analogy. Because there are moral people organized into good (democratic) states and societies, then there can be an international society. For Woodrow Wilson, all that is required for this hope and belief to be realized is for the world to be made safe for democracy—for all sovereign nation-states to be transformed into democratic sovereign nation-states. This isn't the plot of *Independence Day*. But Kegley's way of moving from domestic society to international society is not only in the plot. It is the key to the human victory over the evil aliens. Kegley's move is to argue that domestic society becomes "internationalized" through increased cross-border communications, which are assumed to be good and pure. And what does *Independence Day* give us but the purest form of cross-border communication available to militaries around the world—Morse code. Morse code unites the sovereign nation-states around the world into one just military mission against the evil aliens. The world is now safe from the aliens. "There is an international society."

What is important is that all of this cooperation in the post-Cold War era happens in the scripts of *Independence Day* and neoidealism *not* because the post-Cold War world has been transformed from anarchy to hierarchy—from the absence of an orderer to a world government. International cooperation is the outcome of the coordination of moral efforts by an international society. It is international society that mediates international anarchy in a neoidealist reading of *Independence Day*. It is international society that even promises to take us out of and keep us out of anarchy altogether.

Independence Day supports many of these neoidealist core ideals and moves, but it would be a mistake to conclude that it supports all of them. In particular, it would be wrong to conclude that the film supports the myth "there is an international society." For in addition to rehearsing many aspects of the neoidealist story, the film tells us what makes the myth "there is an international society" function. It does so by adding two vital elements to the neoidealist plot—fear and US leadership.

Fear seems to play a starring role in both of our anarchy myths so far. In the myth "anarchy is the permissive cause of war," fear functions to divide actors in a situation of structural anarchy. Fear leads to conflict. Fear is what makes that myth function. Fear helps the myth "there is an international society" function as well, but to different effect. In this alternative anarchy myth, fear functions to unite people. It is the fear of the aliens that makes humans recognize what they have in common and to draw upon this good moral core to act humanely toward one another.

Even if we accept the film's neoidealist proposition that fear brings out the best in people, we have to wonder what people—even democratically organized people— are like *without fear*. For example, what were all these good US citizens doing prior to the alien invasion? Because the film is set in the US in the present, most of us can judge for ourselves (by looking around US society or by thinking about its depictions in the worldwide media) if the good moral core of these characters might have been expressed prior to the alien invasion—the fear—that brought out the best in them. In my mind a pre-alien invasion US is not full of such widespread benevolent behavior, but of acts of racial prejudice, selfish economic advancement, militia bombings, and school shootings. Without the fear that unites people around the necessary goal of human survival, maybe social interactions are not quite as cooperative as the film suggests that they are in the face of fear. And, of course, this raises the important questions: "Now that the aliens have been defeated and the fear is gone, will there be an international society?" "Will people remain 'united'?" These questions raise serious challenges to a neoidealist reading of *Independence Day*.

While the issue of fear makes us wonder if an international society will last in the aftermath of the defeat of the alien threat, the issue of US leadership makes us wonder if there was ever an international society at all. Think about it. Is there anything truly "international" about the "international society" we see in *Independence Day*? From the opening shot of the US flag waving on the moon until the end of the film in which the lightshow of alien spacecrafts falling from the sky becomes celebratory fireworks for the Fourth of July, *everything* in this film is about how US leadership saves humanity from the aliens. It isn't that the world has united around one cause and collectively decides what to do. Rather, it is the US president who makes all the key decisions for the entire planet! And, according to the script of *Independence Day*, this is precisely what the world is wanting and waiting for, as is made clear in an exchange between two British soldiers when they receive the Morse code message from the US military.

First British Soldier: It's from the Americans. They want to organize a counter-offensive.
Second British Soldier: It's about bloody time.

This isn't a dialogue about equal partners in an international community entering into mutually cooperative relationships. It is a dialogue that suggests a hierarchical relationship between the US leader and the British follower. In *Independence Day*, "international society" is never more than a *global extension of US domestic society*. This could not have been made more clear than it was in the president's speech to US pilots prior to their successful counteroffensive.

President: In less than an hour, aircraft from here will join others from around the world. And you will be launching the largest aerial battle in the history of mankind. Mankind . . . that word should have new meaning for all of us today. We can't be consumed by our petty differences any more. We will be united in our common interest. Perhaps it's fate that today is the fourth of July. And you will once again be fighting for our freedom. Not from tyranny, oppression, or persecution but from annihilation. We're fighting for our right to live, to exist. And should we win the day, the fourth of July will no longer be known as an American holiday, but as the day the world declared in one voice, "We will not go quietly into the night. We will not vanish without a fight. We're going to live on. We're going to survive. Today, we celebrate our Independence Day."

In this speech, the president declares that the US is part of a wider human community—mankind. Mankind must no longer be a divided community. It must be what it really is—an international community. It must speak in "one voice" and fight as one unit if it is going to defeat the aliens. And this is what the film suggests occurs. But there are a couple of troubling turns in the film that make us wonder if what the president "says" is the same thing as what his speech and the film more generally "do."

One of these troubling turns, as I've already mentioned, is that it is the US president who makes all the decisions for "mankind." It is the US government that takes action. It is the US military that unites the state militaries of the world through the pure communication of Morse code. It is always the US government that is acting *on behalf of mankind—on behalf of the community of humans*. This may all be expected. If the US is indeed the most powerful state on earth, then it makes sense that it would have the necessary influence to coordinate global militaries. It would make sense that it would take the lead.

The problem is, however, in taking the lead *the US confuses its leadership and the extension of its domestic influence internationally with an international society*. The president's speech, for example, suggests that the US mission is a mission for all of mankind. This is the same move we found in the opening sequence—with the US flag flying on the moon and the plaque left there by the US astronauts. It reads, "We came in peace *for all mankind*." It is an old habit for the US to imagine (or at least to say) that its acts are acts on behalf of the whole of humanity.

The US acting on behalf of the whole of humanity wouldn't be inconsistent with neoidealism if this US leadership was the first step toward an end to all domestic differences and toward a truly international society. But that isn't how things work out in *Independence Day*. For instead of erasing all domestic boundaries, one domestic boundary remains intact in the film. It is that of the US. Let's return to the president's speech. He declares,

> And should we win the day, the fourth of July will no longer be known as an American holiday, but as the day the world declared in one voice, "We will not go quietly into the night. We will not vanish without a fight. We're going to live on. We're going to survive. Today, we celebrate our Independence Day."

What the president is doing here is extending what is uniquely North American to the whole world. That doesn't mean the US ceases to exist as a distinct political and social space. It means instead that US values, ideals—even holidays—are extended internationally (Figure 3.5).

In *Independence Day*, there is no *international* society. There *appears to be* an international society because US domestic society is extended globally. But this extension of US leadership and US society does not meet the neoidealist terms of

Figure 3.5 How US leadership is extended in *Independence Day*

what an international society is—a formal or informal collective and cooperative set of social relationships among sovereign nation-states. Collective means more than one state must make the decisions. Cooperative means no one state is the leader with all the other states being the followers.

Independence Day encourages us to mistake its combinations of fear and US leadership for an international society that mediates (if not overcomes) international anarchy and ensures moral cooperation. But the world of *Independence Day* is *not* the world of an international society. It is a world in which the US is the leader, the worldwide hegemon. The US is the *orderer* of international life. Anarchy is not replaced by international community. In this film, anarchy is mediated or replaced by hierarchy—by the US as the orderer of international life, even though all the rhetoric that accompanies the action is neoidealist. Might the same series of moves be found in Kegley's neoidealism?

Kegley attributes post-Cold War cooperation to a reorganized international society—one in which increased cross-border communication has led to commonly shared and expressed moral values resulting in more cooperative and moral international behavior among states. But for Kegley's explanation of post-Cold War international cooperation to ring true, it must remain silent on the issues of the unifying effects of fear and, more importantly, on the role of US leadership. It must not acknowledge that the post-Cold War world may be less "anarchical" in the ways that someone like Waltz would think about it not because "there is an international society" but because there is global US leadership. If so, Kegley's neoidealism does not perform a domestic analogy between a domestic society and an international society. It confuses the extension of one state's domestic society with an international society.

Yet the evidence Kegley presents as evidence of a better organized intentional society in a post-Cold War world is the very same evidence others would offer to prove that the US is the undisputed post-Cold War global leader. By leaving US leadership so woefully neglected, we are left to wonder if "there is an international society" that leads to cooperation in the post-Cold War anarchical world and maybe even replaces this anarchy or if, alternatively, post-Cold War cooperation results from the unopposed global spread of US influence. Put differently, might US post-Cold War leadership be so strong that Kegley mistakes it for an international society?

If this is the case, Kegley comes by this confusion/exclusion honestly. It is the same one Woodrow Wilson made in the aftermath of World War I—another post-conflict era in which the US emerged as a world leader (if not *the* world leader). And maybe that is what explains why Wilson's idealist program seemed to fail and Kegley's neoidealist program (at least in the immediate aftermath of the Cold War) seems to succeed.

Overall, though, it is only by leaving unaddressed the presumably unifying function of fear and the question of US global leadership in a post-Cold War era that Kegley's myth "there is an international society" (and the international effects it promises) *appears* to be true.

Suggestions for further thinking

Topic 1 Cooperation under anarchy

The idealist and neoidealist stories of how international society mediates or even supersedes the effects of international anarchy are not the only IR stories about cooperation in relation to international anarchy. Other stories about the relationships between anarchy and cooperation abound. They are found in the so-called "English School" tradition, in neorealism, and in neoliberal institutionalism. For example, Hedley Bull's *The Anarchical Society* (1987) contributes to the anarchy/cooperation debate from the perspective of the misnamed English School (misnamed because its key figures were Welsh and Australian in addition to English and because the cornerstone of this tradition is arguably the writings of the Dutch legalist Hugo Grotius). Robert Keohane's *After Hegemony* is an important contribution from the neoliberal institutionalism position, while Stephen Krasner's edited collection *International Regimes* carries on the debate about international cooperation under anarchy by bringing together theorists from neorealist and neoliberal perspectives.

Suggested reading

Hedley Bull (1987) *The Anarchical Society*. London: Macmillan.

Robert O. Keohane (1984) *After Hegemony*. Princeton, NJ: Princeton University Press.

Stephen D. Krasner (ed.) (1983) *International Regimes*. Ithaca, NY: Cornell University Press.

Topic 2 Morality and ethics in IR

While we often associate ethics and morality with the tradition of idealism, this is a bit of a problem for a couple of reasons. First, idealism is more complicated than I have presented it here, as there are lots of variants within it. For example, there is the cosmopolitan thought of someone like Charles Beitz (1999) and the communitarianism illustrated by Michael Waltzer (2000). Second, morality and ethics actually inform all IR traditions in one way or another, as the collection by Terry Nardin and David Mapel (1993) evidences. Finally, as the discipline of IR becomes more interdisciplinary, it is useful to bring discussions about the politics of moralizing more generally to bear on contemporary international life, as do Jane Bennett and Michael Shapiro (2002) in their collection.

Suggested reading

Charles Beitz (1999) *Political Theory and International Relations*, revised edition. Princeton, NJ: Princeton University Press.

Jane Bennett and Michael J. Shapiro (2002) *The Politics of Moralizing*. New York: Routledge.

Terry Nardin and David Mapel (eds) (1993) *Traditions of International Ethics*, revised edition. Cambridge: Cambridge University Press.

Michael Waltzer (2000) *Just and Unjust Wars: A Moral Argument with Historical Illustrations*, 3rd edition. New York: Basic Books.

Media note

Tim Burton's *Mars Attacks!* counterposes the sanctimoniousness of *Independence Day* with sarcasm. Instead of tempting viewers to embrace a neoidealist script in which "there is an international society," it shows aliens with a sense of humor playing with the language of neoidealism to hilarious (if disastrous) effect.

Classroom activity

An interesting teaching exercise would be to give a lecture (or reading assignment) on neoidealism to a class. Then divide the students into two groups—with one group viewing *Independence Day* and the other *Mars Attacks!* Have each group come up with a report or short essay on what they think about the myth "there is an international society" in the context of neoidealism based on their viewing of their specific film. Then assemble the class as a whole and have them present their views to each other. A follow-up discussion and/or lecture on the influences of cultural mediations for mythologizing international relations "truths" might offer an interesting conclusion to this teaching exercise.

Chapter 4

Constructivism

Is anarchy what states make of it?

Our third and final anarchy myth, "anarchy is what states make of it," proposes a way out of the dilemmas faced by IR scholars thinking about the effects of international anarchy deterministically. If the myth "anarchy is the permissive cause of war" suggests that anarchy means international politics is likely to be conflictual and the myth "there is an international society" suggests that, mediated by international society, anarchy should be cooperative, then this new myth holds that the effects of international anarchy are not quite so predictable as either of these first two anarchy myths suggest. Anarchy is neither necessarily conflictual nor cooperative. There is no "nature" to international anarchy. "Anarchy is what states make of it." If states behave conflictually toward one another, then it appears that the "nature" of international anarchy is conflictual. If states behave cooperatively toward one another, then it *appears* that the "nature" of international anarchy is cooperative. It is what states do that we must focus on to understand conflict and cooperation in international politics, according to this myth, rather than focusing on the supposed "nature" of international anarchy. States determine the "nature" of international anarchy. And, most importantly, *what states do depends upon what states' identities and interests are, and identities and interests change.*

The myth "anarchy is what states make of it" is associated with a branch of the constructivist tradition of IR theory. Constructivism argues that identities and interests in international politics are not stable—they have no pre-given nature. This is as true for the identity of the sovereign nation-state as it is for the identity of international anarchy. The important thing is to look at how identities and interests are constructed—how they are made or produced in and through specific international interactions (Onuf, 1989; Wendt, 1994).

Constructivism is among the most influential IR tradition of the late 1990s and early 2000s (Walt, 1998). This is in part because what it says seems to be just common sense. We know from our own individual experiences that today we are not *exactly* who we were yesterday, and we are unlikely to be *exactly* the same tomorrow. Our identities—who we are—change, as do our interests—what is important to us. Constructivism is also so influential because its myth "anarchy is what states make of it" seems to "build a bridge" between neorealist "truths" and neoliberal/neoidealist "truths." There is something for everyone in constructivism. It provides the answers to all our IR problems.

The success of constructivism, however, depends upon an important move. The myth "anarchy is what states make of it" means that states decide what anarchy will be like—conflictual or cooperative. By making the state the key decision-maker of the "nature" of international anarchy, constructivism contradicts its own argument that identities and interests are always in flux. It allows that the *interests* of states, conflictual or cooperative, change. But by making the character of international anarchy dependent upon what states decide to make it, constructivism produces the *identity* of the state as decision-maker, *and this identity cannot* be changed. If the identity of the state as decision-maker were questioned (as it is in some myths about globalization and empire; see Chapters 6 and 7), the constructivist myth "anarchy is what states make of it" would not function.

The myth "anarchy is what states make of it" was proposed by one of the leading constructivist IR theorists of the 1990s and early 2000s, Alexander Wendt, in his 1992 essay "Anarchy is What States Make of it: The Social Construction of

Power Politics." In this chapter, I will summarize the argument Wendt makes in support of his myth and focus explicitly on how Wendt stabilizes the decision-making character of the state to functionally guarantee the "truth" of his myth. I will turn to the film *Wag the Dog* as my interpretive guide for a functional critique of Wendt's myth.

Wag the Dog is a comic film about producing a phony war to distract the US public's attention from the troubles of its president. As such, the film illustrates how the producing function of identities and interests works. Production works by not letting people see the moves behind the scenes that make what is produced—whether that is a phony war or an IR myth—appear to be true. Production, in other words, works though seduction—through "withholding something from the visible" (Baudrillard, 1987: 21), even though there may be nothing to see.

The neorealist anarchy myth is a seductive myth. With its emphasis on the structure of international anarchy, it seems to withhold from view the *authors* of this structure of international anarchy. Seduced by neorealism, Wendt asks the obvious question, "who is the author of international anarchy?" And he gives us his answer: socially constructed states. But, as the film *Wag the Dog* implies, maybe asking "who is the author?" is the wrong question. Maybe a more interesting question is "how do practices work to make us believe there is an author of international anarchy?"

What does the myth say?

In his 1992 essay "Anarchy is What States Make of It," Alexander Wendt takes as his point of departure the classic dispute between realists and idealists—updated as neorealists and neoliberals—over the behavior of states in international politics. Must state behavior be conflictual, as neorealists argue, or might it become increasing cooperative, as neoliberals hope? A lot of how you think about state behavior, Wendt tells us, depends upon how you think about the "nature of international anarchy." Is it a structure that puts constraints on state behavior so that competition and conflict are guaranteed and much cooperation is ruled out (Waltz, 1979; see Chapter 2) or is it a place in which processes of learning take place among states in their everyday interactions so that more cooperative institutions and behaviors result (Kegley, 1993; see Chapter 3)? Wendt claims that the debate about international anarchy boils down to a debate about which of these two aspects of anarchy theorists decide to stress—structure or process.

Yet however much neorealist and neoliberal scholars divide on the issue of structure vs. process, they share three things in common. Wendt claims that all of these theorists agree that (1) states are the dominant actors in international politics; (2) rationalism is the theoretical disposition through which they explain international state interactions; and (3) security is defined in "self-interested" terms (Wendt, 1992: 130; see Table 4.1). While Wendt doesn't seem to find any problems with the state-centricism of these traditions, he does have worries about their rationalism and the very different ways in which they think about self-interest.

Wendt worries that the neorealist and neoliberal commitment to rationalism restricts how theorists can think about international change. He suggests that "rationalism offers a fundamentally behavioral conception of both process and

Table 4.1 What do neorealists and neoliberals agree and disagree about?

Agree	Disagree
1 States are the dominant actors in international politics	Whether to emphasize structure (as neorealists like Waltz do) or process (as neoliberals like Kegley do) when explaining state interactions in international anarchy
2 Rationalism is the theoretical disposition through which international state interactions are explained	
3 Security is defined in "self-interested" terms	

institutions: they change behavior but not identities and interests" (Wendt, 1992: 129–30). The problem with rationalism, then, is that it takes the identities and interests of states as given, thereby welcoming questions about changes in state behavior but *not* being open to questions about changes in state identities and interests.

This is a problem for Wendt because it restricts how IR theorists are able to think about the notion of "self-interest." Neorealists think of self-interest in terms of "self-help." As we saw in the Waltzian myth "international anarchy is the permissive cause of war," self-help defines the behavior of states in a system of structural anarchy—one in which there is no orderer. Self-help flows from the structural arrangement of international politics. According to Waltz, it is not an institution that can be changed. Therefore, states cannot learn to overcome the limits of international anarchy—the deterministic structure of anarchy that makes states look out for themselves in order to survive. All they can learn to do is to adjust to these limits of anarchy. As Wendt puts it, in this system "only simple learning or behavioral adaptation is possible; the complex learning involved in redefinitions of identity and interest is not" (Wendt, 1992: 130). This limit to state learning is imposed by thinking about international anarchy in neorealist terms *which are also rationalist terms.*

Wendt suggests that these limits on thinking about changes in state learning are found in "weak" liberal arguments as well because such liberals "concede to neorealists the causal powers of anarchical structure," even while they argue that processes of learning can take place within neorealist-defined anarchy. But other liberals—who he terms "strong liberals"—want to move away from simple learning to complex learning, from thinking only about changes in state *behavior* to theorizing changes in state *identities and interests.* Wendt's sympathies lie with these "strong liberals." Yet he laments that because of their commitment to rationalism, "neoliberals lack a systematic theory of how such changes occur and thus must privilege realist insights about structure while advancing their own insights about process" (Wendt, 1992: 131; see Box 4.1). If only there were a theory that would allow them to take structure seriously by recognizing that "transformations of identity and interest through process are transformations of structure" (Wendt, 1992:

Box 4.1 What's wrong with rationalism?

1　Rationalism takes the identities and interests of states as given because it only recognizes changes in states' behavior but not in states themselves (i.e., their identities and interests).
2　Rationalism also takes the identities of and the interests generated from international anarchy as given. For rationalists, neither the structure of international anarchy nor the self-help system it is said to produce can be changed.
3　Overall, rationalism limits theoretical understandings of change in agents and structures because it only examines changes in behavior and excludes an examination of changes in identities and interests.

---

131). And, guess what? There is such a theory—Wendtian constructivism (Wendt, 1992: 131–2).

Constructivism might not only offer neoliberals the theory of change they need to be able to privilege process over structure, but because it takes structure seriously it might also be able to "build a bridge" between neorealism and neoliberalism (Wendt, 1992: 132; Wendt, 1994). And if that can be done, then maybe we won't have to choose between defining the character of international anarchy as either predominately conflictual or predominately cooperative any longer. But to get to this place, we have to recognize that the character of international anarchy is not pre-given but the outcome of state interactions and that self-help is not an immutable feature of international anarchy. Wendt puts it like this: "There is no 'logic' of anarchy apart from the practices that create and instantiate one structure of identities and interests rather than another; structure has no existence or causal powers apart from process. Self-help and power politics are institutions, not essential features of anarchy. *Anarchy is what states make of it*" (italics in original; Wendt, 1992: 132).

How does Wendt make his argument that there is no logic of anarchy and that self-help is an institution that can be changed rather than one that determines the behavior of states? He does so by challenging the neorealist logic of anarchy, a logic which makes self-help an unalterable aspect of international anarchy that leads to competition and conflict. And he does this by reclaiming a place for *practice* in international politics (see Figure 4.1).

Wendt argues that, whatever one may think of Waltz's overall argument in *Man, the State and War* (1954), this early attempt by Waltz to understand international anarchy left a place for state practice that was written out of Waltz's *Theory of International Politics* (1979). In Waltz's early book, international anarchy is what allowed wars to occur, but something else always had to happen—some first or second image practice by states. But in the later book, international anarchy became a structural principle that made states behave competitively and often conflictually, making first and second image explanations of war seem unnecessary (Wendt, 1992: 133–4; see Chapter 2). According to Wendt, the place of practice can and must be reclaimed within this "neorealist description of the contemporary state system as a competitive, self-help world" (Wendt, 1992: 134). And, if practice is recovered, we

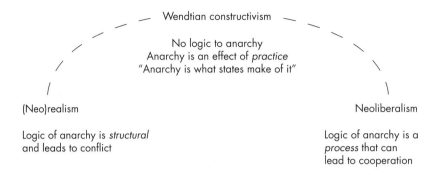

Figure 4.1 Wendt's constructivist bridge between neorealists and neoliberals

can accept this description of the world *without* accepting its explanation of competitive and conflictual state behavior as a necessary structural outcome. Put differently, by restoring an emphasis on *practice* among states, Wendt believes he will be able to recover *process* among states—processes that may transform international anarchy from being either necessarily conflictual (for neorealists) or cooperative (for neoliberals) into "what states make of it" (Wendt, 1992: 134).

How Wendt recovers practice and process within this neorealist description of international politics is by arguing that there are at least two structures that explain state behavior in international politics. The first, which has been Wendt's focus so far, is international anarchy. The second is "the intersubjectively constituted structure of identities and interests in the system" (Wendt, 1992: 138). If we acknowledge only the first structure of international anarchy, we pretty much end up with Waltz's neorealist explanation of international politics or, alternatively, a "weak liberal" argument that even within structural anarchy, some cooperative behavior is possible. If, however, we include the second intersubjectively constituted structure of identities and interests, then international anarchy is not necessarily either conflictual or cooperative.

So, how does Wendt think about this intersubjectively constituted structure of identities and interests? Wendt takes the state as his point of departure. States are the fundamental actors in international politics. These state actors "acquire identities—relatively stable, role-specific understandings and expectations about self" (Wendt, 1992: 135) through their relationships with other actors and the meaning structures in which they find themselves. "Identities are the basis of interests" which are once again constructed relationally (Wendt, 1992: 136). Moving from actors to identities to interests, we finally end up with institutions. "An institution is a relatively stable set or 'structure' of identities and interests" (Wendt, 1992: 136). "Institutions are fundamentally cognitive entities that do not exist apart from actors' ideas about how the world works" (Wendt, 1992: 136).

Wendt is not trying to make a "which came first" argument—identities or institutions. He is trying to say that identities, interests, and institutions all result from interactive, social processes and that they are "mutually constitutive" (Wendt,

1992: 137). We may think institutions are "already there" because we rely upon them to orient our behavior, but institutions are not pre-given. They are constituted through social interactions among identities. Similarly, identities are not pre-given either, but are formed through interactions with other identities and with collective social institutions.

What does this mean for Wendt's myth "anarchy is what states make of it"? It means that even if we accept the neorealist description of the world as an anarchical, self-help world, by supplementing this anarchical structure with the intersubjectively constituted structure of identities and interests, then neither anarchy nor self-help are meaningful terms prior to the social interactions of states. Anarchy and self-help only become meaningful once social interactions have taken place. And, because "people act toward objects, including other actors, on the basis of the meanings that the objects have for them" (Wendt, 1992: 135), and because the objects of "anarchy" and "self-help" have no meaning prior to state interactions, we will only know if anarchy and self-help will lead to conflict or cooperation once we know what states do socially (Box 4.2).

Taking these two structures together, what can we say about state behavior in a competitive, self-help anarchical system prior to social interaction? We *cannot* say it will be necessarily conflictual or cooperative. We can say, according to Wendt, that states will try to survive (Wendt, 1992: 139). But how they will achieve that survival is an open question.

With all this in mind, Wendt invites us to think of an example in which two actors have no prior social contact, stumble upon one another, and both want to ensure their continued survival. His example is the arrival of aliens to earth. Wendt asks, "Would we assume, *a priori*, that we were about to be attacked if we are ever contacted by members of an alien civilization? I think not" (Wendt, 1992: 141–2). Yes, we'd be cautious, he argues, but we would probably not want to appear to be threatening to the aliens unless they were first threatening to us, as we would want "to avoid making an immediate enemy out of what may be a dangerous adversary" (Wendt, 1992: 142). We would read the aliens' social signals before deciding whether we would behave conflictually or cooperatively. And, importantly, Wendt argues "we would not *begin* our relationship with the aliens in a security dilemma; security dilemmas are not given by anarchy or nature" (Wendt, 1992: 144).

The same is true of sovereign states in their social interactions. On first meeting, two states (which Wendt refers to as "alter" and "ego") have no reason to

---

Box 4.2 Three fundamental principles of constructivist social theory

1. "People act toward objects, including other actors, on the basis of the meanings that the objects have for them": SOCIAL KNOWLEDGE
2. "The meanings in terms of which action is organized arise out of interaction": SOCIAL PRACTICE
3. "Identities [and interests] are produced in and through 'situated activity'": SOCIAL IDENTITIES AND INTERESTS

assume the worst of one another. Yes, they each want to survive and to preserve their own unique ways of being states—of organizing their systems of governance. But none of this suggests that they are in a "security dilemma" in which self-help principles prevail. States do not *necessarily* have to increase their power to increase their security because every other state poses a threat to them. "Social threats are constructed, not natural" (Wendt, 1992: 141). Prior to social interaction, there is no such thing as a social threat. It is identities that produce collective meanings like social threats, and "identities are produced in and through 'situated activity'" (Wendt, 1992: 144).

If, in this particular situated activity, the only prior interest states have is to survive, then this means that it is not *a priori* in a state's interest to make a social threat. A state (alter) may choose to make a social threat, or ego may interpret alter's actions as threatening. But prior to social interaction, alter and ego are not in a security dilemma. Wanting to survive in no way guarantees that alter or ego will behave conflictually toward one another. Nor, of course, does their interest in survival guarantee they will cooperate. Anarchy is what alter and ego make of it (see Table 4.2).

Additionally, Wendt adds, "If states find themselves in a self-help system, this is because their practices made it that way. Changing the practices will change the intersubjective knowledge that constitutes the system" (Wendt, 1992: 144). So even if alter and ego make anarchy conflictual by creating a self-help system, they can always escape this self-help system by changing the ways they think about and then act in this system. This is why Wendt argues "that the meaning in terms of which action is organized arise out of interactions" (Wendt, 1992: 140). And Wendt goes on to make this point explicitly, by illustrating how "identities and interests are transformed under anarchy: by the institution of sovereignty, by an evolution of cooperation, and by intentional efforts to transform egoistic identities into collective identities" (Wendt, 1992: 133).

But probably the most important move Wendt makes in his essay is not found in his critique of rationalism or in his critique of self-help. Rather, it is in his *lack* of a critique of state-centrism. He acknowledges that making the state the focus of his analysis may strike some theorists, especially postmodernists, as "depressingly familiar" (Wendt, 1992: 163). But, of course, it is only by keeping the state as the central decision-maker in his constructivist explanation of international politics that Wendt can conclude that "anarchy is what states make of it."

Wendt defends his state-centricism on the grounds that "the authorship of the human world" must not be forgotten. For to forget the author is to risk reifying the world—to make it an object that is already there that actors relate to rather than to recognize it as a "world of our making" (as another constructivist with a different take on constructivism, Nicholas Onuf, puts it: Onuf, 1989) (Wendt, 1992: 147). Wendt is critical of realists for reifying the structure of international anarchy. He puts it like this: "By denying or bracketing states' collective authorship of their identities and interests . . . the realist–rationalist alliance denies or brackets the fact that competitive power politics help create the very 'problem of order' they are supposed to solve—that realism is a self-fulfilling prophecy" (Wendt, 1992: 148). But anarchy is not a problem external to states. It is produced through the "competitive identities and interests" states create through their everyday activities. "It is what

Table 4.2 Three stories of international anarchy

	Realism	Idealism	Constructivism
Actors	States	States	States
Goals	Survival	Survival	Survival
Actors' behavior in anarchy	Increase power to ensure survival	Promote social learning through: • institutions (e.g. UN) • ideas (e.g. democracy and liberal capitalism)	Unpredictable prior to social interaction
What mitigates state behavior?	Self-help because • no world government (anarchy) • cooperation among states unreliable	International society	Intersubjectively constituted structure of identities and interests • if state identities and interests produced as competitive → competition • if state identities and interests produced as cooperative → cooperation
Logic of anarchy	Conflictual	Cooperative	Anarchy is what states make of it

states have made of themselves" (Wendt, 1992: 148). This is a strong argument for accepting the authorship of the state—for viewing anarchy as a product of state activities rather than as a self-help, competitive structure that traps states into behaving conflictually toward one another.

The film *Wag the Dog* illustrates the moves in Wendt's constructivist myth. It demonstrates how identities, interests, and institutions are intersubjectively constituted. And it seems to support Wendt's point that reifying or forgetting the authorship of acts can have dangerous consequences—even leading to war (or the perception of war at least). Either way, real people die. Authorship, it seems to suggest, must be transparent for democratic institutions to operate properly. It must withhold nothing from view. It must not be seductive.

Wag the Dog also makes us wonder if production/authorship can ever be effectively separated from seduction—if authorship can ever be transparent. If not, then we have to ask what the seduction of authorship does. Wendt's answer, as we know, is that authorship reifies what authors supposedly make (like anarchy). *Wag the Dog*'s answer is more complicated. Its answer is this. Yes, seduction reifies production, not just of what authors supposedly make, but of authors themselves. And, this answer goes on, this reification of authorship is terribly clever because there is no guarantee that practices can reliably be traced to authors.

Wag the Dog

Wag the Dog opens with a joke that appears on the screen.

"Why does a dog wag its tail?"
"Because a dog is smarter than its tail. If the tail were smarter, the tail would wag
     the dog."

The film then cuts to a less-than-slick television commercial, in which a couple of jockies discuss why they will support the president in the up-coming election—they know it is unwise to "change horses in midstream." Cut to exterior of the Whitehouse. Cut to interior of White House. A man in a rumpled hat, raincoat and suit has arrived. He looks ordinary enough (apart from the fact that he is Robert DeNiro). He makes his way into the bowels of the White House, into a safe room in which he is the focus of a crisis meeting. He is Conrad Brean or "Mr Fix-It," as the president's assistant Winifred refers to him. Conrad/Connie is briefed on the current crisis. A Firefly Girl has alleged sexual misconduct against the president while she was alone with the president in the Oval Office.

    The president's campaign opponent, Senator Neal, already has word of the story and is ready to run a new campaign commercial. Connie and his team view the new spot in the crisis room. The spot pans a crowd of what we suppose are the president's supporters, cheering. Underneath is a question that is spoken in a voiceover, "In the final days of the campaign, has the president changed his tune?" The commercial cuts to the exterior of the White House as we hear Maurice Chevalier singing "Thank Heaven for Little Girls." The commercial cuts back and forth between this exterior shot and an interior shot of the president's empty desk chair in the oval office. The voiceover continues, "The Presidency is about honor, it's about principles, and it's about integrity. This tune has got to change. On election day, vote Neal for president."

    Mr Fix-It goes to work. The election is 11 days away. All he has to do is distract the public's attention from this sexual crisis long enough to ensure the president is reelected. How he decides to do this is by changing the story—by inventing something the US public will find more gripping than this sexual scandal. He decides to delay the president's return from China and start a series of rumors about non-existent weaponry and a non-existent war to distract the public. He explains his plan to the president's staff in a pretend dialog between a staff member and a newspaper reporter.

Connie: Whoever's leaking that stuff to that geek at the *Post* lets it slip.
     Jees, I hope this won't screw up the B3 program.

Plate 4.1 Stanley, Winifred and others in the Situation Room, plotting how to save the President's election hopes.
Courtesy of the Ronald Grant Film Archive © New Line Cinema.

What B3 program and why should it screw it up?

Well, if the president decides to deploy the B3 before it's fully tested . . .

Deploy the B3 before it's fully tested? Why?

Why? The crisis?

Winifred [interrupting Connie's imaginary dialogue]: "What crisis?"

Connie: Well, I'm workin' on that. [Carrying on with his plan, Connie continues:] At the same time, get General Scott of the Joint Chiefs of Staff and pour him on a plane right away to Seattle. He's all flustered and nervous to talk to the Boeing people.

Winifred: Right [to Connie]. Do it [to an assistant].

Assistant: But, but . . .

Connie: But what?

Assistant: But there isn't a B3 bomber.

Connie: Where did you go to school kid, Wellesley?

Assistant: Dartmouth.

Connie: Then show a little spunk. There is no B3 bomber. General Scott to the best of your knowledge is not in Seattle to talk to Boeing.

Winifred: It won't work, Connie. It won't prove out.

Connie: It doesn't have to prove out. We've just gotta distract 'em, just gotta distract 'em. We've got less than two weeks until the election.

Winifred: What in the world would do that? What in the world would do that?

Connie: I'm workin' on it. I'm working on it.

Plate 4.2
Presidential aide
Winifred and
"Mr Fix-It" (Connie)
visit Hollywood
producer Stanley Motss
in his Los Angeles
home. Winifred feeds
dialogue supplied by
Stanley to a White
House press
spokesperson he is
watching on television
as evidence of her and
Connie's production of
news and events.
Courtesy of the Ronald
Grant Film Archive © New
Line Cinema.

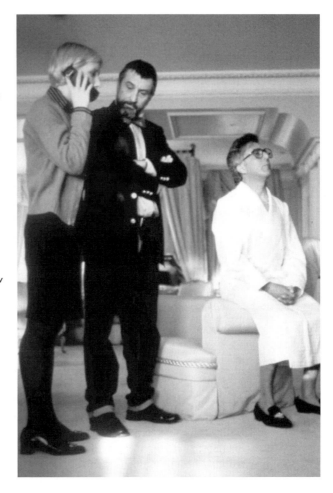

What Connie comes up with is a way to "change the story, change the lead" by creating the "appearance of a war" between the US and Albania—a country about which (at the time this film was made prior to the war in Kosovo) the US public knew very little. He and Winifred fly to Hollywood to enlist the aid of film producer Stanley Motss because, as Conrad puts it, "War is showbusiness." When it becomes clear to Stanley that Connie wants him to help with the "war," Connie tries to explain to him what kind of help he has in mind.

Stanley: And you want me to do what?
Connie: We want you to produce.
Stanley (expressing shock and disbelief): You want me to produce your war?
Connie: It's not a war. It's a pageant. We need a theme, a song, some visuals. We need, you know, it's a pageant. It's like the Oscars. That's why we came to you.
Stanley: I never won an Oscar.
Connie: And that's a damn shame you didn't, but you produced the Oscars.

Stanley (getting the idea):   It's a pageant.
Connie: It's "Miss America." You're Bert Parks.

After Connie has successfully pitched the idea of a US war with Albania to Stanley, Stanley and his team produce the war—its script revolving around Albanian terrorists trying to smuggle a nuclear bomb into the US via Canada in a suitcase, "news footage" of an "Albanian girl" escaping from rebels in Albania that is leaked to the press and run on all the news programs, choreographing the president's return from China at which time he is given an offering of thanks by a small "Albanian girl and her grandmother," not to mention a couple of songs and countless merchandizing tie-ins. And all of it is consumed by television viewers as real.

And then, the "war" "ends."

Senator Neal, the president's electoral opponent, announces on television that he has evidence from the CIA that the war is over. Stanley is upset.

Stanley (angry):   He can't end the war. He's not producing this.
Connie (exasperated):   The war's over guys.
Stanley: No!
Connie (now matter-of-factly):   It's over. I saw it on television.
Stanley: No, the war isn't over 'til I say it's over. This is my picture. This is not the
     CIA's picture . . .

Stanley then devises a scheme to keep productive control of "his picture" even though someone else ended "his" war. He tells Connie, "This is nothing. This is nothing. This is just 'Act I: The War'. Now we really do need an 'Act II'." He continues to spin the war story, now taking place after the war has officially ended. He decides there is a US soldier trapped behind enemy lines who doesn't know the war is over. He has been separated from his troop. US forces will now mobilize to rescue him. Proud of himself, Stanley tells Connie, "Bottom of the ninth (swings an imaginary baseball bat). Alright? Alright? They don't know who they're playing with. They don't shut down our picture."

And so the show goes on, even when the US soldier they "cast" as the hero turns out to be a psychotic imprisoned for raping a nun, even when the hero's return is delayed because the plane in which he, Connie, Stanley, and Winifred are travelling crashes, and even when the "hero" is killed by a shopkeeper because the hero is trying to rape the shopkeeper's daughter. Stanley simply scripts a patriotic funeral for the returned hero. And the story holds long enough to ensure the president's reelection.

What does all of this tell us about the world of *Wag the Dog*? How does this film make sense of the world? What does it say is typical and deviant of that world?

The world of *Wag the Dog* is a made-in-the-media world. TV shows and news broadcasters define reality, even to the extent that they make us believe that the US is at war with Albania. And because television is where reality happens, television is the only place reality can be transformed. For example, early in the film the CIA confront Connie and Winifred with "the facts" that there is no evidence of a war in Albania or of any Albanian nuclear device in Canada. But this is not enough to "end the war." The only way the war can be ended is the way it was started—on television.

Connie articulates this when he declares the war is over because "I saw it on television."

It is through the medium of television that information and ideas are disseminated. And, more importantly, what this practice of dissemination does is construct and reconstruct identities, interests and institutions in the world of *Wag the Dog*. Stanley is reconstructed from a Hollywood producer into a producer of a war with an interest in keeping "his" picture going until he can bring it to some poignant closure. The US public are constructed as patriots with an interest in beating the Albanians and securing the US borders. The institution of war is transformed from something that occurs in places like Albania, the US, and Canada into something that occurs in televisual spaces. All of these identities, interests and institutions co-construct one another. All this seems to illustrate the "inter-subjectively constituted structure of identities and interests" (Wendt, 1992: 136) of which Wendt writes (Box 4.3).

And as the mediatic magic of war replaces both the upcoming Presidential election and the president's alleged indiscretion with a Firefly Girl as the only tale in town, the film seems to invite us to take the notion of tales—and tails—as seriously as it does. What's all this preoccupation with tales, tails, and wagging about anyway?

One way to approach this question is by asking another: "what is typical and what is deviant in the world of *Wag the Dog*?" And seeking an answer to this question takes us back to the joke with which the film opened—"Why does a dog wag its tail? Because a dog is smarter than its tail. If the tail were smarter, it would wag the dog." In light of this joke, the film's title, and the film's plot, it seems fair to conclude that what is typical in the world of *Wag the Dog* is for the tail to wag the dog, and what is deviant is for a dog to wag its tail.

All of this encourages us to ask "who is the dog and who is the tail?" It is this sort of question that Wendtian constructivism gives into. One answer might be that the dog is the US public and the tail is the politicos of Washington who employed Connie, Stanley, and Winifred. Another might be that the media wag the politicos who wag the public. Either way, the US public is constructed as being wagged all the time—as that which is constructed. In contrast, the tail decides how the wagging will be performed. The tail (politics/media) is the author of the tale (story) about the war (see Table 4.3).

One might think of *Wag the Dog* as a clever parable of Wendt's myth "anarchy is what states make of it," rewritten as something like "war is what producers make of it." Whichever way it is phrased, the moral is the same. And this moral is the very one Wendt evoked in his defense of a state-centric/actor-centric approach to understanding international politics. That defense was this: if we forget who the author of practices is, then we cannot hold that author accountable. We end up responding to

---

Box 4.3 How does *Wag the Dog* make sense of the world?

Reality is produced, circulated, and transformed through the media, especially television. It is through the media that identities, interests, and institutions appear to be constructed and reconstructed.

Table 4.3 What seems to be typical and deviant in the world of *Wag the Dog?*

Typical	Deviant
For the tail (spin doctors and policy-makers) to wag the dog (the US public)	For the dog (the US public) to wag its tail (spin doctors and policy-makers)

identities, interests, and institutions as if they were authored by no one. In *Wag the Dog*, we respond to staged events like war as if they were real, which gives them some reality. And in international politics, we respond to "the logic of anarchy" and its accompanying self-help security dilemma as if they were real, thereby giving them some reality.

Identities, interests, and institutions are, however, authored by someone, Wendt suggests. Authorship is always at the bottom of production. It is only by keeping the author in mind that we can hold the author accountable and, maybe even more importantly, recognize that we are the authors of our own lives. Anarchy is what states make of it. War is what producers make of it. Our lives are what we make of them.

Wendt's warnings about the dangers of reification are echoed in the film by Stanley, the Hollywood producer. Stanley asks Connie, "Where do movies come from if nobody produces them, Connie? Where do they come from?" Stanley asks this question because his tale about war, a hero's triumphant return, and the hero's patriotic funeral seem to come from nowhere. But Stanley knows they result from production, and he is the producer. Throughout the film, Stanley waxes philosophically about production.

Producing is problem-solving:

Stanley: If you've got a problem, solve it. That's producing.

Producing is heroic:

Stanley: Producing is being a samurai warrior. They pay you day in, day out for years so that one day when called upon you can respond, your training at its peak, and save the day.

And producing is invisible:

Stanley: Thinking ahead. Thinking ahead. That's what producing is.
Connie: It's like being a plumber.
Stanley: Yes, like being a plumber. You do your job right, nobody should notice. But when you fuck up, everything gets full of shit.

But it is this last aspect of production—its invisibility—that makes it so problematic both for Stanley and for Wendt. According to Stanley, production only truly functions when it is seductive—when it withholds its own acts of production from view. For

Plate 4.3 Stanley admiring an aspect of his production for his fake war.
Courtesy of the Ronald Grant Film Archive © New Line Cinema.

production to work, nobody should notice. While Stanley knows this about production and producers, it is also what bothers him about production. He has never won an Oscar because, as he tells Connie, "There is no Oscar for producing." Producing is never recognized. It is always invisible. So when his "patriotic pageant" is winding up, he quarrels with Connie because he finally wants proper recognition for the work he has done.

Connie: You can't do it.
Stanley: [angrily] Don't you tell me that. Don't you ever tell me that. I'm the producer of this show. [looks out the window at the set where the patriotic funeral of the returned war hero is being shot] Look at that. That is a complete fucking fraud, and it looks one hundred percent real. [contemplatively, softly] It's the best work I've ever done in my whole life, because it's so honest . . . [insistently] I tell you, for once in my life I will not be pissed on. I want . . . I want the credit. I want the credit.

Stanley knows that if he is allowed to have "the credit," the whole picture will fall apart. He just doesn't want to accept what he knows about production when it comes to credit. He knows production is only revealed when there is a problem. When there is no problem, production and the producer are out of sight. And because they are out of sight, we long for them. We want to see the processes of production and the producer who is pulling all the strings. But, as *Wag the Dog* makes explicit, the deal is that we can have our entertaining movie only if we suspend our interest in the processes of production and in the producer.

In this sense, production is always tied to seduction. That's the deal. The story/film/tale teases us into wanting what we cannot see—what is seductively withheld from the visible—while at the same time it promises not to show us too much. For if we knew about all the special effects and all the dramas behind the drama, we would lose interest in the drama itself. That's why it is so hard to be a producer—because the deal is that you can never take the credit. If you do, the audience will be disillusioned with your production, so any "credit" for that job well done will dissolve.

What Stanley knows about production is the same thing Wendt knows. Just as the invisibility of Stanley's role as producer guarantees that his tale about war appears to be true, the invisibility of the state's role as producer guarantees that neorealism's tale about international anarchy appears to be true. By "exposing" states as the producers/decision-makers who make international anarchy, Wendt ensures that the neorealist anarchy tale ceases to function as if no one authored it.

Stanley and Wendt both implicitly understand that production is tied to seduction. But neither of them seems to know that seduction doesn't necessarily conceal an author. *Seduction doesn't just tease us into wanting what we cannot see. It convinces us that there is something there to see.* It fools us not only about what might be a "real" or a "false" tale. *The tale itself tricks us into thinking that there is an author of the tale.*

For Wendt, as for the film *Wag the Dog*, asking "who is the author?" is an important question to guard against the evils of reification. And for Wendt at least, it is a necessary question. For it is by asking the question of authorship that Wendt gets us out of the neorealist anarchy myth by emphasizing state practices in the production of international anarchy. But I wonder if this is where the constructivist emphasis on practice should be placed. Because the film raises another question: "Does the tail wag the dog or does the *tale* wag the tail that *appears* to wag the dog?" Put differently, "is anarchy what states make of it or do *practices* (which Wendt does not consider) make states that *appear* to make anarchy?"

Practice, seduction, and dead authorship

Wendt's myth "anarchy is what states make of it" gets us out of the neorealist anarchy myth in which international anarchy determines that states will compete to ensure their survival relying upon self-help logics. Wendt gets us here by emphasizing practice in international politics—specifically, how the practices of socially constructed states make international anarchy into what it is, whatever that may be. So Wendt emphasizes practice by emphasizing what states *do*. In this sense, Wendt's socially constructed states are the tails that wag international anarchy. They are the authors of anarchy. But there are other practices that Wendt ignores, and these are the practices that construct states themselves as decision-makers who then go on to make international anarchy. This second set of practices concerns tales/stories rather than tails/actors. On this reading, tales or stories construct states as tails/authors who then wag/make anarchy.

It is only by excluding this second set of practices—the practices that construct states as decision-makers or producers of international anarchy—that Wendt can claim states as the authors of anarchy. Put differently, the tale/story must go without saying for Wendt's own constructivist tale "anarchy is what states make of it" to function.

But in the mediatic world of *Wag the Dog* and in the Wendtian world of constructivism, the tale/story is a bunch of practices that no one ultimately controls.

Think about it. Ask yourself the question "who is the ultimate decision-maker in the film?" Several answers present themselves.

The answer is not Stanley. If for no other reason, we know this because when Stanley refuses to let the picture roll without credits—when he makes it clear he cannot abide by the agreement that he can never tell anyone about what he has done—Connie authorizes the government thugs to kill him.

So does that make Connie the author/decision-maker? He certainly seems to be the "real" producer. He is the one who came up with the story. He is the one who initially organized it. He just delegated some of this authority to Stanley. So maybe Mr Fix-It is the real center of decision-making power in the film.

Except this answer doesn't hold up because we know that just as Connie delegated decision-making responsibility to Stanley, the president delegated decision-making authority to Connie. So is the president ultimate decision-maker in the world of *Wag the Dog*? Some might answer yes. I would answer no.

My answer is there is not necessarily a decision-maker behind the scenes. And this answer comes from thinking once again about how the film makes sense of the world. As I mentioned before, the film makes sense of the world through the media. It is the circulation of ideas/stories/tales through the media that constructs reality and tells us what to think. And, throughout the film, the president, Connie, and Stanley are always responding to the mediatic presentation of events, trying to come up with problem-solving solutions to them. But trying to solve a problem—what Stanley calls producing—is only a response. It means that production is driven by *practices*—by the mediatic representation of the tale. The tail/producer, then, doesn't wag the dog/public. The tale/practice wags the tail/producer so that it appears that the tail/producer wags the dog/public (Table 4.4).

Consider these examples. The president needs to bring in Connie to fend off a political crisis before the election because the news media will run the story of

Table 4.4 Reconsidering what is typical and deviant in the world of *Wag the Dog*

Typical	Deviant
For the tale (mediatic practices) to wag the tail (producers/spin doctors/policy-makers) so that it *appears* that the tail (producers) wags the dog (US public)	Either: • For the dog (US public) to wag its tail (producers/spin doctors/policy-makers) or • For the tail (producers/spin doctors/policy-makers) to "really" wag the dog (US public) without being wagged by the tale (mediatic practices) itself

his alleged sexual misconduct with the Firefly Girl the next morning. The tale/story drives the president's decision to employ Connie. Connie understands that tales—not tails—wag dogs. And so he invents another tale to rival the tale of the president's alleged sexual misconduct. His tale is a US war with Albania. Senator Neal, appreciating how tales are wagging tales now, intervenes to put a stop to his electoral opponent's strategy. He doesn't do this by saying "there is no war," even though he clearly has the "evidence on the ground" that there is no war because he has been consulting with the CIA. No, he recognizes that it would be political suicide to speak the "truth" that there is only a mediatic war. So he spins another tale to the tale to the tale—that the war is about to end. By ending the war on television, Senator Neal ends the war. Never mind that Stanley insists this is his war and no one else can end it. The war is over because what happens on television is real.

Examples like these abound in the film. Indeed, the whole film is framed from beginning to end through the media. The film opens with a campaign commercial supporting the president and it ends with the following television special report,

> A group calling itself Albania Unite has claimed responsibility for this morning's bombing of the village of Close, Albania. The president could not be reached for comment, but General William Scott of the Joint Chiefs of Staff said he has no doubt we'll be sending planes and troops back in to finish the job.

What do these two media bookends tell us about the mediatic world of *Wag the Dog*?

Obviously, beginning and ending a film with television spots testifies to the importance of mediatic practices in the world of *Wag the Dog*. But it does more than this. There is a movement depicted in the film from thinking that you can reliably trace the authorship of mediatic events back to an author to knowing that you cannot. The opening campaign spot seems easy enough to trace. It is an advertisement for the president paid for by the campaign to reelect the president. But what about the final special news bulletin? Who authored that? It wasn't Stanley because Stanley is dead. It is unlikely to be either Connie or the president because Connie's job was over when the president's reelection was assured, and that occurred before this special report. So who is the author? Is it the media itself? Maybe in part but never entirely, because as the world of *Wag the Dog* showed us, the media are always responding to stories/tales.

So, as the film ends, we are left with the tale still spinning and no one onto whom we can pin the tale/tail, so to speak. Authorship is unreliable. We'll keep searching for authors because the seductive practices of production make us believe that we might find them one day. But no amount of wanting authors to be findable or authorship to be more reliable will make it that way. Authorship cannot be guaranteed. In the end, we only have a tale—a bunch of practices that gave us not only the illusion of a war but the illusion of an author/producer/decision-maker behind the war.

What does this all mean for Wendt's constructivist myth "anarchy is what states make of it"? It means that however well-intentioned Wendt is in trying to give us an escape from some reified "logic of anarchy," he only succeeds at getting us out of some deterministic conflict/cooperation debate by determining the character of the state. In other words, *Wendt only manages to escape the reification of international anarchy by reifying the state as decision-maker.*

Wendt can allow that states can change roles—from producers of conflict to producers of cooperation, for example, just as Stanley changed roles from producer of films to producer of a war. But Wendt cannot tell us how states get produced as producers. *His constructivism draws the line of taking practice seriously under the state.* States can make practices, but—however much he might claim to the contrary—Wendt's constructivism *does not allow* states to be produced. They are already there. They have to be. They are the producers of anarchy. "Anarchy is what *states* make of it."

Wendt's constructivist myth "anarchy is what states make of it" is a comforting myth. It promises to free us from deterministic logics of anarchy. It claims to build a bridge between neorealists and neoliberals. And, most importantly, it answers the seductive question "who is the author of international anarchy?" and gives us an author—states. IR theorists want all of this. And that is why Wendtian constructivism has been so popular among IR theorists.

By accepting these benefits of Wendtian constructivism, however, we are also accepting its liabilities. And constructivism has at least two major liabilities. First, it fails to deliver on its promise to take us beyond reification, because in order to escape a reified logic of anarchy, it reifies the state. Second, by reifying the state—by insisting on the state as the author/decision-maker of all tales—constructivism misses the opportunity to deliver on another of its promises, to restore a focus on process and practice in international politics (see Table 4.5). *Wag the Dog* suggests to us that it is a more interesting question to ask "how does an actor *appear* to be a decision-maker/producer/author?" than it is to ask the seductive question "who is the real decision-maker/producer/author?"

This constructivist compromise does allow us to hold states accountable for any wagging of international anarchy they may be doing, and that is an important contribution to the anarchy debates. But it prevents us from investigating practices that produce states as producers. With Wendtian constructivism, we think we understand how states as tails function in international politics. But, as *Wag the Dog* reminds us, wagging isn't mostly about tails/states. It's about tales/practices.

Table 4.5 Advantages and disadvantages of the Wendtian compromise

Advantages	Disadvantages
Can hold states accountable for their part in producing anarchy as either conflictual or cooperative	• Cannot escape reification because Wendt replaces a reified logic of anarchy with reified states • Misses the opportunity to restore a broad focus on process and practice in international politics because Wendt must exclude from consideration the practices that produce states as products of anarchy in order for his myth to function

Suggestions for further thinking

Topic 1 Constructivism

Nicholas Onuf was the first to introduce the concept of constructivism into the IR theory debates. Onuf made his case for constructivism in his 1989 book *World of Our Making*. Since then, several theorists have adopted and adapted constructivism, in ways unanticipated by Onuf (as he suggests in his 1999 essay). Wendtian constructivism is the most well known. Recently, Wendt consolidated and clarified his position in his book *Social Theory of International Politics*. Others, like John Ruggie, have applied constructivism to readings of international politics. And the Onuf school of constructivism has carried on apace. It is not surprising, then, to read in the pages of *Foreign Policy* that constructivism is a necessary tool in any IR theorist's toolbox, an argument made by Stephen Walt.

Suggested reading

V. Kublakova, Nicholas Greenwood Onuf, and Paul Kowert (eds) (1998) *International Relations in a Constructed World*. New York: M.E. Sharpe.

Nicholas Greenwood Onuf (1989) *World of Our Making*. Columbia: University of South Carolina Press.

Nicholas Greenwood Onuf (1999) "Worlds of Our Making: The Strange Career of Constructivism in IR," in Donald J. Puchala (ed.) *Visions of IR*. Columbia: University of South Carolina Press.

John G. Ruggie (1998) *Constructing the World Polity*. London: Routledge.

Stephen M. Walt (1998) "International Relations: One World, Many Theories," *Foreign Policy* (Spring): 29–46.

Alexander Wendt (1999) *Social Theory of International Politics*. Cambridge: Cambridge University Press.

Topic 2 Postmodernism

One of the things that makes constructivism so appealing to many IR theorists is that it is *not* postmodernism. Yet it was postmodernist arguments, introduced to IR theory in Richard Ashely's pathbreaking critique of neorealism and through a series of essays by R.B.J. Walker (many of which are collected in his book *Inside/Outside*), that got IR scholars thinking about questions of identity and practice to begin with. While constructivist scholars turned to scholars like Anthony Giddens for their insights about international politics, poststructuralist scholars turned to the works of Michel Foucault, Jacques Derrida, Jean Baudrillard, and Julia Kristeva, among others.

There are long-running debates between constructivists and poststructuralists (both termed "reflectivists" by Robert Keohane) about identity, practice, and politics.

While Wendt's constructivist myth "anarchy is what states makes of it" arguably de-naturalizes the logic of anarchy with its focus on state practice and thereby enables us to hold states accountable for their behaviors which produce either conflict or cooperation, poststructuralists criticize this sort of constructivism because it cannot interrogate the practices that produce states themselves. Some IR scholars have criticized poststructuralism for being apolitical because it does not identify actors and hold them accountable in traditional ways (as Wendtian constructivism does). Yet poststructuralists argue that it is precisely their insistence *not* to ever stop investigating how power is used to stabilize identities that makes their work politics (see George (1994) and Edkins (1999)) and makes some constructivist work politically vacuous in contrast.

As this discussion should make clear, it is a poststructualist position that informs my critique of Wendt's anarchy myth in this chapter. To use this chapter to highlight the differences between constructivist and poststructuralist approaches to states as the authors of international anarchy, a useful poststructuralist work to assign is Michel Foucault's essay "What is an Author?" For more on postmodernism (especially in relation to its debates with neoMarxism), see Chapter 7.

Suggested reading

Richard K. Ashley (1984) "The Poverty of Neorealism," *International Organization* 38(2): 225–86.

Jenny Edkins (1999) *Poststructuralism and International Relations: Bringing the Political Back In*. Boulder, CO: Lynne Rienner.

Michel Foucault (1984) "What is an Author?" in Paul Rabinow (ed.) *The Foucault Reader*. New York: Pantheon, pp. 101–20.

Jim George (1994) *Discourses of Global Politics: A Critical (Re)Introduction to International Relations*. Boulder, CO: Lynne Rienner.

Robert O. Keohane (1988) "International Institutions: Two Approaches," *International Studies Quarterly* 32: 379–96.

R.B.J. Walker (1993) *Inside/Outside: International Relations as Political Theory*. Cambridge: Cambridge University Press.

Gender

Is gender a variable?

What's an IR scholar to do about feminism? This is a question that has troubled IR scholars for decades. While feminist debates engaged people in social and political spaces outside the discipline of IR, IR scholars did their best not to see the relevance of feminism for their own debates. That didn't stop some feminists from rethinking key IR concepts like power through feminism (Carroll, 1972), but such contributions were largely ignored by IR scholars until recently (Murphy, 1996; Pettman, 1998). It was only in the late 1980s when feminist questions pushed their way onto the IR agenda through books, journals, and conferences that feminism suddenly seemed attractive to IR scholars.

And for a few years, IR's affair with feminism flourished. Feminist essays were added to IR journals, feminist panels were added to IR conferences, and feminist jobs were added to IR departments. In the early 1990s, feminist questions—questions about the presumed gender neutrality of international politics from the standpoint of women—seemed to have been added to most aspects of IR.

But IR's affair with feminism did not always go smoothly. Even though IR scholars (mostly men) began to welcome feminist contributions (from mostly women) into their field and even though some men even proclaimed themselves to be feminists, many feminists (mostly female) were not always happy with the terms of this relationship. They kept pointing out to IR scholars (men and women) that feminist questions could not just be added to and stirred in with IR questions in ways that left the core of the discipline unchanged. They stressed that feminist questions changed the very terms in which IR was approached, understood, and studied. Furthermore, they pointed out that feminist questions were every bit as legitimate and important as IR's classical approaches to war and peace.

Needless to say, not everyone welcomed these feminist insights. While the era of dismissing feminists and feminist questions from IR debates without political risk had now passed, surely feminists must realize that the point of feminist approaches to IR was to further IR's core agenda of asking questions about war and peace and not to destabilize the very foundation from which such questions were asked? Sometimes feminists just went too far, it seemed to (mostly male) IR scholars, to the point that feminists seemed to be out of control altogether because they insisted on asking the wrong and the most uncomfortable sorts of questions. Certainly, (mostly male) IR scholars could still advise (mostly female) feminists on how to do feminism in a way that was compatible with IR and comfortable for IR scholars. And so they did (Keohane, 1989; Weber, 1994).

One effect of IR's paternalistic engagements with feminists and feminist questions was to decrease the scope of feminist questions that IR scholars had to take seriously (Zalewski, 1993 and 1995). Feminist questions, it seemed, should not be asked about everything all the time. There seemed to be a place and a time when feminist questions mattered and when feminists should be heard. Feminism deserved a "proper" place in IR debates, but it was (mostly male) IR scholars who placed feminism—who put and kept feminism in its place (Zalewski, 1999). But feminism rarely stayed in its place. And that troubled and sometimes even scared IR scholars. How could feminism more reliably be placed as a compliment to IR questions?

In 1996, a solution for placing feminism presented itself in the form of Adam Jones's essay "Does 'Gender' Make the World Go Round? Feminist Critiques of International Relations." Uniquely for a male IR scholar, Jones seems to argue that the problem with feminism isn't that it is everywhere and has to be kept in its place. Rather, the problem with feminism is that it has limited its own contribution to the IR debates—the gender variable. By "the gender variable," Jones does not mean some quantitative cause/effect quotient. Rather, the gender variable simply expresses what feminists study—or, as Jones argues, what feminists *ought* to study, which is gender.

Jones's use of the gender variable simultaneously expands and contracts feminist IR debates. On the one hand, it seems to open up IR by moving away from what Jones claims are narrow feminist questions about women and the feminine to broader gender questions about all genders. On the other hand, it makes feminism and feminists manageable because it places them within one reasonable realm— gender—and places gender itself within the confines of a variable. Now IR scholars can look at gender as a discrete set of relationships which they can explore qualitatively or quantitatively. And they can do so without forever having to answer feminist charges that they are just adding in gender to IR analyses. After all, it was feminists, Jones tells us, who gave us the gender variable. IR scholars are only putting it to proper use.

Like our neoidealist myth "there is an international society" (Chapter 3), Jones's myth "gender is a variable" is never defended by Jones. What is defended is the need to make feminist engagements with IR more balanced. And to do this, Jones argues, the gender variable must be made more inclusive, especially of the gendered positions of men and masculinities in international relations. In other words, if feminists want "women's issues" and "feminine concerns" to be considered in IR, then (mostly male) IR scholars are right to insist that "men's issues" and "masculine concerns" be given equal time. Yet in making this argument, the gender variable "itself" simply goes without saying. It is simply the basis upon which Jones makes his argument for its expansion.

But is gender a variable? Gender *appears to be* a variable in Jones's essay because its status as a variable is never questioned. But what would it mean for gender to be a variable? It would mean that gender can be placed and contained in some distinct thing called a variable. And, because gender could be so placed, the gender variable itself would be outside of gender (Box 5.1).

All this makes Jones's myth "gender is a variable" attractive to IR scholars because it seems to allow them to stand outside of gender while they analyze gender and the gendered relationships of international politics. Yet many feminists have resisted conceptualizations of gender as a variable precisely because they argue one is never outside of gender. Jones's myth "gender is a variable" only functions so long as it can claim not just a gender-neutral status (equality to all genders) but

---

Box 5.1 What would it mean for gender to be a variable?

1　Gender could be placed and contained in some distinct thing called a variable.
2　This "gender variable" would itself be outside of gender. It would be free of gender.

a gender-free status (being outside of gender altogether). And here Jones runs into a problem, because the effect of his use of the gender variable is to construct a gendered relationship between IR and feminism, a relationship in which feminism is once again placed in the stereotypical feminized position as irrational, unbalanced, and in need of male guidance. Left unchecked and unplaced, feminism threatens to destroy IR's family romance about man, the state, and war.

In this chapter, I will explore how Jones mythologizes the existence of gender as a variable by arguing that "the gender variable" should be more balanced. I will focus on how Jones characterizes feminism, assesses feminism's contribution to the IR/gender debates, and argues for a more comprehensive notion of a gender variable which includes a focus on men and masculinities. Finally, I will reassess Jones's myth "gender is a variable" through the film *Fatal Attraction*.

Fatal Attraction, the 1987 classic horror thriller about a heterosexual affair gone wrong, in many ways parallels IR's relationship with feminism. IR scholars are attracted to feminism just as Dan Gallager/Michael Douglas is attracted to Alex Forest/Glenn Close. But this attraction can be fatal to the classic family romance—in Dan Gallager's case about the heterosexual family; in IR's case about war and peace. It is only by placing the feminine Alex—by keeping her in her place—that Dan survives his fatal attraction to her. And it is only by presenting himself as outside of gender that Dan's placement of Alex seems to be acceptable, so much so that audiences cheer at her demise. But what if neither Dan nor IR can stand outside of gender? Then the myth "gender is a variable" could no longer function because gender could not be isolated from how one sees the world, especially the world of gender.

What does the myth say?

Jones's essay begins with a common IR theme—that the classical tradition of international relations (realist–idealist debates that focus on questions of war and peace; see Chapters 2, 3, and 4) is experiencing challenges from a number of alternative approaches to IR, including feminism (1996: 405). Jones's project is to assess whether or not the feminist challenge to the classical tradition has made a contribution to our knowledge of IR. His conclusion is mixed. On the one hand, he credits feminism for its "seminal 'discovery' of . . . the gender variable in international relations" (1996: 407). On the other hand, however, Jones argues that "feminism's standard equation of *gender*, an inclusive designation, with *women/femininity*, a narrower and more restrictive one" unduly limits what the gender variable is and should be in IR (1996: 407). The gender variable, Jones argues, needs to be expanded to include other aspects of gender, notably men and masculinity (1996: 420–9). Jones spends his essay making his case for the need to expand the gender variable.

If Jones is to argue convincingly that the gender variable needs to be expanded, however, he must demonstrate that feminism's application of it is too restrictive. In making this case, Jones offers answers to three key questions:

1   What is feminism?
2   How have feminists made use of the gender variable in IR?

3   How should feminists and other IR scholars apply the gender variable in future?

What is feminism for Jones? Jones suggests that "few schools of criticism are as diverse and diffuse as feminism" (1996: 405). Even so, he identifies "three essential features of feminist theories", while allowing that some post-positivist feminists might not accept all of these features (1996: 406; see Table 5.1). In terms of their subject of analysis, all feminist theories "focus on women as historical and political actors" (1996: 406). In terms of how they conduct their analyses, all feminists share "an epistemological foundation in the realm of women's experience" (1996: 406). Finally, in terms of their normative outlook, all feminists contend that "women and the feminine constitute historically underprivileged, under-represented, and under-recognized social groups and 'standpoints'; and this should change in the direction of greater equality" (1996: 406).

Later in his essay, Jones adds a fourth point to his list of feminist features. He writes, "It is fair to say that a very common motif, one that almost deserves inclusion on a list of feminism's defining features, is of *men as an international ruling class*, their internal squabbles secondary to the basic challenge of suppressing women" (1996: 408).

What is wrong with feminism is also what, for Jones, is wrong with feminism's application of the gender variable in IR. Feminism's concern with women and the feminine make it too narrow, and its research program is normatively based. It not only attempts to improve women's lives, it seems to place the blame for the difficulties women face squarely on men (if Jones's fourth point is taken into account). And all of this adds up to suspect scholarship because it means that feminism is driven by a normative agenda. And this has no place in proper scholarship, according to Jones. Allowing a quote from Sara Ruddick to speak for all feminists, Jones argues that "feminists are partisans for women" (Ruddick, 1989: 235, quoted in Jones, 1996). But Jones reminds us that "partisanship and scholarship do not always mix easily" (Jones, 1996: 407).

Table 5.1 What is feminism for Jones?

Subject of feminism	Women as historical and political actors
Epistemology of feminism	Grounded in the realm of women's experiences
Normative agenda of feminism	1 Seek global transformations toward greater equality of women and the feminine because both are historically underprivileged, under-represented, and under-recognized
	2 Equality for women and the feminine must overcome suppression of women by men as "an international ruling class"

To make his point that feminist IR scholarship's partisanship makes its use of the gender variable unbalanced—because it includes positive analyses of women and femininity, but primarily negative, if any, analyses of men and masculinity—Jones offers a few examples of what he sees as feminist IR scholar's use of the gender variable. These serve as his answer to question 2 above, "How have feminists made use of the gender variable in IR?" Jones's answer is, restrictively (Table 5.2).

Table 5.2 How have feminists made use of the gender variable?

Topic/theme	Feminist argument	Contribution to IR?
Opposed dualisms	Male and masculine structures privilege men and exclude women. These structures must be supplemented "by incorporating the gender variable," thereby creating more opportunities for women	No, because it blames men and masculinities for how the world is
Realist state	1 The state as either masculinist or male (radical feminist argument)	No, because it is an extreme and essentialist view of the state
	2 "The personal is political" (liberal feminist argument)	Yes, and it should be added to the three other levels of analysis – individual, state, and international
Rational-actor model	Labels of Western-style rationality as a peculiarly male/masculinist phenomenon reflecting and perpetuating patriarchal power. Can be corrected with stereotypical "Mother Earth" essentialist ways of thinking about actors	No, because the argument boils down to men and masculinity are essentially bad, and women and femininity are essentially good
Realist conceptions of power and security	1 Expand the range of power relationships that realism considers	Yes, because gendered power relationships should be included in realism
	2 Redefine power	No, because it sneaks in feminist normative agenda by adding in prescriptions about what power should be rather than descriptions of what power is

Jones's conclusion that "feminist attempts to come to grips with the gender variable remain limited, even radically constrained" (1996: 406) follows from his illustrations of how what he has characterized as feminism has engaged with realism, the privileged pillar of the classical tradition. Jones identifies four themes/topics on which feminists have critiqued realism: (1) opposed dualisms; (2) the realist assumption of the state; (3) the rational-actor model; and (4) realist conceptions of power and security. Jones suggests that feminists are not alone in criticizing realism on these topics. But "what is distinctive about the feminist orientation is the incorporation of the gender variable, and the exploration of its influence on women and (to a lesser extent) society as a whole" (1996: 409).

So on the topic of opposed dualisms, when feminists critique realism for being "inextricably bound up with a hierarchical world order," what feminists focus on is "the extent to which realist discourse perpetuates gender hierarchies along with hierarchies of class and state" (1996: 410). Notwithstanding post-positivist feminist critiques that examine realism's construction of and construction through hierarchies, Jones places his emphasis here on liberal feminist engagements with realism because, as he argues, "there are signs that it [liberal feminism] may be staging a comeback as some of the more paradoxical and stifling aspects of post-positivism become evident" (1996: 410).

What do liberal feminists say about realism and gender hierarchies? According to Jones, these feminists argue that "what is male/masculine is standard, universal, the measure by which everything *other* is judged" (1996: 410). This has the effect of privileging men and masculinities in politics, economics, and academics. And so liberal feminism "concentrates its efforts on *supplementing* classical frameworks by incorporating the gender variable" (1996: 410). In practice, this means opening up structures that have "ordinarily been a male preserve" to women (1996: 410).

Turning to feminist analyses of the realist state, Jones (using the work of radical feminist Catherine McKinnon) argues that feminists describe the state as either masculinist or male, which implies that the state cannot provide security for all of its citizens (Jones, 1996: 412; McKinnon, 1989: 163). Jones dismisses feminists like McKinnon for overstating their case (an argument, it should be added, made by many feminists as well). In contrast to radical feminism, Jones finds the liberal feminist argument that "the personal is political" so persuasive that he recommends that it should "supplement the triumvirate of 'levels' guiding classical analyses of international affairs [individual, state, international, or as Waltz puts it, man, the state, and war; see Chapter 2]" (1996: 413).

Concerning the rational-actor model that realism relies upon, Jones argues that again "the distinctive feminist contribution here is the labeling of Western-style rationality as a peculiarly male/masculinist phenomenon reflecting and perpetuating patriarchal power" (1996: 413). All he sees feminists offering to counter it are stereotypical "Mother Earth" essentialist ways of thinking about actors. And so, Jones concludes that feminists claim all women are good and all men are bad.

Finally, concerning realist conceptions of power and security, Jones claims that feminist contributions here take two forms. "They may seek to illuminate the power relationships that standard commentary has overlooked; or they may propose a radical redefinition of what actually constitutes 'power'" (1996: 414). Jones approves of the former feminist way of engaging realist conceptions of power and security because, as Jones argues, they rightly draw attention to how the realist model that focuses exclusively on states or state elites "misses a wide range of power relationships that discriminate against women" (1996: 414). But he objects to feminist attempts to redefine power because he sees these as "more prescriptive than descriptive" (1996: 415), thus sneaking in feminism's normative agenda once more.

When these feminist critiques of realism are applied to questions of war and peace, Jones tells us, "the plight of embodied women is front and centre throughout, while the attention paid to the male/masculine realm amounts to little more than lip-service" (1996: 412).

What all of this tells us is that feminists' use of the gender variable has been biased from the start against men and masculinities. This is not surprising considering that feminism, as Jones characterizes it, is a tradition that makes a gender-biased argument for a more femininely and womenly engendered world from the beginning. Feminism is unbalanced, even irrational, because of its normative, prescriptive agenda.

So, if this is the problem, how can it be corrected? How should feminists and other IR scholars apply the gender variable in future? Jones's answer is to offer "more balanced and fertile theories of the gender variable's operation in international relations" (1996: 423) by supplementing the partiality of feminist gender analysis with an analysis of gender focused on men and masculinities. He puts it like this, "My suggestions are feminist-grounded in that they seek to apply a core feminist methodology—isolation of the gender dimension of an issue or phenomenon. But they move beyond presently existing feminist approaches by directing the analytical beam equally toward the gender that is, so far by definition, under-represented in feminist commentary" (1996: 424). Jones argues that his focus on men and masculinities is "a necessary first step towards synthesis: a blending of gendered perspectives that will allow the gender variable and its operations to be examined in more multi-dimensional terms" (1996: 424).

Jones offers a list of "issue-areas and phenomena that could help generate real-world research agendas" for his more multi-dimensionally conceived notion of gender in IR. These include mostly "public" topics—like how men are displaced as refugees during war, how men are the victims of murder and suicide more than women, and how state violence including torture and incarceration overwhelmingly affects men rather than women. They also include a couple of "private" topics like men taking risky and/or badly paying jobs to support their families and being the victims of ethnic attacks (1996: 424–9; see Table 5.3).

Overall, Jones's point is that men suffer disproportionately to women in international relations, and feminism occludes the gendered suffering of men because of its biased research focus on women and the feminine. Feminism's contribution of the gender variable is a good one, but it has been badly applied to investigations of IR because feminist prescriptions about how the world *should be* for women detract attention from how the world *is* for men.

The merits of Jones's argument—not to mention the (in)accuracy with which he characterizes feminism—are hotly debated, a point I will come back to later (see Carver et al., 1998; Jones, 1998; Zalewski, 1999). Yet however right or wrong Jones's argument about feminism's uses of the gender variable may be, all Jones's points assume the myth "gender is a variable."

Table 5.3 How should feminists and non-feminists use the gender variable in the future?

Public issues and phenomena concerning men to be included	Private issues and phenomena concerning men to be included
1 Men as displaced war refugees	1 Men taking badly paid and/or dangerous jobs to provide for families
2 Men as victims of murder and suicides	2 Men becoming political victims because of ethnic conflicts
3 Men as victims of state violence, including torture and incarceration	

Writing of the gender variable, Jones suggests that gender can be "isolated" (1996: 410, 424, 424), "incorporated" (1996: 420), "blended" (1996: 424), "balanced" (1996: 423), and "broadened" (1996: 406, 407, 429). In other words, gender is a discrete phenomenon that can be placed in IR. And it is those aspects of feminist IR scholarship which Jones can "add" to IR—like the feminist emphasis on personal politics or feminist attempts to expand the range of power relationships that realism should consider—that Jones credits as genuine contributions to the world of understanding gender relations in international relations. These have a place in IR scholarship, unlike feminist attempts to disturb structures of realism and rationality or to redefine power, according to Jones (see Table 5.2).

Because some feminist insights can be added to/placed within IR scholarship, then "the gender variable" can also be added. It can be expanded to include aspects of gendered international politics that Jones claims feminists ritually neglect. All of this is consistent with Jones's myth that "gender is a variable." That feminism has unduly restricted the place of gender in IR does not detract from Jones's myth that "gender is a variable." All it means is that the gender variable's placement and place must be reconsidered in view of gender studies of men and masculinities.

What if "placing" gender is not as easy as Jones suggests? *What if gender is not something to be placed or added to but something through which the world is viewed?* If gender is a way of seeing the world—a worldview—then it cannot be a variable, because a variable is something that is placed in a world. And it is as a worldview that feminist and gender scholars regularly describe gender. For example, consider the definition of one feminist, V. Spike Peterson, that Jones includes in his essay. Even though Jones quotes Peterson as evidence of his myth "gender is a variable," Peterson instead writes of gender as a worldview.

> Feminist scholarship, both deconstructive and reconstructive, takes seriously the following two insights: first, that gender is socially constructed, producing subjective identities *through which we see and know the world*, and, second, that *the world is pervasively shaped by gendered meanings*. That is, we do not experience or "know" the world as abstract "humans" but as embodied, gendered beings. As long as that is the case, accurate understanding of agents—as knowable and as knowers—requires attention to the effects of our "gendered states" (my italics; Peterson, quoted in Jones, 1996: 406).

Table 5.4 Jones's characterization of feminism vs. Peterson's characterization of feminism

Jones	Peterson
Feminism = normative program	Feminism = worldview
Characteristics of feminism: 1 Feminist subjects are women and the feminine 2 Feminist epistemology is grounded in women's experiences 3 Feminist normative agenda is to promote women's equality and to blame men and masculinity for global injustices	Characteristics of feminism: 1 Gender is socially constructed, producing subjective identities through which we see and know the world 2 The world is pervasively shaped by gendered meanings; therefore, we "know" the world as gendered beings

Peterson's discussion of feminist scholarship and its conceptualization of gender have nothing in common with Jones's list of "essential feminist features" (see Table 5.4). Furthermore, she discusses gender not as something that can be placed but instead as something that helps us to place things—events, people, ideas—that we encounter in our everyday world. If gender is a worldview, a perspective on the world, then no amount of arguing for the expansion of gender as a variable will make gender something that can be placed or, for that matter, kept in its place.

So why do IR scholars like Jones try so hard to "place" gender? Could it be that they fear that their own privileged perspectives on international politics and their own centralized questions might be displaced—if not replaced—by feminist ones? Put differently, if left unchecked, might disruptive and inappropriate feminist questions disturb IR's traditional worldview, in which we see primarily "man, the state, and war"?

The urgency to place gender—especially the feminine—and the question of whether gender can be placed are explored in the film *Fatal Attraction*. *Fatal Attraction* works hard to distinguish between good expressions of the feminine (mother/wife) and bad expressions of the feminine (vengeful lover) in order to leave undisturbed a worldview that makes us sympathetic to the plight of the male lead, a character who fears unbounded femininity. Yet to achieve these things, isn't the film told from a gendered point of view? And if this is the case, then the film raises the more general question, "isn't any 'placing' of gender always a gendered placing?" Put differently, "isn't it impossible to stand outside of gender, especially when trying to put gender in its place?"

Fatal Attraction

Fatal Attraction is a horror thriller in which what is at stake is the survival of the Gallager family, composed of Dan, his wife, Beth, and their daughter, Ellen. The horror genre of the film is established from the very first frame. The credits and title of the film appear on a black background. No music plays. The background becomes the New York sky, and soon we see a very industrial skyline, unlike the typical New York cityscape filmgoers would recognize. Subdued city sounds are heard. As the camera takes us across the skyline to focus on the window of one apartment, the eerie city sounds are replaced by family sounds. We hear a children's television program in which a woman and a small girl are conversing. Cut to interior of the apartment.

Beth Gallager, in T-shirt and underwear, is rushing about the room picking things up and encouraging Dan to hurry. Beth and Dan are going out to a party connected to Dan's work. Dan, also dressed in a shirt and underwear, is stretched out on a couch, listening to music through headphones while working on some papers. On an adjacent couch, daughter Ellen in pajamas and robe watches the television. The family dog rests its sleeping head on Ellen's lap. The wife of another couple, who wants to know what Beth will wear to the party, rings. They coordinate outfits. Ellen plays with her mother's makeup, and Beth cleans her up. Dan asks where his suit is, Beth tells him, and there he finds it freshly dry-cleaned.

The contrast between what is outside the Gallager's apartment and what is inside could not be more stark. Outside is danger, represented by scary sounds and eerie landscapes. Inside is the comfort and routine which comes with a traditional family arrangement. Everything outside is unsettling. Everything inside is safe and secure, made possible by Dan's work outside the home and Beth's work as a homemaker.

Plate 5.1 Dan's wife, Beth, reads to their daughter.
Courtesy of the Ronald Grant Film Archive © Paramount Pictures.

Insecurity is quickly introduced into the Gallager family, however, through Alex Forest, a single woman whom Dan meets briefly at the party that evening and who, we learn later, lives in the eerie warehouse part of the city. We first see Alex when Dan's friend, Jimmy, makes a pass at her. Alex gives him the coldest of looks. Jimmy says to Dan (who sees all this), "If looks could kill . . . (giggling)", foreshadowing the danger Alex embodies. Later, Dan and Alex meet by chance at the bar. They are surprised, a bit embarrassed, and they laugh nervously as they recognize one another.

Dan [laughing]:   No, I'm not sayin' anything. I'm not even gonna look.
Alex [also laughing]: Was it that bad?
Dan [still laughing]:   Well, let's just say I was glad I wasn't on the receiving end of that one.
Alex [lightly]:   I hate it when guys think they can come on like that.
Dan: Ah, Jimmy's ok. He's just a little insecure like the rest of us.

Dan begins this last comment looking straight ahead, but when he gets to the part about insecurity, he turns and looks right at Alex. The move is charming, even seductive, as revelations of male insecurity often are. Alex clearly finds Dan to be charming. Dan introduces himself, and Alex and Dan begin a conversation. Then Beth beckons Dan from the corner of the room.

Dan: I have to go.
Alex: Is that your wife?

Plate 5.2 Dan and Alex meet at a party.
Courtesy of the Ronald Grant Film Archive © Paramount Pictures.

Dan: Yup.

Alex [coyly, making a joke of it]:   Better run along [giggles].

Dan and Beth leave. When they get home, Beth, undressing in the bedroom, says to Dan, "Aren't you forgetting something?" Dan, like us, seems to take Beth's words as a sexual advance. Beth then points to the dog who needs walking. When Dan returns, he finds his daughter Ellen in bed with Beth. Dan looks disappointed, and Beth, smiling, tells him, "It's just for tonight, honey." The price of domestic bliss is stereotypically spelled out for us, as it is for Dan, and that price is passion.

The next morning, Beth and Ellen go off to the country to look at a house Beth is interested in. She has long wanted to move the family to the country. She and Ellen will be away for the night. Dan stays behind because he has a rare Saturday meeting. As it happens, Alex is also at the meeting. She is the editor of a publishing company Dan's law firm is representing. Alex and Dan again by chance run into one another after their meeting. Caught in the rain and unable to get a taxi, Dan suggests they go get a drink together. They end up having dinner and discussing the possibility of taking the evening further.

Alex: Where's your wife?

Dan: Where's my wife [surprised by the question]? My wife is in the country visiting her parents for the weekend.

Alex: And you're here with a strange girl being a naughty boy.

Dan: I don't think having dinner with somebody is a crime.

Alex: Not yet, anyway.

Dan: Will it be?

Alex: I don't know. What do you think?

Dan: I definitely think it's gonna be up to you [laughing nervously].

Alex: We were attracted to one another at the party, that was obvious. You're on your own for the night, that's also obvious. We're two adults. . . .

Dan [hardly able to get out the words]:   I'll get the check.

And so their passionate weekend begins. First we see the famous scene in which they have sex on top of Alex's kitchen sink full of dirty dishes (and we think, Beth just uses her sink to clean the dishes). They move into the bedroom, and when they finally speak, Alex says "That was great." And Dan keeps saying, more to himself than to her it seems, "Thank God. Thank God." They go out dancing, return to Alex's apartment, and have sex in the elevator. Dan spends the night. He returns home and learns that Beth won't be home that night as expected. And so, with Alex's persuasion, he spends the day with her, bringing the family dog with him. But as Dan goes to leave after dinner and sex, Alex asks him to stay. When he won't, she slits her wrists and tells him she is sorry if she upset him. Dan stays to look after her.

From this point on, the cool, collected, careerist Alex turns increasingly weird. She starts by harassing Dan with phonecalls and visits, behavior which is not out of the question for someone who feels hurt and scorned and who wants to let Dan know their brief affair has left her pregnant. But then her behavior turns dangerous when Dan rejects her. Alex pours acid on Dan's car, kidnaps his daughter for an afternoon, and, in a scene reminiscent of Hitchcock, boils his daughter's bunny. In the film's climax, the over-the-top Alex attacks Beth in the bathroom of the family home, only to be nearly drowned by Dan and finally shot and killed by Beth. The film's closing shot is of the family photo of Dan, Beth, and Ellen. Family life for the Gallagers has finally been rescued.

Even though it is Alex who is killed in the film, it is Dan who is portrayed as the film's fearful victim. Indeed, *Fatal Attraction*—like any good horror film—is a paranoia picture, and the paranoia belongs to Dan. But, unlike classical horror films, Dan's paranoia is not introduced into the plot in reaction to something Alex has done. It is something Dan has felt since he was a small child. The film discloses this early on. As Dan and Alex share an evening together during their weekend-long affair, they listen to the opera *Madame Butterfly*. They both agree that this is their favorite opera. And then Dan reminisces, "My father told me she was gonna kill herself. I was terrified."

While Dan's confession foreshadows Alex's suicide attempt and her ultimate suicidal gesture of attacking Beth which results in Alex's death, it does more than this. It asks the question, "why was he terrified?" Terror seems like an unlikely response—even for a young boy—to the information his father has given him. Sad, sorry, upset, even relieved. But terrified? What did this boy have to fear? What does Dan have to fear now? And why—if the conclusion to this opera was so terrifying for young Dan—is it his favorite opera as an adult?

As the film jumps from romance to suspense to horror, it answers these questions. What Dan fears is what the film stereotypes as unbounded female emotion—an irrationality that turns Dan into a victim of Alex's vengeful anger when Dan tries to end their affair. But this unbounded female emotion also releases Dan's passion, something the film shows him experiencing only with Alex and never with his wife Beth (Conlon, 1996). This makes his attraction to Alex understandable. Yet because of his affair with Alex, Dan's family romance with Beth and Ellen is nearly shattered. For Dan, all of that is pretty scary. His attraction to Alex could be fatal to his sense of family.

All of this points to how the film makes sense of the world (Box 5.2). The world of *Fatal Attraction* is a world in which there is no higher value than living in a secure heterosexual nuclear family. This legitimate family gives meaning to one's life. This is the case as much for Alex as it is for Dan. For without a legitimate family (a marriage, a child), a woman like Alex is not valued. She is someone with whom a married man like Dan can have an affair and discard—or at least she *should* be and *would* be if she respected the implicit rules pertaining to affairs with married men. But Alex is not your typical woman. She is located outside of the reasonable limits of the heterosexual nuclear family—the only context in which reasonable behavior is portrayed in the film.

Fatal Attraction works hard to present Alex as irrational. Never mind that Alex is a successful New York editor, a woman who controls her own life and her own body. None of this gives her life meaning because, the film tells us, legitimate meaning comes only from legitimate family. When Alex discovers she is pregnant with Dan's child, her hopes for a legitimate family seem to compel her down the path of increasingly bizarre behavior. Remember the acid, boiled bunny, kidnapping, and attempted murder. Each irrational gesture has its basis in her lack of a legitimate place in a legitimate family. Woman on her own, the film tells us, is a mess.

> ### Box 5.2 How does *Fatal Attraction* make sense of the world?
>
> By valuing the traditional heterosexual nuclear family.
>
> There is no higher value than living in a secure family.
>
> This legitimate family gives meaning to one's life.

This is in contrast to how the film portrays both Beth and Dan. If Alex is irrational because she is a woman out of place, Beth is a reasonable woman struggling to hold onto her legitimate place in the heterosexual family. She is a good wife and a good mother. She seems to have no responsibilities beyond those created by the marriage and the marital home. She makes Dan's life easy, and for this she is rewarded with legitimacy. By killing Alex, it is Beth who rescues her family (see Table 5.5).

Dan, too, is a character in place. Forget his (irrational?) fear and attraction to a woman out of place. Dan is a rational man with a successful career as a lawyer and a traditional marriage. Even though he has an affair with Alex, he makes it clear from the beginning that this affair is not to interfere with his marriage. This is a reasonable position. And he falls back on "adult agreements" and "rules" whenever he finds it necessary to keep Alex in her place.

Plate 5.3 Dan comforts Alex after her suicide attempt.
Courtesy of the Ronald Grant Film Archive © Paramount Pictures.

Table 5.5 The place of woman in *Fatal Attraction*

	Legitimate woman (Beth Gallager)	Illegitimate woman (Alex Forest)
Place	Within the heterosexual nuclear family	Outside the heterosexual nuclear family
Characteristics	Good wife Good mother	Independent personally and professionally. This independence is coded in the film as barrenness and failure
Behavior	Rational	Irrational

As long as Alex seems to be safely in her place, Dan feels free to pursue his affair with her. We see this in a scene in which, shortly after their weekend together, Alex appears in Dan's office to thank him for "not running away" when she slit her wrists and to invite him to the opera as a way of saying "thank you." Dan refuses. Alex accepts this refusal, gets up to leave, and extends her hand for Dan to shake in good-bye. But Dan embraces her instead while (in the director's cut of the film) Alex utters, wonderingly, "When does 'no' mean 'no'?" It seems that "no" only means "no" when Dan fears he cannot keep Alex in her place.

That fear of not being able to keep Alex in her place begins during their lovers' weekend. Dan gushes on about his family life, explaining to Alex how lucky he is. Alex asks, "So what are you doing here?" Dan's only reply is "Boy, you know how to ask the wrong thing." This is illustrated in another scene, this time after Alex turns up at Dan's apartment, meets his wife, and secures his unlisted phone number and new address. Afterwards, Alex (who Dan now knows is pregnant with his child) tells Dan, "I'm not gonna be ignored," and she asks Dan "what are you so afraid of?" Dan gets increasingly agitated and casts Alex as hysterical.

Dan: You're so sad, you know that, Alex.
Alex: Don't you ever pity me, you bastard.
Dan: I'll pity you. I'll pity you because you're sick.
Alex: Why? Because I won't allow you to treat me like some slut you can bang a couple of times and throw in the garbage?

Dan says nothing in reply.

In contrasting Dan's and Alex's responses to their affair, the film tells us what is typical and deviant in the world of *Fatal Attraction* (Table 5.6). What is typical is for the heterosexual nuclear family to be respected as the only legitimate—and therefore reasonable—source of meaning. What is deviant is for this family romance to be disturbed by outside, irrational, and illegitimate forces—like a pregnant discarded mistress. This does not mean that a man like Dan cannot have the occasional affair. It does mean that whatever he does, his behavior must not pose a threat to his family life with Beth, Ellen, the dog, and that poor bunny. This point is

Plate 5.4 Alex attacks Dan.
Courtesy of the Ronald Grant Film Archive © Paramount Pictures.

emphasized in Dan's confessional scene to Beth. Beth does not get angry when she learns that Dan had an affair with a woman he does not love. But she is irate when she learns that Dan has impregnated Alex because Alex's illegitimate claim to a family with Dan now threatens Beth's legitimate family.

Dan's mistake is not that he had an affair. His mistake is that he had an affair with *Alex*—a woman who does not respect reasonable limits, a woman who does not stay in her place, a woman who does not behave as Dan assumed she would. And for this viewers generally feel sorry for him. Poor Dan. Ok, he might not be the best guy in the world because he cheats on his wife. But this Alex woman is a maniac!

The film tells us that femininity must be kept in its place. One way of placing femininity is by securing it within a traditional domestic setting through a traditional marriage. This is where we find Beth. The only other rational ways to place it, the film tells us, are either to ignore it (which Dan fails to do) or to kill it. And of course, the demanding, irrational Alex, as a woman out of place trying to weasel her way

Table 5.6 What is typical and what is deviant in the world of *Fatal Attraction*?

Typical	Deviant
To respect the heterosexual nuclear family as the only legitimate and reasonable source of meaning	To disturb the heterosexual nuclear family though outside, irrational, and illegitimate influences

into the Gallagers' traditional family, ends up dead. By concluding with the family photo, the film tells us that family life—what is traditional—can be rescued, so long as the feminine is kept in its place one way or another.

Fatal Attraction is a popular, anti-feminist response to feminism. Its message is that women like Alex—independent, demanding, and out of place—have gone too far. When woman and the feminine are out of place, all hell can break lose. And when it does, it is at the expense of things traditional (like the family) and of the traditional leaders of things traditional (men).

Fatal Attraction also tells us that if we now have to take gender issues seriously—like those of a "liberated" woman like Alex Forest—then we had better not forget that gender is a problem for men like Dan Gallager as well. Put differently, if Alex's "personal is political," then so is Dan's. Dan has a family to support. That can be boring and passionless sometimes, and, because of this, Dan seeks sexual excitement with Alex. But he is first and foremost a family man who wants his family life to be respected, unthreatened, and unchanged.

Dan's mistake is that he thinks he can "add" Alex/passion/unbounded feminine emotion to his life without changing it. Dan's mistake is the same mistake IR makes with feminism. IR thinks it can "add" feminist and gender issues to IR without upsetting the core issues of the discipline of IR and how they are studied. *Fatal Attraction* is very clear about why Dan thinks he can get away with keeping Alex in her place. It is because the film is told from Dan's point of view, made legitimate by the film's coding of the traditional heterosexual nuclear family as the only legitimate source of meaning. We are introduced to events through Dan's family. We follow Dan's life. We sympathize with Dan's character. *Fatal Attraction* is Dan's story. Feminists would argue that, told from Dan's point of view, *Fatal Attraction* is far from a gender-neutral tale. It is the tale of one man's reaction to unbounded feminine emotion (the film's symbolic equivalent for feminism) which he views as unbalanced and excessive. And his reaction is a reasonable one—and one with which we sympathize—because it is grounded in Dan's (and many viewers') respect for the traditional family. If you doubt this, recall that Alex has a very different story to tell about her affair with Dan, one that the film works hard to delegitimize.

Because *Fatal Attraction* is only able to place Alex as the symbol of feminist excesses by telling its story from the point of view of Dan Gallager, the film raises the question, "Does IR theory tell its story about feminism and the gender variable from a particular point of view?" And, if so, "What is Jones's point of view?"

Placing feminism in IR?

Jones believes that "the gender variable" needs to be more balanced because it occludes objective consideration of issues concerning men and masculinities in international politics. Jones credits feminism for introducing gender issues into IR. But he faults feminists for restrictively analyzing gender in IR. Their normative focus on women and the feminine means that they either neglect or disparage men and the masculine. For Jones, feminism has a gendered perspective—women and the feminine. And that gendered perspective is what limits the contribution feminism could make to IR debates. By "adding" men and masculinities to the gender variable, Jones claims to be correcting feminism's unbalanced perspective.

If Jones's myth "gender is a variable" (not to mention his claim that feminists' use of the gender variable is unbalanced) is to function, it must be indebted to no particular gendered point of view. It must stand outside of gender and of any potentially gendered or genderable perspective. It must be neutral, a partisan for no one and nothing. It must be objective and non-normative. In other words, it must be all those things Jones accuses feminism of not being.

Just as *Fatal Attraction* tells its story about placing gender from a particular perspective, however, so too does Jones. Of course, Jones tells the story of feminism and IR's implicit need to place it in a variable from his own perspective. But what makes Jones's perspective so compelling? What gives it meaning? What makes us think, "yea, this guy has a point"? Just like Dan Gallager's story, Adam Jones's story is told in defense of a cherished tradition. For Dan, it is the traditional heterosexual nuclear family. For Jones, it is IR's classical tradition of realist/idealist treatments of questions of war and peace. *It is only because the classical tradition is the only place in which legitimate meaning is located that Jones's story about feminism's meaningless and unfair excesses makes sense.* And it is only because feminism is taken to be full of excesses that it must be placed in "the gender variable" and replaced with what Jones sees as a more balanced gender variable—one balanced by attending to men and masculinities, by the way the world of IR really is, rather than how feminists wish it would be (see Table 5.7).

Table 5.7 Gendered perspectives in *Fatal Attraction* and traditional IR theory

	Fatal Attraction	*Traditional IR theory*
Point of view	Dan Gallager's	Adam Jones's
Perspective	Traditional – legitimate meaning is based on the legitimacy of the heterosexual nuclear family	Traditional – legitimate meaning is based on the legitimacy of the classic IR tradition's treatment of questions of war and peace
How feminine/feminist "excesses" are managed	• added through an illegitimate affair • ignored • killed	• added through the "gender variable" • feminist work inconsistent with Jones's character-ization of the "gender variable" is ignored • feminine/feminist "gender variable" replaced by (killed off with) a more "balanced" gender variable that reempha-sizes men and masculinities

Jones is relatively up-front about his privileging of the classical tradition in IR as the standard against which any feminist "contributions" will be judged. His article opens by reminding us that "In the last two decades, the classical tradition in international relations has come under sustained attack" and he wants to evaluate the merits of the feminist attack (1996: 405). He couches the objective of his article in relation to the classical tradition: "This article seeks to provide an overview of some major contributions and features of feminist IR thinking, with particular attention to the problem of war and peace that has attracted adherents of the classical approach more than any other" (1996: 406). And then he evaluates feminism in terms of what it has "added to" the classical approach (1996: 408–20).

What is so interesting in Jones's article, though, is that the article itself refuses to recognize that "the classical approach" might not be a neutral point of view. It is like Dan's view of the traditional family and an affair in relation to it. *Any* reasonable person would see things exactly as Dan sees them, the film suggests. Similarly, Jones seems to suggest that any reasonable person would see the classical tradition's approach to questions of war and peace as just what IR is about. Consider our first three myths. All of them are firmly within the classical tradition, focusing as they do on questions of war and peace among sovereign nation-states in international anarchy. But none of these myths questions the classical tradition itself—the institutionalized context which makes questions of war and peace and mainstream approaches to investigating them meaningful.

Yet that is exactly what feminism does. It questions the classical tradition *itself*. Like Alex Forest, it is not content to simply accept the "rules of the game" as already established by traditional social arrangements. Feminism, like Alex, asks of the classical tradition the "wrong questions," like "what makes these questions and approaches meaningful?"; "how are these meanings related to one another hierarchically?"; and "how do these meanings enable us to make value judgements that help us to place people and things as legitimate or illegitimate?" (see Box 5.3).

These sorts of questions are dangerous to the classical approach to IR because they expose IR's classical tradition as not (necessarily) value-neutral or as partisan for no one. And it is Jones who warns us that "partisanship and scholarship do not always mix easily" (1996: 407). Just as a feminist perspective has a normative agenda, feminists would argue, so does the classical approach. And that

---

Box 5.3 The "wrong" questions feminism asks of traditional IR theory

1　What makes traditional IR questions and approaches meaningful?
2　How are these meanings related to one another hierarchically?
3　How do these meanings enable us to make value judgements that help us to place people and things as legitimate or illegitimate?
4　What is traditional IR theory's normative agenda, and how does it use gender to secure this agenda while *appearing to be* gender-neutral and gender-free?
5　Should normatively masculine understandings of the world be the only legitimate ways of seeing the world?

normative agenda, they would argue, is one that privileges subjects and sexualities that are constructed as "normal"—heterosexual married men would be one example; masculinist understandings of reason, another. And feminists go further than this. They ask, "Is this the way things should be?" "Should normatively masculine ways of understanding the world and judging the value of things in the world continue to be the only legitimate ways of seeing the world?" By posing these questions, feminists would argue, they are not ignoring men and masculinities but thinking about them critically. As such, they would argue, feminism provides a corrective to the tendency in IR to see *only* men and masculinities and see them in an unreflective light. Feminists have made a political choice to take a self-aware, "biased" view of the world to compensate and, it is to be hoped, transform traditional ways of seeing the world that occlude women and femininities as well as non-normative men and masculinities. At least they are open about their "partisanship," they would argue, unlike proponents of the classical tradition.

By being unapologetic about its normative claims and by suggesting that all traditions have normative claims (disclosed or undisclosed), feminism jeopardizes everything near and dear to the hearts of proponents of the classical tradition. They can no longer ignore feminism, because that would be "politically incorrect." But they can still do their best not to take it seriously. How Dan refuses to take Alex seriously in the film is by caricaturing her as a stereotypical female hysteric. She is a nutcase. Unsurprisingly, Jones does the very same thing (if in milder terms) to IR feminists. He casts them as "unbalanced," a nicer way of saying they are "irrational" (1996: 423). And, in the terms in which they must be understood from the perspective of the classical approach, they "are."

That, however, is one of feminism's points. It is only because the classical tradition has a particular gendered point of view—one that necessarily sees most feminist questions as threatening and therefore stereotypes them as femininely unbalanced—that its proponents like Jones can "place" feminism at all. Recall Peterson's description of feminism. For Peterson, feminism is a worldview that investigates how "gender is socially constructed, producing subjective identities through which we see and know the world" and "that the world is pervasively shaped by gendered meaning" (1996: 406). If one cannot know the world except from a gendered perspective, as feminists argue, then it is impossible for there to be either a gender-neutral or a gender-free standpoint from which to view the world. How Jones *sees* feminism—as unbalanced and in need of guidance from the classical tradition (guidance he provides)—betrays that Jones's way of seeing the world, *especially* the world of gender, is itself traditionally gendered.

If gender is not a place but a worldview, then it is not surprising that Dan Gallager cannot keep Alex Forest in her place outside the marital relationship any more than Adam Jones can keep feminism in its place inside a "gender variable" in it relationship with IR theory. Alex will not stay in her place because her "role" is a disruptive one in the Gallager's traditional family romance. It isn't that Alex has anything against the traditional family. Clearly not, for she wants to have one herself with Dan. But once Dan crosses the line and invites her into his life, Dan cannot manage her as "a discrete relationship" (Jones, 1996: 423) that can be added to his life when he wants it and forgotten about when he doesn't. For better and for worse, Alex changes everything about Dan's familial relationships. Interestingly, it is not

Dan but Beth (the good, antifeminist girl) who ultimately deals with Alex (the bad, feminist girl) and resecures the Gallager's traditional family.

It's similar for feminism and IR. IR's attempts to place gender are doomed to fail because gender is not a discrete relationship which can be added to IR when (mostly male) IR scholars decide that they can control it and ignored when they decide that they can't. Feminist questions are scary for IR scholars in the classical tradition because they don't allow IR scholars to ignore their own normative—and gendered—perspectives. And for this, Jones gives them "the gender variable" as their "'seminal' discovery" (1996: 423)—a place within IR from which they can reasonably get on with the work of doing gender in IR. Jones's move is a sort of proposal to IR feminists. You can join the classical tradition on legitimate terms and enter the traditional family as full, legitimate members, he seems to tell them, so long as you give up on your destabilizing behavior. Be Beth, a domesticated but happy antifeminist. Don't be Alex, a "free" but unhappy (and ultimately dead) feminist. What irks feminists most about Jones's "proposal" is that he claims it is "feminist-grounded" (1996: 424), when the only ground it protects is that of the classical tradition.

Even so, feminists point out that Jones's gendered moves to domesticate feminism in a variable all evidence what makes Jones's myth "gender is a variable" function. Jones only recognizes the gendered claims of feminism—claims feminists never try to conceal. Jones, on the other hand, fails to recognize his own gendered claims—claims that give meaning to the classical tradition's approach to feminist questions. And, of course, these must go without saying. Because if Jones's own position (and that of the classical tradition) are themselves gendered, then Jones fails to offer a gender-neutral, much less gender-free, account of gender. Gender, it seems, has no place in IR theory—*not* because it is "unbalanced" and therefore out of bounds, but because it is something we see the world though and therefore no "home" can hold it.

Suggestions for further thinking

Topic 1 Feminism

The best way to get a sense of what feminism is and the impact it has had on IR theory and international politics is to read feminist IR theorists themselves. This approach also helps readers to stay focused on feminist questions about international politics rather than on disciplinary IR questions about feminism of the sort someone like Jones asks of feminism (Zalewski, 1995). Elshtain's *Woman and War* and Enloe's *Bananas, Beaches and Bases* are the traditional starting places for an encounter with feminist IR theory. Accessibly written and full of illustrations, they provide lively introductions into the literature, as do a number of books that either look to IR theory most specifically (Tickner, 1992; Sylvester, 1994) or that provide collections of feminist IR writings (Grant and Newland, 1991; Peterson, 1992).

Suggested reading

Jean Bethke Elshtain (1987) *Women and War*. New York: Basic Books.

Cynthia Enloe (1989) *Bananas, Beaches and Bases: Making Feminist Sense of International Politics*. Berkeley: University of California Press.

Rebecca Grant and Kathleen Newland (eds) (1991) *Gender and International Relations*. Milton Keynes: Open University Press.

V. Spike Peterson (ed.) (1992) *Gendered States: Feminist (Re)Visions of International Political Theory*. Boulder, CO: Lynne Rienner.

Christine Sylvester (1994) *Feminist Theory and International Relations in a Postmodern Era*. Cambridge: Cambridge University Press.

J. Ann Tickner (1992) *Gender in International Relations: Feminist Perspectives on Achieving Global Security*. New York: Columbia University Press.

Marysia Zalewski (1995) "Well, What is the Feminist Perspective on Bosnia?," *International Affairs* 71(2): 339–56.

Topic 2 Masculinity

Feminists have long argued that their concern is not only with women (although that is a central focus of their research) but on how gender (femininity *and* *masculinity*) construct, constrain, and empower all gendered bodies. They are no strangers to works like Connell's *Masculinities* and other classic texts of masculinity (as Carver et al. argue in their reply to Jones, 1998). Feminist IR scholars have not only argued that "gender is not a synonym for women" (Carver, 1996). They have theoretically and empirically raised the "man" question in international relations (Zalewski and Parpart, 1998).

Suggested readings

Terrell Carver (1996) *Gender is Not a Synonym for Women*. Boulder, CO: Lynne Rienner.

Terrell Carver, Molly Cochran and Judith Squires (1998) "Gendering Jones: feminisms, IRs, and Masculinities," *Review of International Studies* 24(2): 283–97.

Robert W. Connell (1995) *Masculinities*. Cambridge: Cambridge University Press.

Marysia Zalewski and Jane Parpart (eds) (1998) *The "Man" Question in International Relations*. Boulder, CO: Westview.

Globalization

Are we at the end of history?

It is appropriate that a book examining IR as a site of cultural practices imbued with conscious and unconscious ideologies should examine a myth that claims that ideological struggles are over. This is precisely what Francis Fukuyama claims in his famous 1989 essay "The End of History?" and later elaborates on in his book *The End of History and the Last Man* (1992). Fukuyama argues that liberal democracy as a system of governance has won an "unabashed victory" over other ideas to the point that liberalism is the only legitimate ideology left in the world. Not only are there no coherent ideological challengers to liberalism, liberalism itself is free of irrational internal contradictions which lead to the collapse of ideologies. Having no internal contradictions means that liberalism is a finished idea. For Fukuyama, all this marks "the end point of mankind's ideological evolution" and means that liberalism is "the final form of human government" (1989: 271). Because the history of the conflict of ideas in the form of ideological struggle is now over, all that remains to be done is to spread liberal ideology throughout the world as a material way of life, through social, political, and economic institutions.

Fukuyama's argument could not have been more timely. Published the summer before the Berlin Wall came down, Fukuyama's essay appeared to have predicted the thawing Cold War's final melting, a melting made possible by the absence of any credible rivals to liberalism. The supposed predictive power of Fukuyama's myth was not the only thing that made it popular with IR scholars. If Fukuyama had predicted the end of the Cold War, mainstream IR scholars surely had not. Left bewildered and embarrassed, they looked around for something meaningful to say. Debating the insecurities of anarchy (Chapters 2, 3, and 4), for example, just wasn't as gripping as it used to be, now that the US was considered by most to be the uncontested global hegemon and world police officer. IR scholars and their traditional theories were beginning to look obsolete. But, thankfully, Fukuyama's myth not only foretold the death of the classical Cold War strategic paradigm, it made possible an entirely new realm of research—the study of "globalization."

Globalization became the trendiest craze in IR theory at the turn of the century. What is globalization? That's a good question, and one with which scholars in and out of IR have had difficulty grappling. Globalization has been described as "a term which can refer to anything from the Internet to a hamburger" (Strange, 1996: xiii). That's because theorists disagree on just about everything regarding "globalization." They disagree about when "globalization" started. Some date its beginning after World War II (Leyshon, 1997: 133), while others argue it is as old as capitalism itself (Hirst and Thompson, 1996: 2). They disagree about what it expresses (economic, geographic, social, political or cultural phenomena) and whether or not one or more of these phenomena should be emphasized over the others. And they disagree about whether "globalization" is a process, an ideology ("globalism") or a "state of being" ("globality") (Marchand, 2000: 219). Given all these disagreements, it is not surprising that one theorist described "globalization" as simply "a floating sign of many different problematics" (Ó Tauthail, 1998: 85).

Among these many problematics, two stand out. They are two traditions of international political economy—neoliberalism and historical materialism and their expressions of globalization (Table 6.1). Neoliberal expressions of globalization are based in classical liberal economic arguments that see international economic processes as harmonious realms in which economic exchange processes like free trade spread wealth and increase the quality of life for all who participate. And not only does economics bring economic benefits, it brings political benefits as well, primarily through the spread of liberal democratic institutions in which liberty, freedom, and justice for all are to be guaranteed because the people hold political power. This is why classical liberals believe that economic processes should drive political processes.

In an era of "globalization," classical liberal principles become neoliberal expressions of "globalization," in which three processes occur simultaneously and for the good of humankind—economic liberalization (like free trade), political democratization (power to the people), and cultural universalization (some would say the "Americanization" of the globe; see Strange, 1996). For neoliberals, "globalization" is about the benevolent spread of liberal economic, political, and cultural processes, institutions, and practices throughout the world.

Table 6.1 Neoliberal and historical materialist takes on globalization

	Neoliberal	Historical materialist
Nature of international economic relations	Harmonious	Conflictual
Distribution of economic goods	All who participate in economic processes benefit	Capitalist economic processes redistribute wealth so that the rich get richer and the poor get poorer
Relationship between politics and economics	Economics *should* drive politics. Why? Because harmonious, beneficial economic processes can "spill over" and create harmonious, beneficial political processes like democracy within and among sovereign nation-states	Economics *does* drive politics. Because economic processes are conflictual, this means that political processes are conflictual within and among sovereign nation-states
Take on globalization because	Globalization is good because it spreads the economic, political, and cultural benefits of liberalism	Globalization is bad it does not result in an equitable distribution of global wealth
Globalization's place in history	It is the "end of history"	It is the capitalist stage of history. History ends at the next stage, when socialism or communism is realized

In contrast, historical materialist expressions of "globalization" have their roots in classical Marxism. For historical materialists, economic processes drive political and cultural processes. Unlike neoliberals, historical materialists regard international economic processes as conflictual, primarily between economic classes (owners and workers). These conflicts among economic classes are what lead to historical changes in institutions, ideas, and everyday life. History, therefore, is the history of the class struggle (as Marx put it), and history will not end until the class struggle ends. That can only happen when capitalism (our current global economic system) is transcended by communist economic, political, and cultural processes.

Historical materialists generally agree with neoliberals that "globalization" is a process, ideology, and/or way of living that spreads capitalist ideas, institutions, and practices throughout the world. But historical materialists strongly disagree with neoliberals on two important points. First, they disagree with neoliberals in thinking that capitalist economics and liberal ideology are not themselves premised on contradictions. They are not the final, complete expressions of economics and politics that someone like Fukuyama claims they are because economic classes are still at odds with one another. Second, this means that liberalism is not the final stage of history. It is not "the end of history." Rather, it is a step on the way to communism, the real end of history. As these criticisms make clear, historical materialists don't disagree with Fukuyama that history will have an end. They simply disagree with Fukuyama that *liberalism* is "the end of history."

Neoliberal expressions of globalization are by far the most influential in IR theory and in policy circles. They seemed to be the most "historically accurate" in the wake of the post-Cold War collapse of socialist and communist states and ideologies. They clearly complemented post-Cold War theories of neoidealism (Chapter 3). And they informed policies that create regional free trade organizations like the European Union and the North American Free Trade Agreement (NAFTA) and which affect "global" institutions like the World Trade Organization.

There are lots of problems with neoliberal and historical materialist expressions of "globalization," but this is not the place to debate the shortcomings and merits of each (see Herod et al., 1998). Instead, my interest lies in what these debates and disagreements about "globalization" have to do with Fukuyama's myth "it is the end of history." *Fukuyama's myth cleared the ideological ground for neoliberal expressions of globalization to go virtually uncontested.* By arguing that the history of ideological struggle was over and liberalism had won, Fukuyama put liberalism itself beyond debate in two important ways. First, because liberalism had "won" out over ideological challengers, this meant that any critiques of liberalism from "old leftist" ideological traditions like socialism and communism (as well as from the "old right" of fascism) were regarded as outdated and need not be taken seriously by IR scholars. Second, because liberalism was presented in Fukuyama's work as a finished ideology, scholarly attention should be directed away from analysis focused on possible contradictions *within* liberalism and toward analysis of the global spread of neoliberal processes, institutions, and practices that follow from the "globalization" of liberal ideology.

In this chapter, I will explore how Fukuyama's myth "it is the end of history" makes liberalism the global stage on which international politics in an era of "globalization" unfolds. By Fukuyama's own account, for his myth to function liberalism must be a finished ideology with no credible external rivals. In other words, liberalism must be free of contradictions, both internally and externally. Fukuyama makes the case that liberalism has no credible external ideological threats. But, in directing our attention toward the ideological challengers of liberalism, Fukuyama deflects our attention away from liberalism's own internal contradiction—the contradiction between its creation of boundless desires within individuals for the good life and its failure to fully satisfy or control these desires. It is only by substituting economic consumption for personal satisfaction that liberalism defers and displaces individual encounters with what Fukuyama admits is "the empty core of liberalism" (1989: 281)—its inability to deliver a meaningful life.

We see these processes of endless substitution, displacement, and deferral acted out in the 1998 film *The Truman Show*. Not only is Truman Burbank, the "on the air, unaware" star of a television program "The Truman Show," offered a utopian world in which his material desires are met as a way to control his personal desires and keep him on the set that is his hometown of Seahaven. So, too, are Truman's post-historical viewers offered substitutes for their desires. In place of their desire for history, they are offered "The Truman Show"—a place where history as an ideological struggle between good (Truman) and evil (the show's producer, Christof) is staged for them.

But when Truman escapes Seahaven and "The Truman Show" ends, post-historical liberalism's ability to displace individual desires for history onto "The Truman Show" no longer functions. And this makes us wonder if Fukuyama's promise that liberalism's post-Cold War "triumph" over ideological challengers means that we are at "the end of history." For, if we accept Fukuyama's argument, liberalism may have dealt with ideological challengers. But, as *The Truman Show* suggests, it has not (and I would suggest, it cannot) resolve its own internal contradiction between creating and fulfilling desires, desires that propel Truman out of history and possibly lead his viewers back into history.

To make sense of all of this, we need to examine Fukuyama's claim that "it is the end of history." I will do this by focusing on three questions: "What does Fukuyama mean by the end of history?"; "What does liberalism as a post-historical ideology look like to Fukuyama?"; and "How does Fukuyama appear to resolve liberalism's internal tension between creating unfulfillable desires and attempting to fulfil them so that his myth 'it is the end of history' appears to be true?"

What does the myth say?

In his essay "The end of history?," Fukuyama begins by reflecting that "something very fundamental has happened in world history" and this something is usually described as post-Cold War peace "breaking out in many regions of the world" (1989: 270). But Fukuyama laments that analyses of the end of the Cold War tend to be "superficial" because they lack a "conceptual framework for distinguishing between what is essential and what is contingent or accidental in world history" (1989: 270). Fukuyama takes as his task to investigate "a process that gives coherence and order to the daily headlines" and, he claims, this process is "an unabashed victory of economic and political liberalism" (1989: 270).

As Fukuyama puts it, "What we may be witnessing is not just the end of the Cold War, or the passing of a particular period of post-war history, but *the end of history as such*: that is, the end point of mankind's ideological evolution and the universalization of Western liberal democracy as the final form of human government" (my italics; 1989: 271). But while the "victory of liberalism" is an ideological victory—in that no other ideas or ideologies pose a challenge to it—its victory "is as yet incomplete in the real or material world" (1989: 271). That is why we don't see every state in the world practicing liberal political and economic principles. But Fukuyama argues that "there are powerful reasons for believing that it is the ideal that will govern the material world *in the long run*" (italics in original; 1989: 271). In other words, it is only a matter of time until liberalism is "globalized" as both an unchallenged ideology and as a material way of life.

How does Fukuyama make his argument? He does so by privileging a particular way of understanding history. History, for Fukuyama, is "a dialectical process with a beginning, a middle, and an end" (1989: 271). A dialectical process is a process though which the contradiction between a dominant truth (thesis) and its opposite (antithesis) are reconciled to produce a higher truth (synthesis). This higher truth or synthesis becomes the new thesis, which will necessarily be opposed by a new antithesis. This process continues until "all prior contradictions are resolved and all human needs are satisfied" (1989: 272). From this point onward, "there is no struggle or conflict over "large" issues . . . ; what remains is primarily economic activity" (1989: 272). And when we reach this point, history is over.

This way of describing history draws upon Fredrick Hegel's notion of dialectical history (see Figure 6.1). For Hegel, "history culminated in an absolute moment—a moment in which a final, rational form of society and state became victorious" (1989: 271). For Hegel, this moment arrived in 1806, when, after the French Revolution, "the basic *principles* of the liberal democratic state could not be improved upon" (1989: 272). Now, as then, liberalism's "theoretical truth is absolute

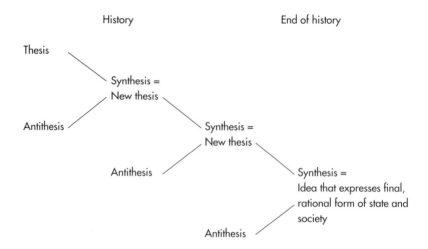

Figure 6.1 The Hegelian dialectic

and could not be improved upon" (1989: 274). All that remains to be done is to spatially extend liberal principles throughout the world (1989: 272).

Many of us are familiar with this Hegelian way of thinking about history because Karl Marx borrowed Hegel's dialectic to make his argument about how contradictions among economic classes would "drag history ahead" and culminate with the realization of communism. Marx was interested in material economic forces of history. But this isn't the way Hegel thought about dialectics. Hegel, in contrast to Marx, was interested not in the progress of material well-being first and foremost but in the progress of the idea. In Hegel's dialectic, it is not economic classes that are in conflict; it is ideologies that are in conflict (see Table 6.2). For Hegel, ideology or consciousness about the world is what causes the world to change materially. As Fukuyama puts it, "consciousness will ultimately remake the material world in its own image" (1989: 274).

For Fukuyama, ideological consciousness is "the real subject underlying the apparent jumble of current events in the history of ideology" (1989: 273). In other words, it is the triumph of liberalism that made the end of the Cold War possible, not, for example, the economic collapse of the former Soviet Union that made liberal consciousness possible. Yes, modern free market economics underwrites and helps to stabilize this liberal consciousness. And so Fukuyama claims the end of history is marked by "the universal homogenous state as liberal democracy in the political sphere combined with easy access to VCRs and stereos in the economic" (1989: 275). But underwriting and stabilizing should not be confused with causing something to happen. For Fukuyama, as for Hegel, ideological consciousness—not economic materiality—is the cause of change, not its effect (1989: 273).

How can Fukuyama argue that liberalism's "theoretical truth is absolute and could not be improved upon" (1989: 274) to the point that we are now at the end of history? He does so by posing a question: "Are there . . . any fundamental 'contradictions' in human life that cannot be resolved in the context of modern liberalism, that would be resolvable by an alternative political-economic structure?" (1989: 275). His answer is "no."

Fukuyama gets to this answer by considering the historical status of ideological challengers of liberalism in the twentieth century—fascism and communism (see Table 6.3). He argues that "fascism was destroyed as a living ideology by World War II. This defeat," he concedes, "of course, was on a very material level, but it amounted to a defeat of the idea as well" because no ideological movements based on fascism have survived long in the post-war era (1989: 275). Communism's challenge to liberalism, Fukuyama argues, "was far more serious"

Table 6.2 Hegelian and Marxist understandings of history

	Hegel	Marx
Understanding of history	Dialectical	Dialectical
Nature of dialectic	Idealist	Materialist
What clashes in the dialectic?	Ideologies	Economic classes

Table 6.3 Ideological challengers to liberalism

	Critique of liberalism	Why challenge fails
Fascism	Political weakness, materialism, anomie, and lack of community of West = fundamental contradictions in liberal society	Destroyed as a living ideology both materially and ideologically by World War II
Communism	Liberal contradiction between capital and labor/owner and workers cannot be resolved	• State commitments to communism in China and the Soviet Union only rhetorical • Bourgeois consumerism embraced internationally • No state offers genuine communist alternative to liberalism
Religion	Liberal consumerism means core liberalism is hollow, meaningless	Offers no universalizable political alternative to liberalism
Nationalism	Offers no generalizable critique of liberalism. Only critical of some particular expressions of liberalism through specific non-representative governments	Because it has no generalizable critique of liberalism, nationalism is not necessarily incompatible with liberal ideology

(1989: 275). Communism claimed that liberalism could not resolve its own internal contradiction between capital and labor, between the owning class and the working class (1989: 275). Fukuyama claims that "classless society" has been achieved in the United States. By this, he does not mean that the gap between the rich and the poor is not growing, but that "the root causes of economic inequalities do not have to do with the underlying legal and social structure of our [US] society" (1989: 275–6). As a result, "the appeal of communism in the developed Western world . . . is lower today than any time since the end of the First World War" (1989: 276).

But what about the rest of the world? To make the argument that liberal consciousness pervades the West tells us nothing new. And Fukuyama recognizes this, arguing that "it is precisely in the non-European world that one is most struck by the occurrence of major ideological transformations" (1989: 276). He cites the example of Japan, a country that had liberal political and economic principles imposed on it after World War II. What is important in the Japanese case, according to Fukuyama, is "that the essential elements of economic and political liberalism have been so successfully grafted onto uniquely Japanese traditions and institutions," thus ensuring their long-term survival (1989: 276). In the case of the newly industrialized countries (NICs) in Asia, the evidence is even more compelling because "political liberalism has been following economic liberalism" as a result of "the victory of the idea of the universal homogenous state" and not because of external imposition as in the case of Japan (1989: 277).

Fukuyama even manages to cite communist China as an example of the triumph of liberalism because "Marxism and ideological principle have become virtually irrelevant as guides to policy, and that bourgeois consumerism has a real meaning in that country for the first time since the revolution" (1989: 278). As a result, "China can no longer act as a beacon for illiberal forces around the world" (1989: 278).

But, of course, "it is the developments in the Soviet Union—the original 'homeland of the world proletariat'—that have put the final nail in the coffin of the Marxist–Leninist alternative to liberal democracy" (1989: 278). The demise of the Soviet Union seals the triumph of liberalism for Fukuyama. As he puts it, since Gorbachev came to power there has been "a revolutionary assault on the most fundamental institutions and principles of Stalinism, and their replacement by other principles which do not amount to liberalism *per se* but whose only connecting thread is liberalism" (italic in original; 1989: 279). And so communism joins fascism as a "dead" ideology. This does not mean that Fukuyama would describe the former Soviet Union as liberal or democratic, and he is clear that this is beside the point. For "at the end of history it is not necessary that all societies become successful liberal societies, merely that they end their ideological pretensions of representing different and higher forms of human society" (1989: 280).

Concluding that fascism and communism are dead, Fukuyama looks around for alternative ideologies that might challenge liberalism in the future. He identifies two—religion and nationalism (see Table 6.3). Of religious fundamentalism, Fukuyama contends that while this may well be a response to "the emptiness at the core of liberalism," it is unlikely to represent a political response. "Only Islam has offered a theocratic state as a political alternative to both liberalism and communism," but because this has little appeal for non-Muslims, Fukuyama argues it lacks "universal significance" (1989: 281; for an alternative view, see Chapter 8). Nationalism, on the other hand, does not represent a clear "irreconcilable con-tradiction in the heart of liberalism" (1989: 281). And because nationalism is generally an ideology about independence from another group, people, or state, Fukuyama concludes that it does "not offer anything like a comprehensive agenda for socio-economic organization" (1989: 281–2).

Having considered the ideologies past and future that could challenge liberalism, Fukuyama concludes that "the present world seems to confirm that the fundamental principles of socio-political organization have not advanced terribly far since 1806" (1989: 282). That doesn't rule out the possibility of some "new ideology or previously unrecognized contradictions in liberal societies" to challenge liberalism, but none of these were apparent to Fukuyama at the time he wrote his essay (1989: 282).

Assuming we have reached "the end of history," Fukuyama asks what all this means for international relations. What will international politics look like in a "de-ideologized world"? (1989: 282). "The end of history" does not mark the end of material conflicts, only ideological conflicts. Conflicts will still rage in "the vast bulk of the Third World [which] remains very much mired in history" (1989: 282). But "international life for the part of the world that has reached the end of history is far more preoccupied with economics than with politics or strategy" (1989: 283). And so in the de-ideologized world, "we are far more likely to see the 'Common

Marketization' of world politics" than we are to see the resurgence of large-scale conflict among sovereign nation-states, "international anarchy" notwithstanding (1989: 284). This does not mean that there will be no conflict among sovereign nation-states. This is likely between "historical states" and "post-historical states" (1989: 285). Nor does this mean that Marxist–Leninism won't try to stage an ideological comeback (see Chapter 7), but, as far as Fukuyama is concerned, it "is dead as a mobilizing ideology" so presents little threat for dragging us back into history (1989: 285).

Overall, Fukuyama concludes that "the end of history" will be rather boring. If ideological struggles made us live risky, purposeful lives that called for "daring, courage, imagination, and idealism," the "de-ideological" age of post-history will be marked by "economic calculation, the endless solving of technical problems, environmental concerns, and the satisfaction of sophisticated consumer demands" (1989: 285–6). It will be "just the perpetual caretaking of the museum of human history" (1989: 286). All this seems to depress Fukuyama, for he writes, "I can feel in myself, and see in others around me, a powerful nostalgia for the time when history existed" (1989: 286). And he concludes by wondering if "centuries of boredom at the end of history will serve to get history started once again" (1989: 286). But, if it does, then Fukuyama cannot claim that liberalism's post-Cold War "triumph" over all ideological challenges marks the end of history.

It is easy to see how Fukuyama's description of the post-Cold War era as "de-ideological," low-conflict, and post-historical set the stage for neoliberal expressions of globalization to become the "next big thing" in IR theory. Since ideological struggles, much less large-scale political conflict, were now a thing of the past, all that remained to be done was to explore the many ways in which liberalism was being spread world-wide in economic, political, and cultural forms. Or was there?

Fukuyama supports his myth "it is the end of history" by making the case that there are no "living" ideological challengers to liberalism. While the "facts" of Fukuyama's case have received a lot of attention and are hotly debated, what goes without saying in Fukuyama's myth is that liberalism itself is free of internal contradictions. Fukuyama simply asserts this and leaves it up to fully expressed, coherent ideological rivals to make the case that he is wrong. Instead, *he* makes the case that *they* are wrong.

But what happens if we look *inside* liberalism? What if we ignore the challenges posed by "alternative ideologies" like fascism, communism, religious funda-mentalism, and nationalism and simply focus our attention on what makes liberalism itself function? If we do our attention is drawn away from liberalism's would-be challengers to that unresolvable tension within liberalism—its creation of unful-fillable desires that (by definition) it can only fail to fulfil. By Fukuyama's own admission, for his myth "it is the end of history" to function, liberalism must be free not only of external challengers but of internal contradictions as well. But liberalism's relationship to the creation and fulfillment of desires always threatens to unravel not only liberalism's promises for the good life but Fukuyama's claim that "it is the end of history."

This tension is exquisitely explored in *The Truman Show*. The film is set in a post-historical era, in which economic concerns and cultural nostalgia have replaced political and ideological struggles. What makes this post-historical world function is the success of the television program, "The Truman Show" to stage history for its viewers and substitute viewers' desires for historical and ideological engagement with their consumption of "The Truman Show." But when Truman reaches his "end of history" by escaping Seahaven, his viewers are left with empty airtime that might represent "the empty core of liberalism" (1989: 281). And we may wonder if the ending of "The Truman Show" also marks the end of Fukuyama's myth "it is the end of history."

The Truman Show

How's it gonna end? That is the question that grips viewers of the 1998 film *The Truman Show*—not for the usual reasons about cinematic climaxes and suspense but because the film *The Truman Show* is about a television program called "The Truman Show." Nothing terribly strange about that. But there is a twist. Truman Burbank/Jim Carrey, the star of "The Truman Show," is the only person in the world who does not know that "The Truman Show" is a television show and that Seahaven Island where he has lived his entire life is an elaborate television set. And one day he is bound to find out. When he does, "The Truman Show" (at least in its current form) will end.

How could anyone be so duped about the "reality" of his life? Easily! As Christof/Ed Harris, the "creator" of "The Truman Show" tells us in an interview, "We accept the reality of the world with which we're presented. It's as simple as that." And for Truman Burbank, "The Truman Show" is the only reality he has ever

Plate 6.1 Truman captured by "bathroom cam" as he draws on the mirror and makes silly faces.
Courtesy of the Ronald Grant Film Archive © Paramount Pictures.

known. From before his birth, Truman has been on television. His whole life—from the exciting to the mundane—has been recorded by hidden cameras (about 5000 cameras to be exact) and transmitted non-stop world-wide as "The Truman Show." First placed in Truman's birth-mother's womb, cameras were later hidden throughout Seahaven—not only in streets and houses but also in buttons, vending machines, a pencil sharpener, and even Seahaven's moon. By the time we meet the 30-year-old Truman, the entire island of Seahaven has been built as a television stage housed in an enormous dome, including a complete town, sea, and sky. It is so big, the film tells us, that like the Great Wall of China, it is the only other unnatural object visible from outer space.

Not only is Truman's "natural" environment unnatural, so too is his social environment. Everyone on the show has been cast into their roles, including Truman's mother, wife, best friend, and an entire town of neighbors, acquaintances, and strangers who inhabit Seahaven. The television viewing audience knows that all of the people in Seahaven are playing roles in "The Truman Show"—all of them but Truman himself. But for Truman, he and everyone he meets and everything he encounters is real. The woman cast as Truman's mother, for example, is the only mother Truman has ever known. Truman does not know that his was an unwanted pregnancy and that his birth coincided with a pre-set airtime for "The Truman Show," making him the child selected as its star. Nor does Truman know that he is the first person in the world to have been legally adopted by a corporation—the corporation that broadcasts "The Truman Show."

Why go to these lengths to produce a television show? As Christof explains,

We've become bored with watching actors give us phoney emotions. We're tired of pyrotechnics and special effects. While the world he inhabits is in some respects counterfeit, there's nothing fake about Truman himself. No scripts, no cue cards. . . . It isn't always Shakespeare but it's genuine. It's a life.

And watching Truman's life has glued viewers to their television sets for 30 years. As we learn from the television program "TruTalk," a "forum for issues growing out of the show," "One point seven billion were there for his birth. Two-hundred twenty countries tuned in for his first steps." "The Truman Show" is a truly global phenomenon.

To emphasize the impact "The Truman Show" has on its viewing public, the film cuts back and forth between action on "The Truman Show" and scenes of its viewing public. We see viewers in the busy Truman Bar, a theme bar packed with "Truman Show" paraphernalia and dotted with televisions that broadcast only "The Truman Show." We see two elderly women clutching pillows with Truman's grinning face on them engrossed in an episode of the show. We see a man who seems to do nothing but watch "The Truman Show" while lying in his bathtub. And we see two parking attendants glued to "The Truman Show" throughout their shifts.

Why is "The Truman Show" so popular? What are audiences looking for in "The Truman Show," and what do they find?

Christof tells us that viewers find not only an escape from boredom but they find "the way the world should be." This is, Seahaven, the world Christof has created for Truman. Seahaven is nostalgically modeled after a 1950s' American television

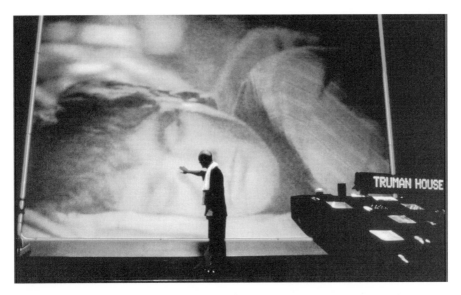

Plate 6.2 Christof admires his creations—Truman and "The Truman Show".
Courtesy of the Ronald Grant Film Archive © Paramount Pictures.

show. Not only do the costumes and sets have a 1950s' feel to them, but everyone on set seems to have a 1950s' attitude. In this economically prosperous community, everyone is friendly and caring toward their neighbor, family life is stable, and crime is at a minimum if it exists at all. Seahaven, then, is a slice of the past made present. And because Truman lives his real life in Seahaven—his only real world—Seahaven is a living museum. Never dead or static, Seahaven is where the action is, even if that action is the tedious daily routines of an insurance salesperson. Seahaven is where living history takes place. Tuning into "The Truman Show" is like turning on history.

Seahaven is where living history takes place not primarily because it is stylistically and attitudinally a throwback to the 1950s. As in Fukuyama's explanation of history, Seahaven is a site of living history because it is a site of ideological struggle. This ideological struggle is between Truman and Christof. It is the final ideological struggle between liberalism and some form of totalitarian ideology (like communism or fascism). Truman represents liberalism; Christof, totalitarianism.

Why is such a struggle necessary in the idyllic world of Seahaven? To put it differently, what could Truman possibly want that he cannot have in Seahaven? The simple answer is freedom. Once Truman realizes he is living in a controlled environment, he does what Fukuyama says one must do when in the grip of ideological struggle. He breaks out of his own boring daily routines and lives a risky, purposeful life that calls for "daring, courage, imagination, and idealism" (1989: 285–6). But how does Truman get to the point that he wants his freedom more than he wants the world of Seahaven in which Christof claims all of Truman's needs are met? Truman gets there because not all of his desires are met.

Plate 6.3 Truman's "world"—the television set—is literally falling apart, as a set light falls from the "sky".
Courtesy of the Ronald Grant Film Archive © Paramount Pictures.

Christof admits that Truman's desire to explore the world around him had to be controlled, for if Truman left the set, the show would be over. As Christof puts it, "As Truman grew up, we were forced to manufacture ways to keep him on the island." And so Christof offers Truman a loving family, a secure job, and a friendly town to live in place of a life of adventure beyond Seahaven. Whenever Truman expresses a desire to leave Seahaven, this substitution of stability for adventure is activated. Truman's mother shows him family albums and has him watch the television program "Show Me the Way to Go Home," which celebrates the small-town values of a place like Seahaven and which emotionally manipulates Truman to stay where he is.

The struggle to control Truman's desire, however, has not always been so easy. This is best illustrated in the film in a flashback in which Truman the college student falls for an "extra," Lauren, which complicates Christof's plans to have Truman marry Meryl, the character Christof has cast to be Truman's future wife.

Truman: I'm Truman.
Lauren: Yeah. I know. Look, Truman, I'm not allowed to talk to you. You know.

Truman notices that Lauren is wearing a pin that says "How's it gonna end?"

Truman: I like your pin. Was wondering that myself.
Lauren: Mm.
Truman: Would you wanna maybe, possibly . . . sometime go out for some pizza or something? Friday? Saturday? Sunday? Monday? Tuesday? . . .

Plate 6.4 Truman nostalgically looks at the family photo album.
Courtesy of the Ronald Grant Film Archive © Paramount Pictures.

Lauren writes on a notepad "NOW."

Lauren: If we don't go now, it won't happen. Do you understand? So what are you gonna do?

The cameras lose them for a while as they sneak out of the library. The cameras discover them going to the beach together. Cut to the beach.

Lauren: We have so little time. They're going to be here any minute.
Truman: Who are they?
Lauren: They don't want me talking to you.
Truman: Then don't talk.

Truman kisses Lauren. A car speeds onto the beach.

Lauren: They're here. Truman.
Truman: What do they want?
Lauren: Listen to me. Everyone knows about . . . everyone knows everything you do. 'Cause they're pretending, Truman. Do you . . . Do you understand? Everybody's pretending.
Truman [looking perplexed]:   Lauren.
Lauren: No, no, no, ah, my name's not Lauren. No, no. My name's Sylvia.
Truman [confused]:   Sylvia?

A man gets out of the car claiming to be Lauren's father.

Lauren: He's lying! Truman, please! Don't listen to him! Everything I've told you is the truth! . . . This . . . it—it's fake. It's all for you.

Truman: I don't understand.
Lauren: And . . . and the sky and the sea, everything. It's a set. It's a show.

Father intervenes.

Truman: I really would like to know what's going on!
Lauren's Father: Schizophrenia. It's episodes. . . . You forget it, forget everything.
Lauren: Don't do it! Don't Truman! . . . Truman, he's lying! Get out of here. Come
        and find me.

But then Lauren's father tells Truman that he is moving his family to Fiji, and he and
        Lauren exit in the car.

Truman is left on the beach with Lauren's/Sylvia's forgotten sweater, which he keeps
as a memento. In future episodes, we see Truman dreaming about Sylvia while
looking at her sweater, trying to construct a composite of her face from pictures in
women's magazines, and expressing his desire to go to Fiji. All of this illustrates
Christof's bind. He must produce desires in Truman, like the desire for a heterosexual family, in order for the show to go on. Indeed, Christof boasts in an interview
that he is determined to deliver to his viewers the first on-air conception. And in the
world of Seahaven, for Truman to be involved in such a conception it must take place
within the confines of a legitimate union. So Truman must marry. But what Christof
cannot control is who Truman wants to marry. He wants Lauren/Sylvia.
    At this point, Truman doesn't follow Sylvia off the set, in part because—despite
Sylvia's attempt to enlighten him—he doesn't understand it is a set. And even if he

Plate 6.5 Truman at the travel agent in front of a poster showing a plane being struck by lightning.
Courtesy of the Ronald Grant Film Archive © Paramount Pictures.

did, Christof has instilled in Truman a fear of flying and a terror of water, the natural boundary around Seahaven Island. Truman's terror of water was "produced" in the "episode" in which Truman's father was drowned in a sailing accident for which Truman feels responsible. Not only does this make Truman give up sailing, he won't take a ferry across the bay, nor will he even drive his car across the bridge.

So what is Christof to do with Truman's desire for Sylvia and the emotion that creates in Truman? Displace it, of course. Immediately after Lauren's/Sylvia's exit from the show, Truman's mother is scripted with an illness, and Truman must remain in Seahaven to care for her. And in place of Lauren/Sylvia, Christof gives Truman Meryl, who Truman is encouraged to marry on the rebound.

What does all of this tell us about the worlds of "The Truman Show" and *The Truman Show*? How do they makes sense of their worlds, and what do they say is typical and deviant in those worlds? It is important to ask these questions for both the television problem "The Truman Show" and for the film *The Truman Show* because the ability of each world to function is related to the smooth function of the other.

Let's start by answering these questions for the television program "The Truman Show." "The Truman Show" makes sense of the world by celebrating history. While on the surface the show's celebration of history is stylistically and attitudinally nostalgic, more fundamentally the show's celebration of history is ideological. Or, to combine the two, "The Truman Show" is nostalgic for ideology. It celebrates the ideological struggle between good and evil, between an "on the air, unaware" Truman and his creator and controller Christof. Truman and Christof represent different ideological positions. Truman represents the desire for freedom and the right to make choices for his own life (a desire for liberalism fully expressed), and Christof represents the desire to maintain totalitarian control over Truman's life and world. Truman's and Christof's ideological positions are locked in a dialectical contradiction (see Figure 6.2).

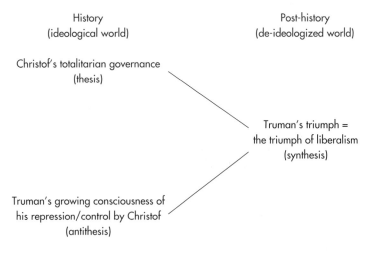

History
(ideological world)

Post-history
(de-ideologized world)

Christof's totalitarian governance
(thesis)

Truman's triumph =
the triumph of liberalism
(synthesis)

Truman's growing consciousness of
his repression/control by Christof
(antithesis)

Figure 6.2 The dialectical struggle in "The Truman Show"

What is typical in the world of "The Truman Show" is for Truman to be blissfully ignorant of his situation. A typical day is one in which Truman has yet to awaken to the ideological struggle for his freedom from Christof that awaits him. Such typical days are produced for Truman by Christof by containing Truman's desires within the utopian world of Seahaven, usually by substituting the category of what Truman wants (a wife and a loving marriage, for example) for the specific thing/person Truman wants (Lauren/Sylvia). So Truman gets a wife, for example, but that wife is Meryl, not Sylvia.

What is deviant in the world of "The Truman Show" is for Truman to become ideologically aware and to ultimately exit his prison, thereby exiting history. What leads to Truman's ideological awakening is Christof's inability to fulfil Truman's desires. Loyal viewers (who seem to be everyone outside of Seahaven) know that Truman's ideological awakening is imminent. Knowing this, they know the answer to the question "How's it gonna end?" "The Truman Show" ends with Truman's "unabashed victory" over Christof's totalitarianism, a victory driven by Truman's unfulfilled desires (Table 6.4).

What about *The Truman Show*? How does it make sense of the world? What does it say is typical and deviant in that world? To answer these questions, we must look beyond the world of the television program "The Truman Show" and think about the relationship in the film between the television program and those who watch it. If "The Truman Show" the television program represents a nostalgia for ideology and is therefore the place where history takes place, what does this tell us about how the viewers of "The Truman Show" are positioned historically? It tells us that they are positioned in a post-historical, de-ideological era. And, as Fukuyama tells us, that must mean these viewers live in a world in which liberal capitalist ideology has triumphed over all challengers.

Think about it. We never see any conflict—ideological or otherwise—in the world beyond "The Truman Show" that isn't about "The Truman Show" itself. The only mention of politics and political struggle occurs when Sylvia (Truman's true love) phones into the program "TruTalk" to berate Christof for his imprisonment of Truman. Beyond that, there is no politics in the film. It is "The Truman Show" that creates any sense of politics for its viewers as nothing else in the film can or does.

If the world beyond Seahaven is the world of post-history—free of ideological struggle and politics as they would be understood in an historical world—then this post-historical world is also a place where desire cannot trouble this de-ideological world in the ways that Truman's desire troubles and ultimately ends his ideological world. Put differently, there are no internal contradictions within the post-historical, de-ideological world of the viewers that cannot be resolved from within liberal

Table 6.4 What is typical and deviant in the historical world of the television program "The Truman Show"?

Typical	Truman is unaware of his ideological struggle with Christof because his desires are contained within the utopian world of Seahaven
Deviant	Compelled by unfulfilled desires, Truman becomes ideologically aware and frees himself from Christof and from Seahaven

capitalism. From the point of view of someone like Fukuyama, this is because the viewers of "The Truman Show" are free, whereas Truman is a prisoner.

That does not mean that we don't see the viewers of "The Truman Show" expressing desire all the time. They do, and they do so in relation to the television program. In addition to expressing their desire for the world of "The Truman Show" by watching it, viewers of "The Truman Show" literally buy it. Everything on the show is for sale—not just the products the cast use (which are plugged in the show through product placement advertisements) but the clothes they wear and the homes in which they live. All this can be ordered from the Truman Catalogue. For the viewers of "The Truman Show," Truman is not just a character in a television program. Truman—or should we call him "Tru(e)man"—is a commodity. Like any commodity, he can be consumed. By consuming Truman, his viewers seem to be happy.

Like Truman's desires, then, the desires of the viewing audience of the show are encapsulated within the confines of the world of Seahaven. So long as these post-historical viewers have an outlet for their "politics" and their "desires"—the ideologically nostalgic space of Seahaven and the economic ability to substitute the political ideology of "The Truman Show" with economic products from "The Truman Show"—then their desires for history as the history of ideological struggle are met.

This is what is typical in the cinematic world of *The Truman Show*—for the televisual actions of "The Truman Show" to fill any nostalgic longings the viewers have for politics and ideology through their daily practices of consumption (either by watching "The Truman Show" or by purchasing products from it). Like Truman's world in which desires are satisfied with substitutes (families, finances, friends), the world of this viewing audience has their desires for history and ideology satisfied with consumable substitutes (viewing time and show memorabilia). What is deviant in the world of *The Truman Show* is for there to be no space—no Seahaven or Truman Burbank's life or Truman Catalogue—onto which viewers can safely project their desires for history and ideology (Table 6.5).

And, of course, this is precisely where the film leaves us. When Truman exits history, his post-historical viewers are left with nowhere to project their desires for history. Certainly, they can fill the empty airtime by changing channels (as the parking attendants do in the film's final scene), but where else will they find "real history" as the struggle of a genuine character in a genuine struggle with a genuine totalitarian in control? Nowhere. As Christof told us, that is why "The Truman Show" was staged in the first place and has had a growing audience ever since—because it is real. And that means there is no substitute for "The Truman Show."

Table 6.5 What is typical and deviant in the post-historical world of the film *The Truman Show*?

Typical	"The Truman Show" is the space in which its viewers consume history as the history of ideology (by watching the ideological struggle between Truman and Christof and by owning a piece of that history though the purchase of goods from "The Truman Show")
Deviant	There is no space for viewers to safely project their desires for history and ideology because "The Truman Show" goes off the air permanently

All this has to make us wonder, "With Truman's history over, might viewers' desire for history now be fulfilled with a return to ideological struggle—not in the form of a televisual substitute but in less apparently mediated ways?" Or, to put it somewhat differently, "Is the end ever really the end?"

Liberalism's internal contradiction, or is the end ever really the end?

The Truman Show aptly displays an unresolvable contradiction within the ideology of liberalism. Liberalism forever attempts to fulfil the desires it creates for individuals by offering them substitutes. These substitutes are often (but not always) economic. Whether this is "the economic good life" in "The Truman Show" or the ability to consume "the ideological good life" for viewers of "The Truman Show," these substitutions generally satisfy individuals for a while. But ultimately, they fail. The trick to making liberalism work—to making liberalism function—is to delay any sense of disappointment its subjects experience when economic desires fail to satisfy personal desires. Capitalism does a very good job in helping liberalism to succeed on this score because the message of capitalism is that economic enjoyment can equal personal fulfillment so long as one keeps on consuming.

The Truman Show reminds us that these substitutions are not only necessary; more importantly, it reminds us that they are limited. There are limits to how happy Christof can keep Truman, no matter how hard he tries. And there are limits to how long Truman Burbank can keep his viewers satisfied. Yes, most of them cheer for his liberation from Christof. But when Truman achieves his "unabashed victory" over Christof, where does that leave his post-historical viewers? It leaves them wallowing in the "emptiness at the core of liberalism" (Fukuyama, 1989: 281) searching for something to fill it (even if initially only by changing channels). What we don't know—and what it seems no one can control—is what form attempts to fill this empty core will take.

Leaving desires unfulfilled—whether they are for "The Truman Show" or for something else—is a problem for liberalism. In the film, a post-"Truman Show" era is a dangerous one, for it is one in which there is no safe space onto which Truman's viewers can project their desire for something to fill the boredom of post-history and "the empty core of liberalism" (1989: 281). This is dangerous because for liberalism to function as an ideology apparently free of internal contradictions, such a space must exist.

What does this tell us about Fukuyama's myth "it is the end of history"? It tells us that it only appears to be true so long as liberalism's claim to be free of internal contradictions *appears to be true*. What our detour through the film *The Truman Show* tells us is that what it takes for liberalism to appear to be free of internal contradictions is the endless deferral of individual encounters with liberalism's empty core. All this suggests that, instead of writing about "the end of history" in which liberalism is triumphant, maybe Fukuyama is writing instead about liberalism's apparent triumph—one that depends on us knowing about but never experiencing its empty core. And Fukuyama's own myth "it is the end of history"—a myth that he evidences by directing our attention away from liberalism's internal contradiction and toward alternative ideological challenges—actually participates in liberalism's process of deferring our encounter with liberalism's empty core.

What does all of this mean for international relations in an era of "globalization"? It means that those determined to study liberalism in a post-Cold War era might be better served by investigating not what alternative ideologies might crop up to challenge liberalism's apparent global dominance but by asking questions like "in an era of 'globalization,' how will liberalism attempt to control and defer our encounter with its empty core?" Or, to put it somewhat differently, "how does liberalism now attempt to control our desires in ways that escape our notice?"

As the protests against the World Trade Organization talks in Seattle in 1999 suggested, these are not unimportant questions. Protesters around the world (but especially in the industrialized West) offered something like a carnival of opposition to global capitalism (using art and performance art mixed with more traditional forms of demonstration), the very global capitalism that gave these protesters "the good life." What they objected to was not only how global capitalism's promise of the good life for some (Western industrialized states) comes at the expense of others (developing states) but also how empty liberalism's offer of economic well-being in place of personal desire is ("the empty core of liberalism"). While the former point of protest is an old Marxist complaint, the latter one requires no alternative ideological challenger to bring it into focus.

Examples like these remind us of the necessary oversights in Fukuyama's myth "it is the end of history." It is not just a coherent ideological challenger that can (in Fukuyama's terms) drag us back into history. It is liberalism's own internal contradiction—that makes us want total freedom but can offer us only economic freedom in its place—that creates historical and ideological struggle as well. And, even though Fukuyama chose not to focus on it when he wrote his essay in 1989, even he admits that this is a contradiction that has been at the core of liberalism from its creation.

Suggestions for further thinking

Topic 1 Globalization

Even though IR theorists cannot agree about what globalization is, they do agree that it is vitally important to our understanding of contemporary international life. Globalization is not a concept that has implications only for what we consider to be the traditional international political economy debates (between liberalism, Marxism, and mercantilism). Globalization impacts upon what we regard as the traditional domain of "politics." For example, IR theorists hotly debate what globalization does to the sovereign nation-state. Does the state "wither away" in an era of globalization, or do forms of state control simply change their form? What is the role of new technologies like the internet in the processes of state control/state retreat? If the territorial state is a thing of the past because of globalization, what (if anything) is taking its place? Is the state being replaced by a truly global cosmopolitanism, for example? Or is globalization nothing more than the (not-so) benevolent spread of US hegemony? These questions defined the cutting edge of IR research at the beginning of the twenty-first century.

Kofman and Youngs (2008) take up these debates about the state, while Baylis and Smith (1997) situate globalization debates in relation to IR theory more generally. For an unabashed liberal defence of globalization, see Micklethwait and Wooldridge (2000). Reading this text in relation to more critical texts on globalization (Herod et al., 1998; Jameson and Miyoshi, 1998; and Hay and Marsh, 2000) is a good way to spark debate.

Suggested reading

John Baylis and Steve Smith (eds) (1997) *The Globalization of World Politics*. Oxford: Oxford University Press.

Colin Hay and David Marsh (eds) (2000) *Demystifying Globalization*. Boulder, co: St. Martin's Press.

Andrew Herod, Gearóid Ó Tuathail, and Susan M. Roberts (eds) (1998) *An Unruly World? Globalization, Governance, and Geography*. London: Routledge.

Fredric Jameson and Masao Miyoshi (eds) (1998) *The Cultures of Globalization*. Chapel Hill, NC: Duke University Press.

Eleonore Kofman and Gillian Youngs (eds) (2003) *Globalization: Theory and Practice*, 3rd edition. London: Continuum.

John Micklethwait and Adrian Wooldridge (2000) *The Future Perfect: The challenge and hidden promise of globalization*. New York: Times Press.

Topic 2 The uses of history

History is another concept that we all seem to understand and accept as given. But, as Fukuyama's myth "it is the end of history" demonstrates, even if we think we know what history *is*, we don't necessarily grasp what history or histories *do*. How does history and temporality more generally function in narrative accounts of international politics? What work does history do in IR theory? How do critical understandings of history and temporality help us to better approach IR theory? Using a text like Ermarth's (1992) as a general introduction to critical under-standings of history is helpful in critically reading how classic IR theory texts (like Modelski, 1987 or Gilpin, 1983, for example) use history. Considering how history is used generally in IR theory, it is even possible to argue that IR theory debates are debates about history/temporality as much as if not more than they are about geography/spatiality, concepts that have more often occupied critical IR theorists (Weber, 1998). For more on the uses of history, see Chapter 7.

Suggested reading

Elizabeth Deeds Ermarth (1992) *Sequel to History: Postmodernism and the Crisis of Representational Time*. Princeton, NJ: Princeton University Press.

Robert Gilpin (1983) *War and Change in World Politics*. Cambridge: Cambridge University Press.

George Modelski (1987) *Long Cycles in World Politics*. Seattle, WA: University of Washington Press.

Cynthia Weber (1998) "Reading Martin Wight's 'Why is there no international theory?' as history." *Alternatives* 23: 451–69

NeoMarxism

Is Empire the new world order?

The end of history sure didn't last long.

As we noted in Chapter 6, a mere ten years after Fukuyama's pronouncement of "the end of history," political discontent began to break out around the world, grabbing international attention with the 1999 Seattle protests at the World Trade Organization meetings. Few would contest the claim that Seattle marked the end of "the end of history." But questions arise as to where this leaves us ideologically. Why were these protestors protesting? An answer suggested by our critical reading of Fukuyama's myth is that the movements begun in Seattle were politics for politics' sake. Bored by the end of history, wealthy, privileged Northerners protested against their own institutions as a way to fill in their own personal empty cores of liberalism. On this reading, anti-globalization protests expressed the internal contradictions inherent within liberalism.

There are other ways to interpret the events of Seattle, however. Maybe Seattle marked not so much a new beginning to history caused by liberalism's own contradictions as it did a reemergence of the sort of active political protest someone like Marx (see Chapter 6) might have predicted. Maybe Seattle was more about the contradictions within the logic of capitalism (the modern means of production and exchange in the global economy) than it was about liberal political guilt. Some on the left initially latched onto this idea. Seattle seemed to these folks like a vindication of their ideological position, for it revitalized the severely wounded if not dead ideology of Marxism for a post-Cold War world.

This reading of Seattle was difficult to support, however, because it didn't look at all like that which Marx had described. Seattle was not about the proletariat rising up against their unjust laboring conditions. Nor was it about the South rising up against the North. Instead, Seattle was about globally (guilty?) conscious Northerners creatively protesting how their own governments and Northern-based IGOs treated not just the South but also the environment and animals, for example. And because the Seattle protestors lacked any coherent group identity, their aims and targets were varied and unpredictable. They did not, for example, all seem to be protesting against the logic of capital as Marx described it, and they certainly did not seem to be protesting against the logic of capital as Marx described they *would*. This is not to say that the Seattle protests were not powerful displays of contemporary political movements. It is simply to say that it is difficult to use these protests to reinvigorate Marxism.

In the months after Seattle, political commentators tended to rally around one of these two explanations—that Seattle was about (youthful) liberal political discontent or that Seattle marked the (nostalgic) reemergence of the Marxist agenda. While the first position was generally too dismissive of Seattle, the second was too optimistic.

And then along came a book called *Empire*. In the early fall of 2000, Michael Hardt and Antonio Negri published a 478-page volume of heavy theory interspersed with emotive political "manifestos" that lent a coherence to leftist ideology which it had lacked since the end of the Cold War. Instantly selling out in shops, *Empire* became the most talked-about book of its times. For what Hardt and Negri accomplished in *Empire* was not just a revival of the left and an explanation for events like Seattle (which the book, in press at the time, seemed to predict). They managed to bring the leftist ideology of neoMarxism into lively conversation with the contemporary postmodern world. They did this in two ways. First, they engaged events like those on the streets of Seattle as the ideological anomalies they were. What happened in such contemporary political protests wasn't strictly liberal or Marxist. It was, they realized, something more complex. To explain this complexity they, second, incorporated the theoretical insights of postmodern political philosophers like Michel Foucault (1990) and Deleuze and Guattari (1987) into their discussion of leftist ideology. Until *Empire*, postmodernists and traditional leftists were very much at theoretical and political odds. In *Empire*, they seem to share similar agendas.

The result was a new myth for a new millennium—"Empire is the new world order."

In a nutshell, their argument goes like this. Contemporary global political life is not an unwieldy, illogical mess. Rather, "there is world order" (2000: 3), and this world order is best described by the term Empire. Empire is the materialization— the tangible actualization—of political, social, and economic global processes of exploitation that repress what Hardt and Negri call "the multitude," a sort of globalized, postmodern proletariat (see Table 7.1).

Hardt and Negri's myth appears to answer what might be *the* fundamental question that has plagued neoMarxists since the collapse of the Eastern bloc in 1989—how is it possible to have a (communist) revolution when there seems to be nothing (coherent) to rebel against *and* in an era in which rebellion itself seems to be so incoherent? By recasting the oppressor as Empire and the oppressed as the multitude, Hardt and Negri restore the basic binarary upon which Marxism has long been based. And, importantly, they do so in a era of so-called globalization in which not only (former) global orderers like hegemonic sovereign nation-states but also (former) rebels like oppressed economic classes seem like the fractured, fluid, foundationless identities that postmodernists have been describing for decades (see Chapter 4, Suggestions for further thinking). Empire is the term that unifies the fragmented nature of global political oppression into a coherent ontology/agency to be opposed—the new enemy of the (communist) left. And the multitude is the term that unifies fragmented, often localized resistance movements into a coherent global ontology/agency to challenge their new enemy, Empire, and thereby transform the nature of global politics.

By applying this "ontological standpoint" (2000: 62) to their assessment of global politics, Hardt and Negri seem to both acknowledge and overcome the

Table 7.1 Marx's vs. Hardt and Negri's understanding of history

	Marx	Hardt and Negri
Understanding of history	Dialectical	Dialectical
Nature of dialectic	Materialist	Materialist
What clashes in the dialectic?	Economic classes	Globalized postmodern ontologies (Empire vs. the multitude)

ontological issues postmodernists have long pointed to. They acknowledge post-modern insights in part by recognizing contemporary global ontology/agency/ identity (which are each slightly different things; see Suggestions for further thinking, Chapter 4) as fragmented, fluid and foundationless. But then they seem to overcome the "proper ontological lack" (2000: 62) of contemporary global agents by unifying Empire and the multitude into proper, coherent agents. In so doing, Hardt and Negri claim to overcome the obstacles postmodern ontologies have posed to global resistance.

What does that mean in practice?

It means that now that the multitude know who they are as the multitude (the globally fragmented resistors of oppression who are unified in their purpose of resistance) and now that the multitude know whom they are resisting (the globally fragmented but unified in purpose new enemy called Empire), global resistance movements across the world become more meaningful. The multitude's efforts may not end in a communist utopia, as Marx predicted. But their actions can now be understood properly to be part of a global revolution that could lead to that end (which is the desired end for Hardt and Negri). All this is possible—or, really, actually happening—because postmodern ontology is no longer a problem to global resistance.

But is the problem of ontology so easily dealt with? Is solving the problems of coherence and direction and even potentially "progress" that postmodernists have pointed to simply a matter of naming the multitude as coherent global resistors of Empire and of naming Empire as their new enemy?

As we saw with Chapter 4's myth "anarchy is what states make of it," just because we may desire a coherent ontology/producer/author behind production (in that case, the state; in this case, global order and resistances to it), that doesn't necessarily mean we can find one. And even if we do find one (like Hardt and Negri claim to find Empire and its global resistor, the multitude), this doesn't mean that this ontology/producer/author is not experiencing "ontological lack," or that it is as coherent or reliable as we wish it to be. Indeed, as we will see in Chapter 8, "ontological lack"—the impossibility of being a coherent identity—may be the only "identity" left in the so-called postmodern world. And, if that is the case, then theorizing "ontological lack" out of existence is not the same as producing the truth about ontology. It is merely symptomatic of a desire to produce such a truth.

What makes such a desire appear to be just the way things really are in contemporary global life? What, in Hardt and Negri's case, makes their desire to produce a truth about ontology appear to be *the* truth?

The 2000 film *Memento* takes the problems of ontological lack and the production of the truth head on. Its hero is Leonard Shelby, a victim of a rare neurological disorder which allows him to retain his past memories but makes him incapable of creating new memories. The past memory that haunts Leonard is of his wife's violent murder at the hands of an unknown intruder. Using a series of mementos like tattoos and photographs as substitutes for his short-term memory, Leonard pursues his wife's murderer until he kills him, again and again and again (because of course Leonard cannot retain the new memory of having killed his wife's killer). In telling its sad tale about a figure attempting to compensate for his ontological lack by producing truth tales that produce enemies, *Memento* engages questions such as "how are the ontologies of enemy and avenger produced?," "why are these ontologies produced?," and "what must go without saying in order for the production of such ontologies to appear to be true?" Reading *Memento*'s selective use of memory back onto *Empire*, we can ask yet another question, "what must Hardt and Negri necessarily exclude from their narration of Empire and the multitude in order for their myth 'Empire is the new world order' to appear to be true?"

In this chapter, I will explore these questions by first asking three additional questions—(1) What is Empire? (2) What is the multitude? (3) What is the relationship between Empire and the multitude?

What does the myth say?

"Empire is materializing before our very eyes" (2000: xi). This is the claim that Hardt and Negri make at the outset of their book *Empire*. What has enabled the materialization of Empire seems to be the end of colonization and the collapse of the Soviet bloc which in turn led to the "globalization of economic and cultural exchange" (2000: xi). So Empire is connected to globalization. But Hardt and Negri are interested in much more than the mere globalization of production and exchange. As their myth suggests, they want to understand what all this implies for world order.

And so, in addition to the globalization of economic and cultural exchange noted by others, they have observed the emergence as well of "a global order, a new logic and structure of rule—in short, a new form of sovereignty" that they call Empire (2000: xi). "Empire is the political subject that effectively regulates these global exchanges, the sovereign power that governs the world" (2000: xi). It is the new sovereignty that has emerged in an era of globalization, at "the end of history." As Hardt and Negri put it, "Empire exhausts historical time, suspends history, and summons the past and future within its own ethical order. In other words, Empire presents its order as permanent, eternal, and necessary" (2000: 11).

These are enormous claims to make, especially when considered within the field of international politics. For Hardt and Negri are insisting that it is not sovereign nation-states alone or in some combination that rule the world but instead that this thing called Empire does. And this, of course, runs contrary to the declared wisdom of many traditional IR scholars from realists (Chapter 2) to Wendtian social constructivists (Chapter 4). Equally, Hardt and Negri imply that the whole anarchy problematic is silly. If Empire is what rules world politics—provides world order—then it doesn't really matter that there is no formal world government ("international anarchy" as anarchy scholars define it; see Chapters 2–4), for according to Hardt and Negri, there is a world orderer—a sovereign political subject who governs the world—and that world orderer is called Empire.

So what exactly is Empire?

Hardt and Negri have an awful lot to say about what Empire is and, just as importantly, about what Empire isn't. Sometimes it seems that the more they explain Empire, the more confusing the concept becomes. Take a look at Box 7.1 which lists just a few of the things Hardt and Negri say about Empire.

Box 7.1 What Empire is and isn't

What Empire is

- "a single logic of rule" (2000: xii)
- the political subject that regulates global exchanges (2000: xi)
- "the sovereign power that governs the world" (2000: xi)
- "an order that effectively suspends history and thereby fixes the existing state of affairs for eternity" (2000: xiv)
- "a virtual center" (2000: 58)
- "a non-place" (2000: 190)
- "a decentered and deterritorializing apparatus of rule" (2000: xii)
- a society of control constructed through biopower (2000: 25)
- an "international disciplinary order" (2000: 261)
- "a single logic of rule" (2000: xii)
- "force" presented "as being in the service of right and peace" (2000: 15)
- the enemy of the multitude (2000: 45)

What Empire is not

- not reducible to the United States of America (2000: xiii–xiv)
- not imperialism (2000: xiv)

So, how do we make sense of all of this?

The first thing to do is to recognize that what makes Empire both so difficult to grasp and such a powerful concept is its mixed character. On the one hand, some of the things Hardt and Negri attribute to Empire seem to have a certainty about them, things like "a political subject" or "a sovereign power." These are the sorts of things about which we might say, "I'd recognize that if I saw it." But, on the other hand, there seem to be just as many things about Empire that are elusive, things like it being "a virtual center" or "a non-place." These sorts of things are really hard to identify—to know them when we see them—because they are defined by their very inability to be pinned down.

This mixed character to the concept of Empire results from Hardt and Negri's mixed theoretical debts. In addition to using the traditional language of international relations theory to explain their myth of world order, Hardt and Negri also rely upon postmodernism and neoMarxism. What this means is that Hardt and Negri's concept of Empire is so complex and (to some) contradictory because it fuses together three approaches to understanding the world—traditional IR theory, postmodernism, and neoMarxism.

What Hardt and Negri take from traditional IR theory are concepts like "world order," "sovereignty," and "political subjectivity," concepts that seem to require no further explanation to students of IR. We understand what Hardt and Negri mean when they say that Empire is a form of world order, a form of sovereignty, a form of political subjectivity. Or at least we think we do. And then they twist the very concepts we thought we understood by combining them with postmodernism and neoMarxism.

They seem to postmodernize this new form of world order by turning to the work of Michel Foucault on biopower and to the work of Deleuze and Guattari on nomadism. World order cannot be understood simply as a clash among sovereign nation-states. States aren't the only important actors in international politics any more. Rather, to understand this new world order, we need to examine not only how international order is created among states but also within states *and within individuals*. Foucauldian biopower is the concept that explains how individuals' relationships to society, economics, and governance are constructed and recon-structed *within themselves* in relation to states and societies so that individuals, too, end up constructing the very orders that construct them. Put very simply, Foucault recognizes that relationships among states, societies, and populations have changed historically, from states at first subjecting populations to the sovereign authority of the state, to societies (usually within states) disciplining populations to behave in accordance with humanitarian norms of conduct, to individuals becoming self-disciplined once they have internalized the lessons (and power relations) circu-lated in and by states and societies.

What this means for Hardt and Negri is that Empire is not something that has been imposed upon us from above (like a bad world government). Rather, Empire is something that an awful lot of us have had a hand in making (examples might be as trivial as buying a McDonald's hamburger and thereby supporting globalization to Western citizens rallying around their national flags during Gulf War I). Because populations in the industrial West have been (self-)disciplined into being good consumers and good citizens, they have also helped to construct Empire as an "*international disciplinary order*" (2000: 261, italics in original).

In trying to explain the location of Empire, Hardt and Negri turn to the work of postmodern philosophers Deleuze and Guattari on nomadism. Following Foucault, Deleuze and Guattari recognize that power is not located in any one place any more; rather, it flows through states, societies, and international orders. Power relations, then, can no longer be described in territorial terms. We cannot say, for example, that the United States of America is where Empire is located, even though we can say that the USA is one of the points at and through which Empire is expressed. This is why Hardt and Negri describe Empire as having a "virtual center" rather than a true center. As a network of power relations, it is both everywhere and nowhere at the same time. So, even though Empire is very real for Hardt and Negri, it is not something we can ever pin down to one place.

What this means is that the agency/ontology of Empire is postmodern. What does that mean, and how does that work? Well, postmodern agency/ontology— postmodern ways of being—differ from traditional agency/ontology in that instead of simply being there (knowing them when we see them), they appear to be foundationless, fluid, and fragmented (things we can't really pin down). What does this mean for Empire? By being located everywhere and nowhere at the same time, Empire is foundationless. It is not, for example, confined within a particular territorial state or group of states. Being foundationless, the forces of Empire flow across boundaries rather than remaining restricted within them. They are more like what Manuel Castells refers to as global networks of informationalized flows than they are like traditional expressions of imperialism, for example (2000: 286). As such, Empire is fluid. And because Empire is located in so many different places in so many different ways all at the same time, Empire has a fractured identity. It isn't any one thing. It is a lot of things taken in combination.

So Hardt and Negri rely upon postmodernism for three specific intellectual debts—to explain how international order is constructed through biopower into an international disciplinary order, to explain the deterritorialized location of Empire, and to express the fragmentary agency/ontology of Empire.

It is on this final debt to postmodernism—its ontological debt—that Hardt and Negri complicate things yet again. They do so by turning to neoMarxism, the key theoretical foundation of their myth of Empire.

Hardt and Negri want to preserve postmodern insights about ontology while insisting that Empire has a concrete character—the character of a world orderer. And so they twist and turn a few more times. For example, very much like (but not identical to) Marx's explanation of the logic of capital, Hardt and Negri describe Empire as "a single logic of rule" (2000: xii). Describing some-thing as "singular" seems to contradict everything postmodernism says about agency/ontology. Yet Hardt and Negri combine this claim with postmodern insights about agency/ontology. They suggest that as a logic and not a place, Empire is empowered by "contingency, mobility, and flexibility" (2000: 200). That sounds very postmodern. But then they go on to argue that Empire is *the* logic that dominates the current international order. "Empire is the new world order." And even though Empire cannot be located in any single state or group of states, as the logical orderer of the world it is "a political subject," "a sovereign power," a (traditional) ontology.

They then go on to describe the character of Empire as a ruler. Empire seems to be a benevolent ruler. It seems to mobilize power relations for good—for humanity, for right, for justice. But, argue Hardt and Negri, the way Empire really rules the world is through exploitation; and those whom they claim are exploited (true to Marxism) are laborers. As Hardt and Negri put it, "Empire is the non-place of world production where labor is exploited" (2000: 210). So just as in capitalism where the rich get richer off the backs of the poor, in Empire the few benefit by exploiting "the multitude." Empire's exploitation is globally performed through political, social, and economic processes. It is through these processes of exploitation that we are able to see Empire, that "Empire is materializing before our very eyes" (2000: xi).

What is important here, however, is that we wouldn't be able to recognize Empire—these global processes of exploitation—if we couldn't identify the victims of Empire's oppression. In other words, it is the material exploitation of the multitude by Empire that makes us aware of the global processes that cause this exploitation. This is one reason why Hardt and Negri claim that "the multitude call Empire into being" (2000: 43). The multitude call Empire into being not only through their oppression. More importantly for Hardt and Negri, they call Empire into being through their resistance to this oppression.

Resistance to oppression is really what neoMarxism is all about. And, indeed, it is what *Empire* is all about. *Hardt and Negri's myth of Empire is less about trying to explain the new world order than it is about striving to understand how resistance to that new world order is happening and how it can be made more effective*. If that is the case, then why have Hardt and Negri gone to such lengths to expound their myth "Empire is the new world order"? Because, they argue, "The first question of political philosophy today is not if or even why there will be resistance and rebellion, but rather *how to determine the enemy against which to rebel*" (2000: 211, my italics). Put differently, in order to make resistance today meaningful, the multitude have to know who or what is to be resisted. In claiming that "Empire is the new world order," Hardt and Negri are in effect also claiming that "Empire is the new world *enemy*" (2000: 57; my italics). Empire is the enemy of the multitude. Empire is what is to be resisted.

Empire, then, may know itself to be at "the end of history." But, in effect, the eternity of Empire can be—and needs to be—challenged by the multitude. As Hardt and Negri put it, "Our political task . . . is not simply to resist these processes [of Empire] but to reorganize them and redirect them toward new ends. The creative forces of the multitude that sustain Empire are also capable of autonomously constructing a counter-Empire, an alternative political organization of global flows and exchanges" and, they claim, these struggles are already taking place (2000: xv).

Linking up our discussions of the agency/ontology of Empire and the character of Empire, what we see in Hardt and Negri is that both postmodern and neoMarxist accounts of agency/ontology are crucial to how they describe Empire. For Empire to be the enemy of the multitude, it has to "be"—it has to be an agent, an ontology "against which to rebel" (2000: 211). Otherwise, fear Hardt and Negri, Empire could not be opposed. But when we look at the contemporary world, we don't see a traditional world orderer. There is no world government. There is no traditional imperial power. All we (might) see is fragmented, fluid, and foundationless Empire. But for Hardt and Negri, this fragmented, fluid, foundationless Empire very much "is." It is a singular a logic, a new sovereign, a new world orderer. And so it can be opposed. But because it is now a singular sovereign ruler, Empire seems to be as modern as it is postmodern.

Ok, so now we know a bit about what Empire is. What about the multitude? How do Hardt and Negri think about them?

The multitude is a concept reminiscent of "the masses" in neoMarxism. Without going into any detail, the multitude—like the masses—represent both exploited labor and (because they are fed up with being exploited) revolutionary potential. In Marxism, the masses are class-based. Hardt and Negri try to complicate the class-based character of the masses in their conception of the multitude. Referring to the multitude as a "new proletariat" (2000: 402), Hardt and Negri emphasize the indefinite identity of the multitude. The multitude is a postmodern agent/ontology. Like Empire, it is not territorially (or even merely class) based. It is fragmented, fluid, and foundationless. Like Empire, it can be composed of seemingly disjointed political elements. For example, global resistance movements under the names of Seattle, Chiapas, and the Intifada might all be part of the multitude (2000: 54–6). The disparateness of the multitude does not mean it is not a powerful agent in contemporary global politics; it just means that it is more difficult to identify the multitude as an agent, which can make political resistance to an enemy (Empire) more difficult.

Global resistance is not impossible, however. Yes, Hardt and Negri claim that what has kept global movements of resistance from becoming unified across regions and movements and from making sense (and, they imply, making progress, i.e., breaking out of the seemingly eternal time of Empire) as a unified global axis of resistance is their fragmented agency/ontology (2000: 54–6). But they also claim that while political movements are of course distinctive and localized— and therefore, when examined as a global whole, seem to be fragmented, fluid, and foundationless—they share two things in common. First, they share the common enemy of Empire (2000: 57); and because they share this common enemy, second, they also share the common identity of the multitude (2000: 393–413; see Box 7.2). The only problem is that they just don't always know this and therefore cannot always organize their resistances as effectively as they could (which is why intellectuals like Hardt and Negri had to write their book to explain it all).

What we see here is that just as "the multitude call Empire into being," Empire calls the multitude into being. The multitude call Empire into being as its enemy to be resisted in the form of an "international disciplinary order" and orderer. And it is only because the multitude—these fragmented resistance groups scattered around the world—have a common enemy in Empire that they know themselves to have a common identity, a common agency, a common ontology, to "be" the multitude.

Who the multitude should be is a force for "counter-Empire" (2000: 207). As Hardt and Negri put it, "Globalization must be met with a counter-globalization, Empire with a counter-Empire" (2000: 207). "The multitude, in its will to be-against and its desire for liberation, must push through Empire to come out the other side" (2000: 218).

In the end, what *Empire* leaves us with is not an unruly world composed of illogical, anarchic, fragmented forces. Instead, we are left with a single logic (the logic of Empire) and a single contradiction (between Empire and the multitude). We are left, in other words, with a classic Marxist encounter between oppressor

---

Box 7.2 Who are the multitude?

"a new proletariat" (2000: 402)

a unified (or at least, unifiable) global axis of resistance (2000: 54–6)

those who share the common enemy of Empire (2000: 393–413)

"counter-Empire" (2000: 207)

"the real ontological referent of philosophy (and, I would add, history" (2000: 48)

contemporary militants (2000: 413)

Source: Hardt and Negri, 2000

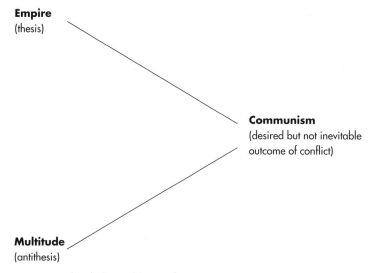

Empire
(thesis)

Communism
(desired but not inevitable
outcome of conflict)

Multitude
(antithesis)

Figure 7.1 The dialectical logic of Empire

and oppressed. And even though Hardt and Negri reject such a reading, their characterization of this contemporary clash between Empire and counter-Empire slots in nicely to a traditional Marxist materialist dialectic (see Figure 7.1). The relationship between Empire and the multitude, then, is dialectical.

Empire (thesis) is opposed to the multitude (antithesis), although Hardt and Negri would insist that this Empire/multitude clash is not dialectical because it is non-teleological (i.e., it is open-ended rather than having a determined endpoint like the realization of communism, 2000: 47, 48, 51) and because (they claim) their ontologies are postmodernized (Table 7.2).

By unifying global forces of oppression into a single logic called Empire, by unifying fractured forces of resistance into a single global resistor called the multitude, and by placing oppressor/Empire and oppressed/the multitude into a neat opposition, Hardt and Negri claim to solve the problem of resistance in our contemporary postmodern era. "Ontological lack" is overcome because Hardt and Negri's ontological standpoint identifies clear ontologies/agents—Empire and the multitude. Without ontological lack, resistance (like oppression) itself becomes "a *political subject*" (2000: 394), "a singularity that establishes a new place in the non-place of Empire" (2000: 395), and "the real ontological referent of philosophy"

Table 7.2 Modernism vs. postmodernism

	Modernism	Postmodernism
Time	Progressive	Non-progressive
Space	Bounded	Unbounded

(and, I would add, of history) (2000: 48). The multitude becomes a kind of (communist) militant fighting not for phony justice (as Empire does) but for real justice. As Hardt and Negri put it, *"This militancy makes resistance into counterpower and makes rebellion into a project of love"* (2000: 413; italics in original). *"This,"* they conclude, *"is the irrepressible lightness and joy of being communist"* (2000: 413; italics in original).

Memento

If ever there were a character who reveled in the joy of resistance and turned rebellion into a project of love, it is Leonard Shelby. We meet Leonard in the opening shot of Christopher Nolan's 2000 film *Memento* (based on the short story *Memento Mori* by his brother Jonathan Nolan).

Memento opens to the sound of a simple note followed by others quietly rippling in the background. Credits fade in and out. As the title appears, the music changes to an ominous chord. Fade in to a close-up of a hand holding a Polaroid picture. The photo vividly shows a blue-jacketed torso face-down amongst blood-soaked white tiles. We see the photo from the point of view of the person holding it. As the camera lingers on the photo, its sharpness fades. The hand shakes the Polaroid. The picture fades some more. This action is repeated until the Polaroid fades to white.

Plate 7.1 Faded Polaroid photo of a dead body.
Courtesy of the Ronald Grant Film Archive © Newmarket Capital Group.

The man holding the photo reaches inside his jacket for his camera and places the photo where the film exits the machine. We hear mechanical sounds as the Polaroid camera sucks up the photo, then flashes.

Cut to a close-up of the photographer's blood-splattered face. He is a white male in his thirties. Cut to quick montage close-ups of what he sees—blood running up the tiles, a bullet shell, blood-splashed glasses, the head of the man in the blue jacket face down.

Cut back to the photographer standing above the dead body. A gun leaps into his outstretched hand. He kneels down. The shell dances on the tiles, the bloodied glasses jump onto the dead man's face, the dead man's head sucks up its spilt blood. As the shell flies into the sparking gun, the victim—a middle-aged white male with a mustache—turns to face the gunman, screaming. We cannot make out what the victim says. The sound is "wrong." All the sounds are wrong, except the music. For they, like the visuals in this opening sequence, are played backwards.

Cut to a black-and-white extreme close-up of the photographer/gunman's face in profile. As the camera moves up his face, we hear his thoughts in calm voice-over. "So where are you? You're in some motel room. You wake up and you're in some motel room." The camera confirms this, showing us a room key, a closet, the gunman sitting on a bed, all in black and white. He continues, "It feels like maybe the first time you've been here, but perhaps you've been there a week, three months. It's kinda hard to say. I don't know. It's just an anonymous room."

Cut to a color Polaroid of a smiling mustached white male in a blue jacket. Beneath his photo is the word "Teddy" and some numbers. The photo rests on a small counter. A hand from behind the counter turns the photo toward the gunman. "This guy," he says to the gunman, tapping the photo with his finger, "he's here alright." The gunman turns around to see Teddy entering the hotel lobby. Teddy sees the gunman and greets him with a friendly, "Lenny."

Lenny/Leonard (dressed as he was in the opening color sequence) drives Teddy to an abandoned building out of town. In their conversation, it is revealed that Leonard has an as-yet-unexplained disability and that he is playing detective (Teddy playfully calls him "Sherlock"). All sorts of small things are unexplained in this scene, like why Leonard has two bloody scratches on his face (scratches he did not have in the previous black-and-white sequence).

Inside the building, Leonard consults his Polaroid of Teddy, turning it over to reveal the words, "Don't believe his lies. He is the one. Kill him." In voiceover, we hear Leonard's thoughts, "I've finally found him. How long have I been looking?" Leonard jumps Teddy, dragging him into a white tiled area of the building. He tells Teddy to beg his wife's forgiveness before he kills him. Teddy protests.

Teddy: Leonard, you don't know what's going on. You don't even know my name.
Leonard: Teddy.
Teddy: That's cause you read it off a fucking picture. You don't know who you are.
Leonard: I'm Leonard Shelby, I'm from San Francisco . . .
Teddy: That's who you were, that's not what you've become.
Leonard: Shut your mouth!
Teddy: You wanna know, Lenny. Come on . . . Let's go down to the basement. . . .
     Then you'll know who you really are.

Plate 7.2 Leonard and Teddy.
Courtesy of the Ronald Grant Film Archive © Newmarket Capital Group.

Leonard looks confused, fearful. He takes aim at Teddy's face.
> At this moment, the film has arrived at the final shot of the first color sequence.
> Teddy turns away and screams, "No," as Leonard shoots him in the head.
> Cut to black.
> Fade into black-and-white sequence. Leonard is sitting on his motel bed, wearing boxers and a plaid shirt, just as in the previous black-and-white sequence. In his voiceover, we hear the beginnings of a long explanation, an explanation that begins where the last black-and-white scene finished.

Leonard [voiceover]:   It's just an anonymous room. . . . You know, you know who you are, and you know kinda all about yourself. But just for day to day stuff, notes are really useful.

Close-up of a tattoo on Leonard's hand that reads, "Remember Sammy Jankis."

Leonard (voiceover):   Sammy Jankis had the same problem. He really had no system. He wrote himself a ridiculous amount of notes but he'd get them all mixed up. You really do need a system if you're gonna make it work.

Quick fade to color scene in which Leonard is writing on the back of a Polaroid, "He is the one. Kill him." The scene continues. . . .

> This is how *Memento* opens.
> Needless to say, this is an unusual opening. First, unlike other films we've discussed, *Memento*'s opening has no clear ending (and, as we will discover, no clear beginning either). As I have related it here, it is composed of four sequences and

the beginning of a fifth, three in color and two in black and white. My selection of four-plus sequences is arbitrary. I could have selected maybe three instead. But selecting just one would have been problematic. For if I selected just the first color sequence—what would traditionally be regarded as an opening sequence—we wouldn't have enough information to go on to grasp what we need to know to analyze the film. This is because, in *Memento, the ordering of sequences is as important as the content of sequences.*

Which leads us to the second difference between this film's and other films' openings. Opening sequences usually tell an audience everything they need to know to understand a film. For example, they introduce central themes and tensions, if not also central characters. *Memento* does some of this. It does introduce us to Leonard and Teddy. It does suggest that Leonard has a disability (although we don't know what this is). And it does give us a murder to solve. But it does all of this with a twist. Instead of standing as a clarifying distillation of codes that we can revisit in our minds to make sense of the action as it unfolds, *Memento*'s opening sequence raises more questions than it answers. Who is Leonard Shelby? Who is Teddy? Why did Leonard kill Teddy? And why did Leonard photograph Teddy once he killed him?

As such, *Memento* is a detective film. It isn't a classic "whodunit" (we know Leonard did it) but a complex "why did he do it?" Who wants to know why he did it is the audience. The audience is *Memento*'s off-screen detective. The audience is trying to make sense of events as they unfold from the first color sequence. This is one of the things that makes *Memento* so compelling. We have to think throughout this film. But, typically, we don't have to think alone. As in any detective film, the audience gets to puzzle through the story with the film's on-screen detective. *Memento*'s detective is Leonard, whom Teddy refers to as "Sherlock" in the second color sequence. Since the film's detective is the very guy who committed the murder, the audience presumes that Leonard knows why he murdered Teddy. All it has to do is hang around for Leonard to explain things to them.

And explain Leonard does. Indeed, this is what happens in the black-and-white sequences. First in voiceover and later in a long conversation to an anonymous telephone caller, Leonard answers the audience's questions about the back story, providing Leonard's motivation for murder. As Leonard tells it, "John G." raped and murdered his wife and, in the process, injured Leonard. When Leonard finds John G., he will kill him.

From the outset, then, the audience immediately identifies with and then relies upon Leonard. It identifies with Leonard as a detective because the audience is itself in the position of detective. And it relies upon Leonard as the seemingly all-knowing narrator of the story who will help the audience solve its puzzle. For the audience, then, Leonard's sense of the world is the sense they most care about.

Having a detective narrator with whom the audience identifies and upon whom it relies is a typical ploy in what is called the film noir genre. But, as Matt Zoller Seitz points out, "*Memento* is built around an amusing reversal of convention: where the typical film noir hero is a talkative wiseacre who thinks he knows more than he does, Leonard is a quiet cipher who knows he understands very little and is desperate to learn more" (2001). This is because, as Leonard explains to everyone he meets, he has a condition that makes him unable to make new memories. As he tells a motel clerk,

Leonard: I have no short-term memory. I know who I am and all about myself, but since my injury I can't make any new memories. Everything fades.

Clerk: That must suck. It's all . . . backwards. Well, like . . . you gotta pretty good idea of what you're gonna do next, but no idea what you just did. [laughs] I'm the exact opposite.

And, indeed, most people are. Most people depend upon their ability to make new memories in order to conduct their lives in a meaningful way. But Leonard is not most people. Leonard's handicap does *not* prevent him from knowing who he *was*—he was Leonard Shelby from San Francisco who, he explains later, used to be an insurance investigator. But Leonard's handicap does prevent him from knowing who he is—a man who not only wants to kill "John G." but is a multiple murderer. Leonard has killed "John G." over and over and over because each time he kills "John G.," the memory of this act fades like a Polaroid developing in reverse. Leonard, then, is a sort of postmodern serial killer who doesn't know he is killing serially because Leonard's life has no seriality. Leonard lives outside of sequential historical time, in a time that seems to be eternal. To the extent that Leonard experiences time, he does so "backwards." He has moments when he knows what he is going to do next, but he cannot hold onto the memories of what he has done since his injury.

Leonard's temporality is the film's temporality. The film takes place outside of historical time, in a seemingly eternal post-history, the time of Hardt and Negri's Empire. Time is post-historical because it is non-progressive. For Hardt and Negri (as for Leonard), this is because time has been postmodernized. Contingency rather than progress best explains temporal relationships. Still, progress may be possible, but it is not necessarily going to occur.

The film identifies with Leonard's perspective and so tells its story just as Leonard experiences it—backwards. The first color sequence is completely backwards, playing the action and all the sound apart from the music in reverse. Indeed, *Memento*'s opening shot shows the audience exactly how Leonard's memory works, for it is of a just-developed Polaroid, fading. Thereafter, the temporality of each color sequence is internally forward (showing events from beginning to end *within* any one sequence) but sequentially backward (showing us the last color sequence at the beginning of the film and the first at the end of the film).

Not only does the film identify with Leonard's sense of time. It also identifies with Leonard's sense of space. Leonard could not live in a more deterritorialized space. Place has little relevance in *Memento*. The film looks like it takes place in California, but this is just a guess. And it doesn't matter. The town doesn't matter. The motel doesn't matter. Even the abandoned building where Leonard murders Teddy doesn't matter. The only place that does matter is the space of Leonard himself. He is the space that we follow throughout the film. But Leonard is as unbounded as the postmodern landscape he occupies, if not more so. Put differently, the physical limits of Leonard's body do little to ground him as a single person, a coherent agent/ontology, a knowable place. The primary question raised by the film is not "Why did Leonard kill Teddy?" but "Who is Leonard Shelby, really?" As the film goes on, this question seems to be less and less reliably answered, especially by Leonard himself.

Box 7.3 How *Memento* makes sense of the world

Memento's postmodern world is uncertain:

- temporally because there is no guaranteed progress through time
- spatially because everything (even individuals) is unbounded.

So this is how the film makes sense of the world. The world is the postmodern temporal and spatial landscape that Hardt and Negri associate with Empire. This space is postmodern because the dual certainties of progress through time and boundedness in space are suspended, even at the most personal level of the individual (see Box 7.3).

What is typical and deviant in this postmodern world of *Memento*? What is typical is for people to be able to make new memories and, in so doing, to hold on to a sense of themselves and thereby live their lives "forward" not "backward." Living "forward" at least opens up the possibility of temporal progress, even though it does not guarantee it. What is deviant is for someone to be unable to make new memories and, therefore, have to re-create their sense of self and "progress" constantly. Such a person (Leonard) experiences time backwards, knowing what he is about to do but not knowing what he just did (see Table 7.3). It is only by supplementing his life with (1) an ordered and disciplined system of habit and conditioning; and (2) a motive to make it all work that Leonard is able to drag himself through his meaningless present. It is only, in other words, by applying a Foucauldian system of biopower to himself that Leonard passes himself off (to himself) as a functioning agent/ontology.

Leonard's system for reordering his world is postmodern not just because it replies upon biopower but also because it is an informationalized world. Leonard uses mementos—instant photography, notes, conceptual maps, files—to orient himself. But Leonard's most important messages are not tucked into his pockets or stuck upon walls. They are the tattoos poked beneath his skin. Having become "a walking text" (Hoberman, 2001), Leonard is himself a memento—a collection of scraps from the recent past, a collage of confused meanings he forgets he has and, upon each (re)discovery of them, desperately tries to decode and (re)assemble.

Table 7.3 What is typical and deviant in the world of *Memento*?

Typical	Deviant
Time moves forward because people make new memories as they pass through time. This makes temporal progress possible and allows individuals to hold onto their senses of self	Time moves backward because people cannot make new memories as they pass through time. This makes temporal progress impossible and means individuals have to constantly re-create their senses of self

Leonard's motive for reordering his world is a horrible injustice. As he tells it, this injustice is the rape and murder of his wife by John G., one of two men who broke into the family home, killed Leonard's wife, and struck Leonard on the head (thus leading to his short-term memory loss). That is the last thing he remembers, his wife . . . dying. Up Leonard's arm, onto his torso and thigh are tattooed "the facts" about John G.—white, male, drug dealer, etc. Across his upper chest are the words, "John G. raped and killed my wife."

It is this character—a vengeful "detective" who admits that the truth about his condition is that he doesn't know anything—who guides the equally confused audience through the story. Put differently, the character who epitomizes ontological lack is the very character to whom the audience turns for its orientation. This gives *Memento* its drive, but also its humor. For even Leonard knows he is the "most unreliable of unreliable narrators" (*Independent Focus*, 2000). As he tells his unknown caller, "You don't believe someone with this condition."

So why would the audience be gullible enough to believe Leonard? Why would the audience identify with and even trust a character as confused as Leonard to sort out their own confusion? The answer lies in another structural feature upon which the film relies, the splicing of black-and-white sequences with color sequences. Marking sequences with different colorings divides a filmic world into two—one imaginary and unreliable and the other real and reliable. Conventionally, it is the color world that is fantastical (not factual) and the black-and-white world that is real and reliable (just the facts). *Memento* seems to follow this convention.

As we already know, the color sequences in *Memento* are confusing. Even though they constitute a complete story which answers the question, "why did Leonard kill Teddy?," these sequences are not presented intelligibly to the audience. They do not seem to be composed of a comprehensible, structured narrative because they mirror Leonard's "memory" by running backwards. What they represent is the postmodern world in which Leonard lives and acts but which is beyond his ability to understand rationally, at least as a series of acts. And yet it is Leonard's understanding of events that compels the action in the color sequences. It is in these sequences that our (and Leonard's) puzzle is introduced, is explored, and (we initially believe) will be solved. But Leonard's "understanding" of his actions in the color sequences is grounded in his motivational fantasy. The color sequences are the sequences in which Leonard either acts on or is compelled to act on his fantasy to kill John G.

Most audience members intuitively get this. They know they don't understand what is going on in the color sequences, and they know Leonard doesn't know what is going on in them either, apart from moment to moment or, really, memento to memento. So the color sequences *do* make the audience identify with Leonard as detectives, asking "What is going on?" and "Who is Leonard, really?" But they *do not* make the audience rely upon Leonard to be their all-knowing narrator because, clearly, Leonard doesn't have much of a clue.

It is in the black-and-white sequences that Leonard appears to have a clue, indeed, to have most of the clues. Unlike the color sequences that run backwards, all of the black-and-white sequences run forward. They form an absorbing narrative in which Leonard not only situates himself physically and mentally, but also situates the audience in relation to what's going on in the color sequences. In these sequences, Leonard is generally in control. Even though he suffers from short-term memory loss and is forever asking questions ("Where am I?"), he has the ability to answer them persuasively based upon the evidence before him ("I'm in a motel room"). As such, these sequences are not part of the puzzle; *they appear to be what we need to know to solve the puzzle*. What Leonard seems to offer is a coherent past-to-present narrative of his old memories—memories of his wife, of her rape and murder, of having been an insurance investigator—that took place in historical time (past to present) and in real places (Leonard's house, San Francisco).

The audience devours these sequences as if they were reliable information because they are so comprehensible in contrast to the color sequences. Unlike the color sequences, what makes the black-and-white sequences make sense are three things—(1) Leonard's certainty about "facts" and "past memories"; (2) a progressive, modernist narrative; and (3) a bounded, modern sense of space (with real places like San Francisco and especially the space of Leonard himself functioning as a meaningful [because meaning-making] agent).

The primary device Leonard uses in the black-and-white sequences to guide the audience through the color sequences and to orient himself through his troublesome life is his narration of the story of Sammy Jankis. Sammy, Leonard tells us, also suffered from short-term memory loss. As the insurance investigator assigned to Sammy's case, it was Leonard's job to investigate Sammy's claim. Was Sammy's illness genuine? And, if so, was it caused by a physical injury or did it have a psychological cause? As Leonard tells the story, the time he spent with Sammy and his wife raised questions for him about Sammy's condition. For example, Sammy could carry out complex tasks like giving his wife her insulin injections because he had learned these skills prior to the onset of his condition. But Sammy could not make any new memories. And, crucially for Leonard, Sammy could not even use routine and conditioning to help him reorder his new life. Physically, patients with short-term memory loss can learn new behaviors, relying upon instinct rather than memory (which is a wholly different part of the brain).

When Sammy failed the instinct-based tests Leonard ordered, Leonard concluded that Sammy's condition was mental and not physical. Physically, Sammy had the ability to create new memories. Psychologically, he did not. Sammy's wife interpreted Leonard's judgement about Sammy to mean that Sammy was faking his condition. So she devised her own test. As before, when she needed her insulin injection, she said to Sammy (whom she knew without doubt loved her and would never harm her), "Sammy, it's time for my shot." And, as before, Sammy rose from his chair, assembled the medication, and gave his wife her injection. A few minutes after receiving her injection, Sammy's wife again told her husband, "Sammy, it's time for my shot," and again, without seeming to know he had just injected her, Sammy went through the same routine and injected his wife. Again she told Sammy, "It's time for my shot," and a third time, Sammy injected her. This time she went into a diabetic coma and died. Sammy, discovering his comatose wife, could not explain what had happened. Sammy passed this test—it showed he wasn't faking his condition—but at the cost of his wife's life.

Throughout *Memento*, Leonard implores himself to remember Sammy Jankis. Indeed, "Remember Sammy Jankis" is the only tattoo on Leonard's body that is not concealed by his clothing. It is this tattoo that leads Leonard to all his other tattoos.

And just as Leonard tells everyone over and over about his condition, he explains his condition to them in relation to his account of Sammy Jankis.

What matters to Leonard is not primarily the similarities between himself and Sammy—they both suffer from short-term memory loss—but their differences. Sammy's condition was psychological; Leonard's, physical. For while Sammy was not able to use instinct to create new behaviors, Leonard is. "Routine and discipline make my life possible," he tells his nameless caller. And it appears that the reason why Sammy could not will himself to behave differently through instinct, routine, and self-discipline is, as Leonard puts it, "He didn't have a reason to make it work. Me, yeah, I got a reason." Leonard's reason is to kill John G.

So what we have here are two characters who suffer from ontological lack—Sammy Jankis and Leonard Shelby. Sammy ends up institutionalized because he has no system and, most importantly, no motivation to overcome his ontological lack—to function as a whole person. Leonard, on the other hand, does have a system (mementos) and a motivation (John G.). Indeed, how Leonard "overcomes" his ontological lack is precisely the same way that Hardt and Negri claim that the multitude overcomes its ontological lack. He constructs an enemy—John G. Being against his enemy is what coheres Leonard into a functioning ontology/agent.

We know this both from Leonard's mementos and from his voiceovers. As we already know, Leonard has tattooed across his torso, "John G. raped and killed my wife." What is interesting about this tattoo is that, unlike all the others, it is inscribed in backward lettering that can only be deciphered when read in a mirror. Why is this tattoo backwards? It is this tattoo more than any other that reminds Leonard who

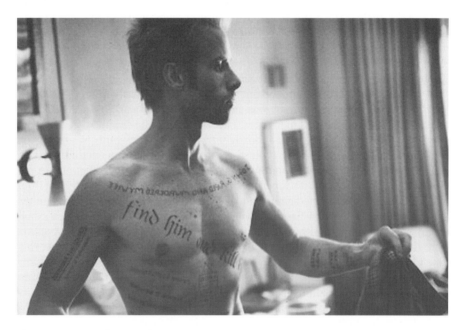

Plate 7.3 Tattooed Leonard.
Courtesy of the Ronald Grant Film Archive © Newmarket Capital Group.

he is *because it reminds him who his enemy is*. As Leonard explains in a voiceover near the end of the film, "We all need mirrors to remind ourselves who we are. I'm no different."

By informationally reordering their worlds, both Leonard and the multitude find themselves opposed to an enemy, and it is this enemy who "calls them into being." The enemy for Leonard, of course, is John G. And the enemy for the multitude is Empire. Without John G. as a coherently constructed ontology who can be opposed, Leonard would not know who he is or what to do. His life would be as aimless and meaningless as that of Sammy Jankis. And without Empire as a coherently constructed ontology that can be opposed, so, too would the resistances of the multitude seem to be aimless and meaningless (at least from the perspective of the modernist narrative of neoMarxism).

What makes Leonard's myth about himself function—that he is on a romantic quest to secure justice for his wife—is precisely the same thing that makes the multitude's romantic quest to secure global justice possible. It is that they have each (with a little help from their friends) constructed an enemy. Teddy, Natalie (the film's femme fatal), and who knows who else help Leonard construct John G., and Hardt and Negri help the multitude construct Empire.

Through the informational reordering of their worlds, then, both Leonard and the multitude seem to have achieved one of Hardt and Negri's maxims. Speaking specifically about truth commissions (but, I would argue, capturing their general attitude toward truth in *Empire*), Hardt and Negri write, "Truth will not make us free, but taking control of the production of truth will" (2000: 156). The truth Leonard tells himself is that John G. exists. The truth the multitude tells itself is that Empire exists. In both cases, truth is what both constructs these fractured ontologies into coherent agents and liberates them by turning them into powerful forces of resistance.

But is this "the truth"? Or is this just what Leonard and the multitude want to believe is true?

Truth, Ontology, and Desire

When *Memento*'s backwards color sequences and forward black-and-white sequences catch up with one another in the film's climax, answers emerge that put all truths in question. The color sequences indeed do answer the question "why did Leonard kill Teddy?" The reason that the audience suspects is, of course, that Teddy is really John G. And he is. His name is John Gammell. Only his mother calls him Teddy. And Teddy is Leonard's John G. He is the man Leonard has been looking for throughout the color sequences. So Leonard is right when he tells himself in voiceover just before he kills Teddy, "I finally found him." But there is a scary twist to *Memento*. What the color sequences also reveal is that *Teddy is Leonard's John G. because Leonard willfully constructed him as such. Leonard lied to himself in order to turn this John G. (Teddy) into his John G.* Why? Because Teddy emerges as an alternative narrative voice in the film, a voice that throws everything Leonard believes into doubt.

There are two things that Leonard firmly believes throughout the film—two things that allow Leonard to be Leonard. The first is that John G. raped and murdered his wife, and Leonard has to give his wife justice by killing John G. The second is that Leonard Shelby and Sammy Jankis are distinct individuals. Put differently, Leonard believe he knows who his enemy is and who he is. But when the dying Jimmy Grantz (the John G. Leonard kills at the end of the forward playing black-and-white sequences) calls Leonard "Sammy" and Teddy explains this to Leonard, the dual certainties Leonard relies upon to be Leonard start to unravel.

Leonard [to Teddy, about Jimmy Grantz]:   He knew about Sammy. Why would I tell him about Sammy?

Teddy: You tell everyone about Sammy. . . . Great story. Gets better every time you tell it. So you lie to yourself to be happy. Nothing wrong with that—we all do. Who cares if there's a few little things you'd rather not remember?

Leonard: What the fuck are you talking about?

Teddy: I dunno . . . your wife surviving the assault . . . her not believing about your condition . . . the doubt tearing her up inside . . . the insulin.

Leonard: That's Sammy, not me! I told you about Sammy. . . .

Teddy: Like you've told yourself. Over and over. Conditioning yourself to believe. "Learning through repetition."

Leonard: Sammy let his wife kill herself! Sammy ended up in an institution!

Cut to Sammy sitting in an institution, then film splices in one or two frames of Leonard as Sammy, sitting in the same chair in the same institution.

Leonard: . . . Sammy's wife came to me and. . . .

Teddy: Sammy didn't have a wife. It was your wife who had diabetes.

Cut to Leonard remembering giving his wife an insulin injection. Cut to Leonard shaking his head to reorder the memory. Cut back to the same scene, with Leonard giving his wife the injection, only this time Leonard is playfully pinching his wife with his fingers rather than poking her with a needle.

Leonard: She wasn't diabetic. You think I don't know my own wife? . . .

Teddy: I guess I can only make you believe the things you want to be true, huh? Like ol' Jimmy down there.

Teddy goes on to explain to Leonard that he helped Leonard kill the real John G. over a year ago, but even though Leonard has the Polaroid of this killing, he can't remember it. And so Teddy finds him more and more John G.'s to kill, to keep him happy. Jimmy Grantz was one of Leonard's many John G.'s.

Teddy: . . . I gave you a reason to live and you were more than happy to help. You lie to yourself! You don't want the truth. . . . So you make up your own truth.

It is at this point that Leonard distracts Teddy long enough to write on the back of Teddy's photo, "Don't believe his lies" and writes another "fact" down to be tattooed onto his body—"Fact 6: Car License Number"—and then he copies the number from Teddy's license plate onto his "fact sheet".

Leonard [in voiceover]:   You're a John G.? Fine, then you can be my John G. Do I lie to make myself happy? In your case, Teddy . . . yes, I will.

Of course, Leonard doesn't remember doing any of this. He doesn't remember lying to himself about John G., about Teddy, about Sammy, or certainly about himself. And so Leonard begins his new quest to find and kill John G., not knowing that Teddy is his John G.

As the temporal timelines of the black-and-white and color sequences converge, it is not only Leonard's "truths" that unravel but the audience's. For, against everyone's advice, the audience believed Leonard and believed in Leonard. Indeed, the film's director encouraged them to, by dividing the film into black-and-white sequences which normally would convey reliable information and color sequences which normally would not. What the audience learns at the film's climax is that they can rely upon nothing that Leonard has told them, except that no one believes someone with his disability. The black-and-white sequences aren't a narrative of "the truth" but a narrative of *the truth as Leonard wishes it to be*. It is a truth that allows Leonard to be Leonard—a coherent, functioning ontology/agent in the fluid, foundationless world he occupies.

Leonard, then, is an ontology/agent caught somewhere between truth and desire. He *desires* to be a coherent agent. But the *truth* is more likely that he is fractured and fragmented. For, if we believe Teddy and the dying Jimmy Grantz, Leonard is at least partly Sammy, too. And, indeed, the director—with his cross-splicing of Leonard into Sammy—suggests to the audience that Teddy and Jimmy got this right. This doesn't mean Teddy is any more of a reliable narrator than Leonard is, though. For Teddy keeps changing his story. One minute he is a cop, another a snitch, another a drug dealer. For all we know, he really could be the original John G. (but, then again, so could Leonard if it is true that he killed his wife).

So the black-and-white sequences do *not* explain the color sequences. If anything, the color sequences explain the black-and-white sequences. They explain that we cannot trust all-knowing narrators because their will to be all-knowing is based upon desire and not (exclusively) truth. We cannot trust Leonard because he lies to himself to be happy. We cannot trust Teddy because he lies to Leonard. And we cannot even trust the film's director because he misled us about the existence of a reliable narrator.

However much we may want them, then, *Memento* offers us no reliable narrators and no reliable truths. What it does offer us is something more important. It offers us an explanation of how something appears to be true. And, in so doing, it tells us how Hardt and Negri's myth "Empire is the new world order" appears to be true.

In the first instance, the stories told in both *Memento* and *Empire* appear to be true because their narrators so desperately need them to be true, because "desire" wins out over "truth" in their ontological tales.

In *Memento*, Leonard tells a tale of a tragic injustice—the rape and murder of his wife—that he needs to make right by killing his wife's assailant. So Leonard constructs an enemy, John G., who he repeatedly tracks and kills. But Leonard's story is not just the story of the loss of his wife. It is also the story of the loss of himself and the loss of his reason to exist. For, as Leonard tells it, John G. not only took Leonard's wife from him, he took Leonard away from himself. By injuring Leonard so that he could no longer lay down short-term memories, Leonard ceased to function as a coherent identity who could make meaning and progress in history.

Plate 7.4 Leonard holding up a Polaroid photo as evidence of his (unreliable) memory. Courtesy of the Ronald Grant Film Archive © Newmarket Capital Group.

John G. gives meaning to Leonard's life as the enemy he must bring to justice. It is John G. who calls Leonard into existence, who fulfills Leonard's desire to be a coherent ontology/agent.

In *Empire*, it is Hardt and Negri who tell a tale of injustice—the injustice of Empire as a new world order that oppresses the multitude. And so they construct Empire as the enemy of the multitude. But, as in Leonard's story, Hardt and Negri's story is not just about the loss of global justice. It is also about the loss of the multitude itself as the maker of meaning in contemporary global political life. And if the multitude doesn't make meaning, then resistance (and, indeed, communism itself) is not meaningful in this post-historical era. And, of course, here is the irony—if communism isn't meaningful, then surely communist intellectuals like Hardt and Negri aren't meaningful either.

In losing the resistive potential of the multitude, Hardt and Negri lose themselves. They cease to be making meaning and potential progress through contemporary history. By writing Empire—a terribly scattered, fractured, contradictory set of propositions and ideas—into "being," Hardt and Negri not only call the multitude into being. They call themselves into being. They, in other words, fulfill their desires to be relevant communist intellectuals.

What we see here, then, is that Leonard's desire to be a coherent ontology/ agent for himself and his strategy for becoming such an identity is strikingly similar to that of Hardt and Negri. Both construct an enemy. And this enemy is not only their reason to exist. It is what makes their very existence as relevant historical figures possible.

If, however, Leonard's ontology/agency and Hardt and Negri's ontology/ agency are really grounded in their desire to be (relevant) rather than the truth of their being (relevant), then why does it appear to be true? How is it that their stories are so compelling, even a story by such an unreliable narrator as Leonard?

The answer to this question is the very theme of *Memento*. It has to do with how memory functions.

What *Memento* tells us is that we do not always remember things as they really are but rather as we wish they were. Leonard remembers John G. killing his wife, not himself killing his wife. He remembers Sammy Jankis as an aimless, psychologically damaged, baffled man whose wife could not accept him, not himself as such a man. And when Leonard's memory is not enough to preserve the consistence of his story (and of himself), he lies to himself to be happy.

I would *not* make the claim that there is any self-aware lying going on in *Empire*. But I would make the claim that Hardt and Negri remember things selectively for the same reason Leonard does—to preserve their relevance. Hardt and Negri's investigations, like those of Leonard, lead them to "discover" Empire as a coherent ontology that can be opposed. But as they describe it, Hardt and Negri's Empire might be just as incoherent and multiple as Leonard's John G. Empire seems to be a moving and multiple target, one that counter-Empire is unlikely to succeed in overthrowing for some time, if ever. This means that the multitude, having been called into being by Empire, will exist as a relevant counter-formation for a long time, thereby insuring Hardt and Negri's continued relevance.

What makes Hardt and Negri's construction of an enemy into a coherent tale function is, just as in Leonard's case, their selective memory of anything that might contradict this tale. For Leonard, Sammy Jankis is the figure who threatens to make his story unravel. For Hardt and Negri, it is postmodernists. Postmodernists didn't just pose the problem of ontology—the idea that agents are fragmented, fluid, and foundationless. They additionally argued two things: (1) that the problem of ontology/agency is not one that can be solved, however much we might desire to solve it; and (2) that the problem of ontology/agency does not need to be solved. We can still have meaningful political resistance in the absence of the kind of coherence modernist narratives promise. Indeed, *political resistance might make more sense if we appreciate it as fractured rather than as singular.*

In *Empire*, Hardt and Negri selectively recall what postmodernists have to say. They borrow Foucault's notion of biopower to describe contemporary global life as an international disciplinary order, and they read Deleuze and Guattari's idea of the nomad onto Empire to emphasize its decentered, deterritorialized character. But they (willfully?) forget that postmodernists never claim that "the problem of ontology" is a problem rather than merely the postmodern condition. They forget how postmodernists describe how political resistance takes place in a postmodern world—through fragmented, foundationless, fluid struggles against fragmented, foundationless, fluid sights of power. What this means is that postmodernists would never say they contributed anything to Hardt and Negri's story about Empire and the multitude because, they would argue, "Empire" and "the multitude" don't exist as the coherent ontologies/agents that Hardt and Negri describe *and they needn't exist as such in order for meaningful global resistances to objectionable uses of power to take place.*

This is what must go without saying in order for Hardt and Negri's myth "Empire is the new world order" to appear to be true. These aspects of postmodernism are things that Hardt and Negri must not remember. For if they remembered them, the very task Hardt and Negri set for themselves and are celebrated for—to make resistance meaningful in our contemporary, postmodern world—would be irrelevant because, as postmodernists tell the story, resistance is already relevant.

The story postmodernism has to tell about global politics, then, is as destabilizing to Hardt and Negri's claim to be relevant contemporary intellectuals as the story Sammy Jankis has to tell is destabilizing to Leonard Shelby. It is only by either forgetting what postmodernism and Sammy have to say or by reordering the information forthcoming from the spaces of postmodernism and Sammy that Hardt and Negri's and Leonard's stories appear to be true.

In fairness to Hardt and Negri (and to Leonard), we all do this. We all remember things selectively and will ourselves to forget what we don't want to know. We all long to be historically relevant, even after our historical tasks (like Leonard's murder of John G. or Marx's critique of capital) have already been achieved. All ontologies/agents are, in other words, caught somewhere between "truth" and "desire."

The warning of *Memento* is that this makes us into unreliable narrators.

Leonard is not an unreliable narrator (just) because he suffers from short-term memory loss. He is an unreliable narrator because he refuses to examine all the evidence, specifically, the evidence about himself. It is because this is precisely what Teddy implores him to do that Teddy must die. Similarly, Hardt and Negri's narration of Empire and the multitude seems unreliable because it refuses to entertain all the evidence. In particular, it refuses to investigate the two further claims post-modernism makes about contemporary ontologies and contemporary resistance— that while some singular sense of ontology is impossible, this does not mean that fractured, fragmented, fluid resistances are meaningless. This is precisely what postmodernists implore Hardt and Negri to consider and why they remain at political odds with neoMarxists.

Overall, then, a willful not remembering and not knowing is indeed useful for constructing a coherent sense of self, for overcoming the loss of the (modern) subject. But in "overcoming" this loss, something else is lost. What is lost is the ability for critical reflection about selves. In Leonard's case, this means he cannot investigate himself and the new "ethical order" which he produced. In Hardt and Negri's case, this means they cannot (further) investigate the fragmentation, fluidity, and foundationlessness of Empire and the multitude, and of the counter-"ethical-order" which the multitude is producing.

For example, by insisting on the ontological singularity of the multitude, Hardt and Negri make it impossible to further investigate the political and moral uniqueness of resistance movements like those in Seattle, and Chiapas. Furthermore, if the multitude is a singular ontology that resists Empire and if (as Hardt and Negri imply) all resistance to Empire is good, then how are we to understand resistances to Empire that even many on the left would disavow? How, in particular, are we to understand the events of September 11? Was this a case of counter-Empire resisting Empire? Or is it correct to think of these events as terrorism? These questions are beyond the scope of *Empire* because they are outside the bounds of the sort of critical self-reflection that would make Hardt and Negri more reliable narrators.

Yet only a year after *Empire's* publication, these were the very questions that dominated the discussions of international politics. And so, not surprisingly, the importance of *Empire* (and Empire) faded from relevance for many as the first commercial jet crashed into the World Trade Center. The myth "Empire is the new world order" seemed to offer too little by way of explanation of contemporary international events, either politically or ethically. And so, a new myth to describe this next new world order emerged—a myth that described a world ordered by "the war on terror."

Suggestions for further thinking

Topic 1 Imperial IR

Hardt and Negri's Empire did not only introduce the myth "Empire is the new world order" into IR theory. It reignited debates about imperialism, the imperial, and the quasi-imperial in international politics. Does imperialism (still) exist? If so, in what form? What does this mean for states, sovereignty, and international order? Does Hardt and Negri's description of Empire capture what the imperial now looks like in international politics? If so, how? If not, why not? These (among other issues) are taken up in a series of essays published in *Millennium*. The debate is kicked off by Tarak Barkawi and Mark Laffey and responded to in the next issue by three theorists with very different perspectives on international politics—a Marxist, a social theorist, and a postmodernist.

Suggested reading

Tarak Barkawi and Mark Laffey (2002) "Retrieving the Imperial: *Empire* and International Relations," *Millennium* 31(1): 109–27.

Alex Callinicos (2002) "The Actuality of Imperialism," *Millennium* 31(2): 319–26.

Martin Shaw (2002) "Post-Imperial and Quasi-Imperial: State and Empire in the Global Era," *Millennium* 31(2): 327–36.

R.B.J. Walker (2002) "On the Immanence/Imminence of Empire," *Millennium* 31(2): 337–45.

Topic 2 Memory in IR

That memory and forgetting are political acts is not news to many social theorists. But actually investigating how memory and forgetting help us to construct orders— be these individual, national, or international—is rather new in IR theory. A lot of the work on memory in IR theory focuses on how to theorize trauma and how to understand and explain particular traumas in international politics. And, of course, in the aftermath of September 11, how memory and forgetting about the events of that day participate in the construction of subjectivities from states to global networks has been much discussed.

Paul Antze and Michael Lambek's edited volume is a good place to start reading about memory and trauma in the wider context of culture and society. Jenny Edkin's work brings these discussions to IR theory, not by working through classical texts on memory, but by applying her analysis to specific case studies like Vietnam, the Holocaust, Kosovo, and of course September 11. Maja Zehfuss's essay "Forget September 11" and Cynthia Weber's essay "Flying Planes Can Be Dangerous" both ponder official Bush administration memories of September 11 and their consequences.

Suggested reading

Paul Antze and Michael Lambek (eds) (1996) *Tense Past: Cultural Essays in Trauma and Memory*. New York: Routledge.

Jenny Edkins (2003) *Trauma and the Memory of Politics*. Cambridge: Cambridge University Press.

Cynthia Weber (2002) "Flying Planes Can Be Dangerous," *Millennium* 31(1): 129–47.

Maja Zehfuss (2003) "Forget September 11," *Third World Quarterly* 24(3): 513–28.

Chapter 8

Modernization and development theory

Is there a clash of civilizations?

And so the world changed, again.

On September 11, 2001, terrorists hijacked four passenger jet-airliners and flew three of them into targets in New York City and Washington, DC—one each into the twin towers of the World Trade Center and another into the Pentagon. The fourth airliner (which some believed was targeting the White House) crashed in a field in Pennsylvania.

Suddenly, US scholars and practitioners of international politics were again caught out by events. Hardt and Negri (Chapter 7) had indeed described the new world order as conflictual, but not in terms that were meaningful to most after September 11. And scholars and practitioners who had celebrated the end of ideology, the end of history, and the benevolent spread of Western (usually US) culture found themselves urgently returning to ideology and culture, albeit very differently. Liberalism, it seemed, had not won the hearts and minds of all the world's population. And even though American intellectuals like Francis Fukuyama recognized that liberalism as the ideal form of political and social organization had not *yet* spread the world over (Chapter 6), he and other triumphalist liberals failed to predict how destabilizing illiberal individuals willing to martyr themselves for what they believed was a higher cause, a greater good, and a purer ideal than anything liberalism had to offer could be when they were unleashed in a direct attack against the mainland of the world's only remaining superpower.

One scholar had, it seemed, provocatively predicted dramatic conflicts between liberal and illiberal forces in a post-Cold War world. This was the American political scientist Samuel P. Huntington, in his 1993 essay "The Clash of Civilizations?" Unlike Fukuyama who expressed his vision of the post-Cold War world in terms of ideas, Huntington translated what some might regard as ideological disputes into what he claimed were cultural disputes. Boldly articulating what he claimed would be the "crucial, indeed a central, aspect" of what "global politics is likely to be in the coming years" (1993: 22), Huntington posited his clash of civilizations thesis.

> It is my hypothesis that the fundamental source of conflict in this new world will be not primarily ideological or primarily economic. The great divisions among humankind and the dominating source of conflict will be cultural. Nation states will remain the most powerful actors in world affairs, but the principal conflicts of global politics will occur between nations and groups of different civilizations. The clash of civilizations will dominate global politics. The fault lines between civilizations will be the battle lines of the future.
>
> (1993: 22).

And so they seemed to be on September 11. Whether or not Huntington's hypothesis accurately described the post-September 11 world, it was to his clash of civilizations thesis that a stunned world turned as it began to make sense of the terrorist attacks on America. This does not mean everyone embraced Huntington's thesis. While American commentators like former Clinton administration Assistant Secretary of State James Rubins immediately translated the September 11 attack into civilizational terms, stating "This was an attack on civilisation. The World Trade Center is the centre of Western civilisation" (Rubins, 2001), cultural theorist Edward Said rejected Huntington's thesis, referring to it as "the clash of ignorance" (Said, 2001: 1).

Attempting to finesse the category "civilizations," President George W. Bush strenuously argued that while it is justified to speak of "civilized" and "uncivilized" people and even states (non-terrorists = civilized; terrorists and their supporters = uncivilized), it is unjustified to make broader generalizations using these terms, especially as they apply to people of different religions or regions (Bush, 2001a and 2001b). Yet whether by endorsement, refutation, or refinement, Huntington's clash of civilizations thesis *had* to be engaged.

What makes Huntington's thesis so compelling—whether contextualized through the "war on terror" or considered more generally in terms of global political life—is that it stands as a contemporary response to "the problem of what to do about cultural difference" (Blaney and Inayatullah, 2002: 104). As David Blaney and Naeem Inayatullah explain, Huntington's problem is also IR's problem. "Instead of accepting that cultural difference offers, not only problems, but also opportunities, IR theory assumes that difference is debilitating to the purpose of establishing order" (2002: 104). IR "solves" this problem by placing sameness within containable political units—sovereign nation-states—and relegating difference to spaces between them (Walker, 1993). Huntington accepts IR's move, preserving as he does the centrality of states as "the most powerful actors in world affairs" (1993: 22). But then he supplements IR's move with his own remapping of IR into larger units of similarity and difference—civilizations (Debrix, 2003). Both IR and Huntington conclude that sameness reduces instability whereas difference produces instability *and* that the best way to manage difference is either to assimilate it within the state or to expel it from the state.

Grappling with the problem of cultural difference and its production of instability is nothing new for Huntington. He did not suddenly start thinking about this problem or even the possibility of categorizing the world through a hierarchy of cultural zones in the aftermath of the Cold War (see, e.g., Weiner and Huntington, 1987). Rather, this problem, the concepts Huntington developed to address it, and the solutions/dilemmas he outlined all figure in his work on the modernization and development of states, work that has preoccupied Huntington since the 1960s.

The modernization and development tradition emerged during the Cold War as the West's economic, political, social, and cultural response to the management of former colonial territories. The dilemma facing Western scholars and practitioners of international politics was twofold. First, they hoped to theorize ideas and then implement policies that would transform newly independent colonies into politically developed sovereign nation-states. But these theorists—the bulk of whom were from the US—were not interested in so-called "Third World states" achieving development according to just any model. Rather, the only acceptable model of development was through liberal processes of politics, economics, and socialization, and the only acceptable model of a fully-developed state was a Western liberal capitalist so-called "First World state." What this means—and this is the second point—is that the modernization and development tradition was consciously conceived as a Western (and predominately US) alternative to Marxist and neo-Marxist strategies of development espoused by so-called "Second World states" such as the then Soviet Union (see Suggestions for further thinking).

As a specifically liberal and specifically US alternative to Soviet-style communism, the modernization and development traditional grounded itself in (among other things) liberal economic theory and a version of Talcott Parsons's sociological theory to explain how developing Third World states would naturally *evolve* into developed First World states. As we saw in Chapter 6, liberal economic theory offers a view of economic relations as naturally harmonious in which the distribution of economic prosperity is shared by all, albeit in different degrees. To share in economic benefits and to receive the promised "spillover" effect of legitimate political institutions like liberal capitalist democracy, Third World states need only avail themselves of the free market. In the classic statement of modernization and development theory by Gabriel Almond and Bingham Powell (1978), such Third World states became like Talcott Parsons's adaptive societies, themselves analogies to organisms in evolutionary biology. In Parsons's structural-functionalist model, increased social stratification (i.e., distribution of tasks and its resulting social inequality) is necessary for progress. And what produces social stratification is the functional transformation of simple inputs into complex outputs. In Almond and Powell's model, inputs are political demands, outputs are political policies, and the functional transformation of inputs into outputs occurs in the state through interest groups, political parties, bureaucracies, and the legislative, executive, and judicial branches of government. While Parsons measures the degree of movement of a society from traditional to modern by the complexity/differentiation of its stratification, so too do Almond and Powell measure the degree of movement from underdevelopment to development of Third World states (Figure 8.1).

Overall, the modernization and development tradition promises that, under the right social, political, and economic conditions, difference will give way to social, political, economic, and cultural sameness, with Third World states modernizing and developing to become more like First World states (Figure 8.2). In so doing, it promises a better standard of living for people in Third World states, and it promises an increasingly secure world for First World states (because the lives of Third World people will improve and because more states will become First World rather than Third World or Second World).

The first wave of modernization and development theorists drew four general conclusions about the development process for all states (Table 8.1). First, change and development are easy. Second, all good things go together (like economic growth, economic equality, political stability, democracy, national independence, and autonomy). Third, radicalism and revolution are bad (because they

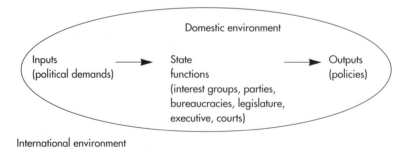

Figure 8.1 Structural-functional model

Figure 8.2 Political development timeline

are unnecessary for political development, following on from points one and two). And, finally, distributing power is more important than accumulating power (because democratic pluralism leads to stability) (Packenham, 1973).

Samuel Huntington is *not* a first-wave modernization and development theorist. He is a modernization revisionist. What this means is that while he accepts the basic principles, values, and arguments of modernization and development theory, he has devoted himself to the refinement and correction of some of the ideas in this tradition. Huntington argues that the modernization and development tradition is too focused on development and insufficiently focused on political order. And it is for this reason that this tradition fails to recognize that development (transforming difference into identity) and political stability are often incompatible. As Huntington puts it, "It is not the absence of modernity but the efforts to achieve it which produce political disorder. If poor countries appear to be unstable, it is not because they are poor, but because they are trying to become rich" (1968: 41). What this means is that, for Huntington, addressing the question of political development also requires theorists and practitioners to address the question of order. For Huntington, establishing a legitimate public order in developing states should be privileged over protecting the political liberty of citizens even when that means supporting authoritarian, one-party governments. Democracy should be a secondary goal because, as he argues, "Authority has to exist before it can be limited" (1968: 8).

Huntington's contentions amount to a rejection of two of the core principles of the modernization and development tradition—all good things go together and distributing power is more important than accumulating power. In addition, what Huntington implies is that the modernization and development approach fails to solve either the problem of cultural difference or its resulting problem of political disorder. If, as most IR theorists believe, difference leads to instability, *and* if modernization and development strategies do not always (if ever) succeed in

Table 8.1 Assumptions of political development

General assumptions	Assumptions Huntington rejects
1 Change and development are easy	
2 All good things go together	2 All good things go together
3 Radicalism and revolution are bad	
4 Distributing power is more important than accumulating power (Packenham, 1973)	4 Distributing power is more important than accumulating power

transforming difference into identity, then the problem of cultural difference and its inherent instability remains. Because few if any Third World states became or are becoming First World states, this means that the social, political, economic, and cultural differences of Third World states are not naturally adapting to the social, political, economic, and cultural identity of First World states. What's more, while striving to become developed, many Third World states experience greater political instability. This has implications not only for the credibility of the modernization and development tradition (which provides unsatisfying recommendations for how newly independent states might achieve development). It also has implications for the order and security of international life. Huntington's contribution to the modernization and development debate was to tackle this issue head-on, focusing on how order could be achieved *within developing states* when identity fails to universalize itself by assimilating difference, when Third World states (and cultures) persist in being different from First World states (and cultures). *His clash of civilizations thesis pessimistically globalizes this problem by suggesting that cultural difference creates disorder not only nationally but internationally in a post-Cold War era.*

In the remainder of the chapter, I will explore what makes Huntington's myth "there is a clash of civilizations" appear to be true. I will do so by analyzing Huntington's 1993 essay "The Clash of Civilizations?" bearing in mind Huntington's earlier responses to the question of cultural difference in order to pose the question "what must go without saying in order for Huntington's myth 'there is a clash of civilizations' to appear to be true?" Huntington's myth, like IR theory in general, assumes that sameness reduces disorder and difference produces disorder. But what if both sameness and difference produce both order and disorder? And what if the distinctions between identity and difference and between order and disorder cannot be so easily maintained as Huntington and IR theory suggest? These questions are raised by the 2000 British film *East is East* (Miramax).

East is East tells the story of how the Khan family—a working class bi-ethnic, bi-religious, and bi-racial family—struggles with the problem of cultural difference in a northern English suburb of Manchester in 1971. Conflict abounds in this family. Caught between their Pakistani father and their British mother, the Khan children appear to be the disputed fault line between Islamic and Western Christian cultures, where their father's and mother's differences meet. Yet it is also possible to read the Khan children *not* as emblematic of the clash of civilizations but instead as symbolizing a British multiculturalism emerging in the wake of post-colonial immigration, where cultural identities do not so much clash as they reshape and redefine one another. By suggesting that the Khan children represent emerging identities rather than clashing ones, *East is East* directs us to look for the sources that motivate conflict in the Khan family elsewhere. Maybe, the film suggests, conflict is not located in the mere existence of cultural difference or even necessarily in attempts to transform cultural differences (bi-ethnic children) into pure cultural identities (either Pakistani or British but not both). Maybe conflict is (also) located in identity itself, in the desire (as we saw in Chapter 7) to be a pure identity but the impossibility of achieving this desire. If this is the case, we have to ask what the implications of this might be for the identities that Huntington claims exist (civilizations) and their post-Cold War relations with one another (clashing).

What does the myth say?

Just as modernization and development theory is interested in the evolution of former colonies from traditional societies to modern states, so, too, is Huntington's post-Cold War clash of civilizations thesis preoccupied with evolutionary processes. These evolutionary processes are not those occurring within states but between them. The change that Huntington's thesis claims to account for is "the evolution of conflict in the modern world" (1993: 22). The history of the modern international system until the end of the Cold War was marked by conflicts between princes, then nation-states, and then ideologies, all of which "were primarily conflicts within Western civilizations" (1993: 23). Huntington claims that, "With the end of the Cold War, international politics moves out of its Western phase, and its centerpiece becomes the interaction between the West and non-Western civilizations and among non-Western civilizations" (1993: 23).

Huntington's thesis poses three questions: (1) What are these civilizations of which he speaks? (2) How precisely is world politics mapped into civilizations? (3) Why will civilizations clash in a post-Cold War world? I will address each of these questions in turn.

First to the definition of civilizations. Huntington defines a civilization as "a cultural entity" (1993: 23). A civilization is not just any cultural entity (nationalities and religions are not civilizations, for example). "A civilization is . . . the highest cultural grouping of people and the broadest level of cultural identity people have short of that which distinguishes humans from other species" (1993: 24). As we try to identify civilizations, Huntington tells us we must look to both "common objective elements" of a people, such as language, history, religion, customs, institutions and to the "subjective self-identification of people" (1993: 24). He gives us the following example.

> People have levels of identity: a resident of Rome may define himself with varying degrees of intensity as a Roman, an Italian, a Catholic, a Christian, a European, a Westerner. The civilization to which he belongs is the broadest level of identification with which he intensely identifies.
>
> (1993: 24)

In defining and identifying what civilizations are, Huntington does not claim that civilizations are discrete or unchanging. "Civilizations obviously blend and overlap, and many include subcivilizations" (1993: 24). As a result of people redefining their identities, "the composition and boundaries of civilizations change" (1993: 24). And sometimes civilizations disappear altogether (1993: 24). Even so, Huntington insists, "Civilizations are nonetheless meaningful entities, and while the lines between them are seldom sharp, they are real" (1993: 24).

By positing civilizations as the "crucial, indeed a central aspect" (1993: 22) of contemporary global politics, Huntington recognizes that IR scholars will contest his claim, arguing that states—not civilizations—dominate global politics (see Chapters 2–4). And while, as noted earlier, Huntington appeases IR scholars with his view that "[n]ation-states will remain the most powerful actors in world affairs" (1993: 22), he implies that states may not be the "principle actors in global affairs"

(1993: 24), at least not over the long run. As he puts it, while states have been the world's principal actors for only a few centuries, "[t]he broader reaches of human history have been the history of civilizations" (1993: 24–5).

So that's what civilizations are generally. How, then, do civilizations map onto the contemporary world of global politics? Mapping the world in terms of civilizations is not just a matter of grouping large numbers of people into this category. Lots of people may compose a civilization, "as with China ('a civilization pretending to be a state' as Lucian Pye put it)" (1993: 24). Or there can be very few people in a civilization, "such as the Anglophone Caribbean" (1993: 24). Nor is mapping the world in terms of civilizations the same as mapping it state by state. While, for Huntington, there are cases of a single state constituting a civilization (Japanese civilization, for example), "civilizations may include several nation-states, as is the case with Western, Latin American and Arab civilizations" (1993: 24). And states may include more than one civilization, like the "torn countries" of Turkey, Mexico, and Russia (1993: 42–5).

Once he gets past all his qualifiers, Huntington claims that there are "seven or eight major civilizations. These include Western, Confucian, Japanese, Islamic, Hindu, Slavic-Orthodox, Latin American and possibly African civilizations" (1993: 25). Huntington does not so much justify his categorization of these seven or eight groupings of states, religious identifications, and philosophical traditions into civilizations as he takes them as historical givens. The existence of civilizations is one thing that goes without saying in Huntington's myth. What he does justify is why these particular seven or eight civilizations will likely end up in conflict with one another now that the Cold War is over. His answer is twofold. First, Huntington tells us that the fault lines among these seven or eight civilizations have historically been where conflicts have occurred. Second, while the ideological struggles of the Cold War contained civilizational struggles, in the aftermath of the Cold War "[t]he Velvet Curtain of culture has replaced the Iron Curtain of ideology as the most significant dividing line in Europe" and has had implications for relations between the West and other parts of the world as well (1993: 31).

So where are these fault lines between civilizations? A primary one is in Europe which, Huntington tells us, has been culturally divided between Western Christianity and Orthodox Christianity and Islam since 1500. This cultural divide accounts for the different historical experiences and contemporary potentials of these civilizations. On the side of Western Christianity, there is a history of feudalism, the Renaissance, the Reformation, the Enlightenment, the French Revolution, the Industrial Revolution, resulting in a present filled with economic prosperity and moving toward increasing economic and democratic consolidation. On the side of Orthodox Christianity and Islam, there is a significantly different history resulting in fewer economic advantages and a lesser chance of developing stable democratic systems. And along this fault line there is a history of conflict (1993: 29–31). Huntington recounts other historical fault lines between civilizations with their different historical experiences and different historical trajectories which either resulted in conflicts (as between Muslims and Hindus, 1993: 33) or which promise to result in conflict in the post-Cold War era (as between China and the US and Japan and the US, 1993: 34). But Huntington devotes the bulk of his attention to the fault line between the West and Islam.

As Huntington argues, "Conflict along the fault line between Western and Islamic civilizations has been going on for 1,300 years" in Europe, Turkey, and North Africa, with Islamic empires battling Christian empires through World War II (1993: 31). The end of World War II saw the retreat of Western colonialism, the appearance of Arab nationalism and then Islamic fundamentalism, Western dependence on Persian Gulf oil, and the increasingly oil-rich Arab states amassing wealth in money and sometimes armaments. During this period, clashes between Islam and the West mostly occurred in the Middle East and in North Africa, involving everything from all-out wars to the bombing and hostage-taking of Western targets.

Writing in 1993, Huntington argued, "This warfare between Arabs and the West culminated in 1990, when the United States sent a massive army to the Persian Gulf to defend some Arab countries against aggression by another" (1993: 31). While Huntington recognizes that the Gulf War does not strictly support his "clash of civilizations thesis" (for it is an instance of infighting within what he calls one civilization, Islam), Huntington marks the *aftermath* of the Gulf War as a moment of consolidation of Islamic civilization, a moment that many post-September 11 commentators point to as one important factor in the events of September 11. He writes,

> The Gulf War left some Arabs feeling proud that Saddam Hussein had attacked Israel and stood up to the West. It also left many feeling humiliated and resentful of the West's military presence in the Persian Gulf, the West's overwhelming military dominance, and their apparent inability to shape their own destiny.
>
> (1993: 32)

And, he argues further, as economic and social developments in many Arab countries lead to the introduction of democratic practices, "[t]he principle beneficiaries of these openings have been Islamist movements. In the Arab world, in short, Western democracy strengthens anti-Western political forces," at least for the time being (1993: 32). Or, translated into the language of the modernization and development tradition, all good things do *not* go together.

Huntington is careful not to argue that Islam's only fault line is with the West. Instead, as Huntington describes it, Islam appears to have fault lines just about everywhere. "[A]long the boundaries of the crescent-shaped Islamic bloc of nations from the bulge of Africa to central Asia, [v]iolence . . . occurs between Muslims, on the one hand, and Orthodox Serbs in the Balkans, Jews in Israel, Hindus in India, Buddhists in Burma and Catholics in the Philippines. Islam has bloody borders" (1993: 35).

While Huntington writes in general terms about civilizations when he predicts "[t]he next world war, if there is one, will be a war between civilizations" (1993: 39), and states that, "[t]he central axis of world politics in the future is likely to be, in Kishore Mahbubani's phrase, the conflict between 'the West and the Rest' and the responses of non-Western civilizations to Western power and values" (1993: 41), his primary focus remains firmly on the confrontation between Islam and the West. This is clear from his choice of expert quotes. Huntington first quotes the observations of Indian Muslim M.J. Akbar, who argues that "[t]he West's next confrontation . . . is definitely going to come from the Muslim world. It is in the sweep of the Islamic nations from the Maghreb to Pakistan that the struggle for a new world order will begin" (1993: 32). He next offers the observations of historian Bernard Lewis who writes,

> We are facing a mood and a movement far transcending the level of issues and policies and the governments that pursue them. *This is no less than a clash of civilizations*—the perhaps irrational but surely historical reaction of an ancient rival against our Judeo-Christian heritage, our secular present, and the world-wide expansion of both.
>
> (my italics; Lewis, 1990: 24–8 quoted in Huntington, 1993: 32)

With Lewis's quote, we realize that it is from Lewis's observations that Huntington got the phrase "clash of civilizations" to begin with. And while Huntington has generalized it beyond the clash between the West and Islam and has done so in work dating back to at least the 1980s (see Weiner and Huntington, 1987), it is now anchored firmly in the West vs. Islam clash in Lewis's remarks and in Huntington's.

So, all this explains why Huntington focuses on his seven or eight civilizations rather than some others in his clash of civilizations thesis—because these civilizations have been and continue to be in conflict with one another. What remains to be explored is the question of why. Why do civilizations conflict with one another, and why should we be focusing on civilizations rather than just states as we try to understand post-Cold War conflict?

Huntington has no shortage of answers to these questions, which is to be expected since his thesis seems to hinge on these issues. We already know Huntington's general answer to these questions—post-Cold War ideologies no longer keep civilizational conflicts in check. But why do we have civilizational conflicts in the first place, and why specifically are they likely to be unchecked in the post-Cold War world?

Huntington offers six specific responses to support his claim that future conflicts will be along cultural fault lines separating civilizations. First, he argues that "differences among civilizations are not only real; they are basic," and "[t]hey are far more fundamental than differences among political ideologies and political regimes" (1993: 25). This is because civilizations, as we saw earlier, "are differentiated from each other by history, language, culture, tradition, and, most important, religion" which leads

> people of different civilizations to have different views on the relations between God and man, the individual and the group, the citizen and the state, parents and children, husband and wife, as well as differing views of the relative importance of rights and responsibilities, liberty and authority, equality and hierarchy.
>
> (1993: 25)

Second, Huntington observes that "the world is becoming a smaller place" (1993: 25). This does not have the effect of turning the world into one big international society, as someone like Charles Kegley has argued (see Chapter 3). Rather, it has the effect of further dividing people into civilizations. "The interactions among people of different civilizations enhance the civilizations-consciousness of people that, in turn, invigorates differences and animosities stretching or thought to stretch back deep in history" (1993: 26).

Third, "the processes of economic modernization and social change throughout the world are separating people from longstanding local identities" as well as weakening their attachments to nation-states as a source of identity (1993: 26). In the place of local and national affiliations, people are increasingly returning to religion to fill this gap (1993: 26). Quoting George Weigel, Huntington claims that "'the unsecularization of the world . . . is one of the dominant social facts of life in the late twentieth century,'" which means that religion currently "provides a basis for identity and commitment that transcends national boundaries and unites civilizations" (1993: 26).

Fourth, "the growth of civilization-consciousness is enhanced by the dual role of the West" (1993: 26). On the one hand, with the West at the peak of its power, it (and especially the US) dominates international life not only politically but culturally, especially through popular culture, something that is often embraced by non-Western masses. On the other hand—and probably as a result—Huntington notes a movement among non-Western elites toward increasing "de-Westernization and indigenization," like the "'Asianization' of Japan, . . . the 'Hinduization' of India, . . . and the 're-Islamization' of the Middle East" (1993: 26–7).

Fifth, "cultural characteristics and differences are less mutable and hence less easily compromised and resolved than political and economic ones" (1993: 27). This is because political and economic differences are about opinions or status which can change, whereas cultural differences are about identity. As Huntington explains, "In class and ideological conflicts, the key question was 'Which side are you on?' and people could and did choose sides and change sides. In conflicts about civilizations, the question is 'What are you?' That is a given that cannot be changed" (1993: 27). This is even more true in the case of religion than in the case of ethnicity, for "[a] person can be half-French and half-Arab and simultaneously even a citizen of two countries. It is more difficult to be half-Catholic and half-Muslim" (1993: 27).

Finally, "economic regionalism is increasing" and "successful economic regionalism will reinforce civilization-consciousness" (1993: 27). This is because "economic regionalism may succeed only when it is rooted in a common civilization," such as the European Community rooting itself in the Western Christian civilization (1993: 27).

Overall, Huntington fully recognizes that "[a]s people define their identity in ethnic and religious terms, they are likely to see an 'us' versus 'them' relation existing between themselves and people of different ethnicity or religion" (1993: 29). This, combined with the end of ideologically-based states, long-standing territorial disputes, and, "[m]ost importantly, the efforts of the West to promote its values of democracy and liberalism as universal values, to maintain its military predominance and to advance its economic interests" all "engender countering responses from other civilizations" (1993: 29 and 39–41).

All of this has implications for the West. Because "the paramount axis of world politics will be the relations between 'the West and the Rest'" (1993: 48), Huntington sets out an agenda of short- and long-term policy recommendations for the West to follow. In the short term, his advice to the West is to consolidate its civilization, with Europe and North America wooing Eastern Europe and Latin America into its civilization and maintaining friendly ties with Russia and Japan. As the West consolidates itself, it should also take steps to defend itself against non-Western civilizations with which it is not friendly, by limiting their military might, exploiting differences among them, maintaining Western military capabilities, and promoting Western interests and values wherever possible. In other words, Huntington counsels the West to consolidate sameness/identity globally where it can while it guards itself against and divides difference wherever it finds it (1993: 48–9).

Over the longer term, the West must be prepared to deal with modern, non-Western civilizations, civilizations that reject Western values and interests but which nonetheless command sufficient power to challenge the West economically and militarily. To deal with these civilizations, Huntington counsels first military and economic protection from them, second, a back-to-comparative-politics Western development of "a more profound understanding of the basic religious and philosophical assumptions underlying other civilizations" and their interests, and finally "an effort to identify elements of commonality between Western and other civilizations" (1993: 49). All this is necessary, Huntington writes at the close of his article, because "[f]or the relevant future, there will be no universal civilization, but instead a world of different civilizations, each of which will have to learn to coexist with the other" (1993: 49).

Taken as a whole, Huntington's attempt to confront the problem of cultural difference is firmly located within both traditional IR theory and within the modernization and development tradition. Read through IR theory, Huntington's myth asks the very question at the center of IR theory—why do we have conflict, and where is conflict located? Recall, for example, that this was Kenneth Waltz's question in *Man, the State, and War* (Chapter 2). And Huntington arrives at the very same answer as IR theory—we have conflict because we have differences, and these differences/conflicts are located between identities. For Huntington, identity is a civilization, and difference is located at the fault lines between civilizations. While it is differently nuanced (for example, it does not get stuck in the levels of analysis problem), Huntington's answer is no different to that of Waltz (identity = states; difference = anarchy between states) or Fukuyama (identity = ideology; difference = dialectical ideological clashes) or Hardt and Negri (identity = ontological singularities of "Empire" and "the multitude"; difference = clashes between them). Nor is it different from the logic implicit in Kegley's myth "there is an international society" (Chapter 3), which accepts that difference leads to conflict and therefore attempts to remap the world as one big identity (international society).

Read through modernization and development theory, Huntington's work tackles this tradition's failure to solve the problem of cultural difference. The modernization and development tradition's attempts to transform difference into identity through development efforts have been most successful at *destabilizing* Third World states internally. During the Cold War, Huntington's clash of civilizations thesis suggests, it was possible to contain Third World destabilizations— the destabilizations of difference—within Third World states. But now that the Cold War is over—now that ideology no longer maps the world and now that globalization (i.e., "the world is becoming a smaller place," 1993: 25) means that the degree of stability of developing states increasingly affects the degree of stability of developed states and global markets—Third World instability is everywhere seeping out of its former political containers (nation-states), collecting into larger units that remap the global without the promise of containment (civilizations), and destabilizing the post-Cold War international order.

For all of his qualifiers, Huntington's conclusion about the problem of cultural difference is no less teleological than are those found in the modernization and development tradition. The only distinction is that while modernization and development theory promised that economic development and political stability could be achieved simultaneously by adapting Third World difference to First World identity because "all good things go together," Huntington's clash of civilizations thesis promises the opposite. Noting how "processes of economic modernization and social change throughout the world" (1993: 26) not only fail to deliver modernization and development but fail to deliver political stability, Huntington's clash of civilizations thesis "ontologizes" global differences—making global differences themselves into identities called civilizations that are not reducible to one another—which promise only increasing global instability because of the inevitable clashes among them.

Huntington is correct that his thesis is an improvement on modernization and development theories that denied non-Western civilizations any historical agency. Writing of the new post-Cold War realities as he sees them, Huntington claims, "In the politics of civilizations, the peoples and governments of non-Western civilizations no longer remain the objects of history as targets of Western colonialism but join the West as movers and shapers of history" (1993: 23). Yet the only agency Huntington allows non-Western civilizations is the destabilizing agency of difference. This is hardly something to boast about.

Given all this, what must go without saying in order for Huntington's myth to appear to be true is that difference is inherently destabilizing, or at least more destabilizing than identity. But is this necessarily the case? It is this question that is considered in the film *East is East*.

East is East

East is East is set in the working-class Manchester suburb of Salford in 1971 against the dual backdrops of the rise of racist nationalism in Britain and war between India and Pakistan over East Pakistan in the Asian subcontinent. Importantly, even though the film takes place during the Cold War, the Cold War plays no role in the film, through plot, characters, or motivation. What this allows is for the world of *East is East* to be mapped not by ideology but by culture. And so it is. *East is East* tells the story of the Khan family—Pakistani father George (Om Puri), white British mother Ella (Linda Bassett), and their seven bi-racial, bi-ethnic children—Nazir, Abdul, Tariq, Saleem, Maneer, Meenah, and Sajid. The film introduces us to all of its major characters and defines the tensions over identity and difference within the Khan family in its title sequence and first post-credits series of scenes.

The film opens in celebratory style. Before we see any action, we hear five drum beats from a marching band, followed by a distorted, twisted note that readies us for comedy. On this note, the screen cuts from black to an aerial view of a Salford street, lined with redbrick terrace houses. A procession led by a priest marches into view from the bottom of the scene as the up-beat marching music is joined by fast-paced, bouncy lyrics.

> So we waved our hands as we marched along,
> and the people smiled as we sang our song,
> and the world was safe as we listened to the band.
> And the banner man held a banner high.
> He was ten feet tall, and he touched the sky.
> I wish that I could be a banner man.

With the camera now at street level, we see the priest, young girls in their white confirmation dresses, and boys in their Sunday suits carrying a ten-foot high banner, all leading the procession as it turns onto the Khan family's street. Cut to a statue of Jesus mounted on a six-foot cross, bobbing up and down as it is being carried. The camera pans down to reveal who is carrying it. It is a smiling teenage girl, Meenah, George and Ella's only daughter. Behind her are her older teenage and twenty-something brothers. Maneer and Saleem are carrying a statue of the virgin Mary holding the baby Jesus, and behind them are Tariq and Abdul each carrying small banners. Tariq is followed by his girlfriend Stella (who follows Tariq everywhere) and her friend Peggy (who follows Stella everywhere). In front of Meenah is their pre-teen brother Sajid (who is eternally dressed in a drab green parka with a fur-lined hood). While his older brothers whisper to one another "Check out the nurses," Sajid gleefully tosses about crêpe-paper petals, as Annie, a woman who works with Ella and George, walks beside him. They are all well back in the procession. It is Whit Week, and this is the Whitsun parade.

Suddenly a frantic Ella enters the scene. Finding Annie, she urgently tells her friend that George is back early from mosque. Cut to George standing on his street, smiling as the parade advances toward him. Annie turns to the kids. "Red alert. Red alert. Red alert." All the kids—still carrying their Catholic statues and banners and Sajid still throwing his petals—plus Stella and Peggy exit the procession just as it is about to turn the corner. Cut to aerial view. We see the kids running down a back alley while Ella rushes down the main road to join her husband. As the camera returns to ground level, we see George and Ella watching the procession now absent of Khan children. George is unaware that his children were ever part of the procession, and an anxious Ella is determined to keep it that way. George waves a greeting to Annie while Ella watches her kids slip behind George's back down the alley. As the procession turns off the Khan family road, the children once again join it.

This is the end of the title sequence.

Cut to the interior of the Khan house. The camera situates the action with its opening shot of a wall containing the family portraits, with George and Ella in the middle surrounded by their seven children. Preparations are underway for a special event. Downstairs, as the children playfully torment one another, Ella, dressed in her best clothes, brushes the hair of complaining Meenah while Saleem fusses with Meenah's sari. Ella hurries Maneer through his kettle-filled zinc tub bath and scolds

Sajid, who wears a fancy waistcoat over his parka, for scratching his head. Upstairs, the atmosphere is solemn. Abdul, Tariq, and George help to prepare eldest son Nazir for the occasion. It is Nazir's wedding day. Abdul helps Nazir with his coat. George paints Nazir's eyes, adjusts his turban, and places a veil of gold tinsel over his face as is the tradition for a Muslim groom. He tells Nazir, "Son, today you making me very proud." Then George straps a watch with Nazir's name in Arabic to Nazir's wrist and leads his son down the stairs, where he presents Nazir to the family, saying to the stunned faces, "Ella, your son."

Outside, the wedding party crowds into a minibus while Enoch Powell supporter Mr Moorhouse (the grandfather of Tariq's girlfriend Stella and Sajid's friend Ernest who has a crush on Meenah) quips, "Look at that, a piccaninny's fuckin' picnic."

Cut to interior of mosque. People assembled for the wedding are cheerful and noisy as they await the ceremony. Nazir and his family take their places at the front of the hall, with veiled Nazir facing the crowd. A hush breaks across the room as the veiled bride is led in by her parents. They join the groom and his family. The bride's mother removes the veil from her daughter's face. At George's signal, Abdul lifts Nazir's veil. Bride and groom see one another for the first time. Both are beautiful. The bride smiles cautiously, as Nazir looks increasingly nervous. The ceremony begins. But Nazir raises his hand and stands.

George: You alright, son.
Nazir [sorrowfully]:   I can't do this, Dad.
George: Nazir . . .
Nazir [insisting]:   No, I can't.
George [urging]:   . . . everything ok.

Nazir rushes down the aisle toward exit.

George [angry]:   Nazir, don't do this. Nazir!
Ella [worried as she rushes after her son who leaves the hall]:   Nazir.

Everyone is stunned.

Cut to interior of Khan house. The camera focuses on Nazir's photo on the wall of family portraits, as it fades to an empty space.

Cut to interior of mosque. George is consulting the Mullah.

George [speaking of Nazir]:   Why he wants to do this thing to me, bring a shame
    on a my family. I no understand. No understand. [pause] Maybe I should have
    take family to Bradford long time ago. More Pakistanis there. No this problem.
Mullah [addressing George by his Pakistani name]:   It will always be difficult for
    you, Zaheer. They're different.

This is the end of the first sequence. The rest of the action takes place six months later.

What do these two sequences tell us about how the film makes sense of identity and difference? How are identity and difference characterized, and where are they located?

Because the film maps the world not through Cold War ideology but through culture, it would come as no surprise to Huntington that the film casts identity and difference in national and religious terms. Nationally, we have British identities and Pakistani identities. From an extreme British nationalist perspective (symbolized by Enoch Powell and characterized by Mr Moorhouse), Britishness is identity and everything else (including Pakistaniness) is difference. From an extreme traditional Pakistani perspective (a position George flirts with and increasingly gravitates toward in the course of the film), identity is Pakistaniness and difference is Britishness. Each national position has a dominant religious position, with Britishness introduced through Western Christianity in the title sequence and Pakistaniness introduced through Islam in the first sequence.

Because they are cast in national and religious terms, identities are located within spaces like nation-states and what Huntington would call civilizations. And because Huntington's civilizations defy Waltz's "levels of analysis" problem by being simultaneously located at the individual, the state, and the international level, it is not surprising that we also find these identities located within the families of Salford and differences located between them. According to the heads of their households, the Moorhouse family is British and belongs to Western Christianity; the Khan family is Pakistani and belongs to Islam. Each clash with the other, with Mr Moorhouse, on the one hand, campaigning for the relocation and repatriation of immigrants like George and George, on the other, running "George's English Chippy" shop down the road from the Moorhouse home while raising his children as Muslims.

Plate 8.1 Ella and Annie having a smoke outside "George's English Chippy."
Courtesy of the Ronald Grant Film Archive © FilmFour.

All of this seems to support Huntington's thesis "there is a clash of civilizations," with two of the world's major civilizations clashing in Salford as the world becomes a smaller place (Huntington, 1993: 35; in the film through post-colonial immigration rather than as in Huntington's myth through globalization, although some might argue that the first is the necessary precursor to the second) and two civilizations (Islam and Hinduism) at war with one another in Asia over the succession of East Pakistan from Pakistan. This is one way to understand how the film makes sense of the world. It claims that civilizations/identities are best kept apart (via repatriation or, as George wishes, by clustering cultures in segregated communities like Bradford which the film refers to as "Bradistan") because when civilizations meet, the differences between them cause conflict (see Box 8.1).

Of course things aren't quite that simple, however. On the one hand, Salford represents the increasing difficulty of keeping different identities apart, while the Moorhouse family and especially the Khan family represent the impossibility of this. Yes, families of different identities do constitute Salford, but individuals of different identities increasingly constitute these families. For example, while the Moorhouse family is led by its ultra-nationalist Grandad, granddaughter Stella has a Pakistani boyfriend, and grandson Ernest not only has a Pakistani best friend, he also greets his friend's father as if Ernest himself were Muslim, with "Salaam-alacum, Mr Khan" to which George replies "Waalacum-salaam." In the Khan family, George represents Islam/Pakistan, Ella represents Western Christianity/Britain, and their seven children represent another fault line where these two civilizations clash. At first, this, too, suggests that Huntington got it right because the question that preoccupies each Khan child is the urgent question Huntington identifies for a world mapped by civilizations, "Who am I?" Caught between two civilizations and therefore between two identities, the Khan children struggle to answer this question because neither their father's nor their mother's answer precisely maps onto any of them. They represent, in Huntington's terms, the ease with which one might simultaneously claim two nationalities but the difficulty of being "half-Catholic and half-Muslim" (Huntington, 1993: 27). Or, to put it in the terms of the film's opening song, they represent how the fulfillment of their desire to "be a banner man"—to be an identity—always seems to elude them.

And yet all of the Khan children are scripted as strong, if stereotypical, characters. Young Sajid cocoons himself from the struggles facing his elder siblings with his parka and his age. For example, when asked by a Pakistani woman how old he is, Sajid replies, "Not old enough to get married, so don't ask me." Meenah is a

---

Box 8.1 How *East is East* makes sense of the world

1 George/Islam and Ella/Western Christianity clash over their bi-cultural children who represent the fault lines between these civilizations; *or*
2 The Khan children do not represent the fault lines between Western Christianity and Islam but foreshadow the multicultural Britain emerging in the post-colonial era.

tomboy. Saleem is an art student passing as an engineering student to his father but out to his mother. Maneer, nicknamed Gandhi by his siblings, follows Islamic traditions more closely than the others, although even he took part in the opening Catholic procession. Tariq/Tony is the clubber who fancies himself a bit of a playboy and certainly not a "Paki." Abdul is the most independent of the children remaining at home, negotiating racism in the workplace and attempting to respect his mother and his father at home so he can hold on to his family. And Nazir, who refused to marry in the first scene, turns up later as a gay hairdresser working in his boyfriend's fancy salon. What this suggests is that the Khan children have strong personalities, but none of their personalities is reducible to the "civilizational" choices available to them.

And, indeed, the Khan children do not want to choose a civilizational identity. They don't think of themselves as either Pakistani or British, as either Catholic or Muslim, much less as belonging to the broader grouping of civilization. In this sense, the Khan children represent less Huntington's fault line between civilizations than they foreshadow the present multicultural Britain.

Plate 8.2 Best friends Sajid and Ernest.
Courtesy of the Ronald Grant Film Archive © FilmFour.

This, then, is an alternative way of reading how the film makes sense of the world. The film suggests that the world is a multicultural place with "culture," defined in national and religious terms, spilling out of its prior boundaries and mixing in and across nations, families, and individuals, not so much creating conflict as it is *redefining identity*. Even so, the film does (as we will see) depict conflict, and this conflict is located primarily around the Khan children. What, then, do the Khan children represent? Are they fault lines between civilizations or are they multicultural sites in the Britain emerging from the 1970s? Or, put differently, which depiction of the world is correct?

For the Khan children to represent fault lines between civilizations, their bifurcated cultural identities must motivate the conflict in the film. For the Khan children to represent an emerging multicultural Britain, their cultural identities still might well be sources of conflict, but the conflict that motivates the film's action would be located elsewhere. And if it is, then Huntington's thesis "there is a clash of civilizations" fails to function.

So, where is the motivation for the conflict in *East is East* located?

As I have already suggested, conflict is located at some fault line, and at first this fault line appears to be between identities where differences meet. But as a second look at the film reveals, this fault line need not be located *between* identities. It can also be located *within* identities. We see it within the Pakistani state, a territorially discontinuous, artificial entity resulting from India's partitioning into Hindu and Muslim communities, now at war with itself. We see it within the British state, a former empire faced with absorbing its colonial subjects as citizens. We see it within the Khan family, in its inability to be either Muslim or Christian, traditional

Plate 8.3 The pork-eating Khan children.
Courtesy of the Ronald Grant Film Archive © FilmFour.

or modern, Pakistani or British, black or white. We see it within the Khan children, a bunch of pork-eating, mosque-educated fans of Bollywood and English football. And we see it within George Khan himself. Indeed, in *East is East*, it is George Khan who is having the central identity crisis, with all the other identity crises either mirrored (Britain, Pakistan) or provoked (his kids) by him.

George has good reason to be in crisis about his identity. George/Zaheer/Ghingus to his kids is a self-made, modernized, Westernized Pakistani immigrant living in the predominately white working-class British suburbs with Ella and their seven children while his traditional Pakistani Muslim first wife, to whom he is still married, lives in Pakistan. Even though "first wife" lives in Pakistan (and "second wife" is determined to keep her there), this does not mean that George has managed to keep his Pakistani and British-Pakistani lives from mixing. Unlike his tea which George enjoys in half cups, his complex relationships to people, nations, and religions refuse to be taken in halves, defying this simple trick of spatial separation. For, as the opening sequences establish, George's identity is daily disputed around nation through local and national racist repatriation campaigns (which double for Britain's own post-colonial identity crisis) and through Pakistan's war with India (which doubles George's double Pakistani identity—"pure" Pakistani and British-Pakistani). And George's crisis of religious (not to mention generational and gender) identity constantly crops up through his kids. It is not contained by his eldest son's refusal of his Muslim bride. Six months later, when the action resumes, the Mullah discovers to George's embarrassment that, due to some oversight, Sajid was never circumcised. To reclaim his honor in the eyes of his religious community, George insists (and Ella agrees, although she later regrets this) that Sajid be "de-hooded." But even this procedure provokes George's anxieties when George discovers that Sajid's surgeon is a doctor of Indian origin.

With this, George has had enough. Despairing, he again consults the Mullah about his family.

George: Just 'cause they mam English no mean they not good Pakistani. I know people think this thing.
Mullah: Zaheer, until your sons join the community fully, they will be a worry to you.

Lack of total integration into any community—the lack of a unified, community-based identity—is precisely George's problem. As a good father concerned about his children, George plots with the Mullah about how to protect his kids from this terrible predicament. The answer—Muslim marriages. George agrees in principle to marry Abdul and Tariq to the daughters of a Bradford Pakistani, Mr Shah. When George lets it slip to Ella that he has arranged the marriages without informing the boys, Ella is angry and demands that George tell them. But George warns Ella to stay out of his business.

Ella: They have a right to know, George.
George: What you mean right? Pakistani believe if father ask son marry, son follow father instruction. I should have sent all bloody kids to Pakistan when young, other wife teach them bloody respect.

Here, George is clear. He is a Pakistani father to Pakistani children from whom he demands respect for his traditions, or at least these are his desires. And while the apparent realization of these desires is something Ella and the kids generally offer him, marriage without consent is going too far, especially in light of the family's history with Nazir.

All this gives indications of what the film says is typical and deviant in the world of *East is East* (see Table 8.2). What is typical is for George's values *and* Ella's values to respectfully co-exist within the Khan family, even if in this patriarchal 1970s' household, Ella's values and the children's respect for them must be concealed. What is deviant is for George to force his children to become fully integrated into his longed-for cultural identity, even if he believes it is for their own good.

This suggests that there is no "clash of civilizations" in the film. George and Ella never compete over the civilizational identities of their children. Ella respects George's wishes when it comes to religious matters, and so do the children (although, like other children, they don't necessarily enjoy themselves in the process or take either their father's or their mother's religion seriously). And while Ella certainly exposes the children to Western Christianity, she does not, cannot, and (we are led to believe) would not insist that the children define themselves through her "civilizational identity." For Ella recognizes that her children embody new, distinct identities. They are the full cups of tea that George only ever takes as halves.

The conflict in *East is East*, then, occurs not because differences cannot peacefully and respectfully co-exist (as they have for the past 25 years of the Khan marriage). Conflict seems to exist because George insists on transforming difference (first his bi-cultural children and later his English wife) into identity (Pakistani Muslims fully integrated into that community). It is only at this point that his children and his wife lose respect for him and his culture.

When the boys find out about their arranged marriages, Tariq breaks into the wedding chest, angrily destroys the apparel, and crushes the watches with his and Abdul's names in Arabic. George discovers the scene as Maneer is trying to return the damaged items to the chest. When Maneer refuses to tell George who is responsible for the mess, George drags him to the shop where Ella is and beats him. Ella intervenes.

George [to Maneer]:   I not finished with you yet, Mr! (to Ella) You just same as you bloody kid. I your husband. You should agreeing with me like proper Muslim wife.

Table 8.2 What is typical and deviant in the world of *East is East*?

Typical	Deviant
For George's values *and* Ella's values to respectfully co-exist within the Khan family, even if in this patriarchal 1970s household, Ella's values and the children's respect for them must be concealed	For George to force his children to become fully integrated into his culture

Plate 8.4 George and his wife, Ella, at the cinema.
Courtesy of the Ronald Grant Film Archive © FilmFour.

Ella: Yeah, right, I'm a Muslim wife when it suits you. I'll stop being a Muslim wife at 5:30 when the shop wants opening, or one of your relatives wants help at the home office. Don't make me bleeding laugh, George.

George: I tell, don't starting, 'cause I fix you, like I fix your baster kids! You all pucking trouble with me.

Ella: They're only trouble because you don't listen to them, you never have.

George: You married me 25 years and know nothing. [very angry] I warning Ella, you not talk to me like this.

Ella: Yeah, you're right, 25 years I've been married to you, George. I've sweated me guts out in your bastard shop and given you seven kids as well. And I'll tell you this for nothing, I'm not gonna stand by and watch you crush 'em one by one because of your pig bloody ignorance.

At this point, George turns on Ella, beating her.

All this still seems to suggest that Huntington got it right. For in his work on modernization and development theory, Huntington argued that difference alone does not cause instability. What causes instability are attempts to transform difference into identity. His solution for the modernization and development tradition was first to recognize this and second to support sometimes authoritarian Third World governments to ensure stability during the transition to development. This is precisely the logic that George follows. When faced with resistance as he tries to transform difference into identity, George becomes increasingly authoritarian in order to retain order within his family. Because Huntington learned this in his early work, in his later work on the clash of civilizations he counsels that identity should stop trying to transform difference. For Huntington, identity is the West and difference is the Rest. Rather than transform difference into identity, Huntington urges separation, segregation, and securitization. All this is necessary because, as we saw earlier, Huntington elevates difference itself into the central source of instability in a world mapped by civilizations. Therefore, the best approach identity (the West) can take in relation to difference (the Rest) is to steer clear of it.

In *East is East*, it is the Rest (Islam) that is trying to secure itself from the West (Western Christianity). But, from Huntington's perspective, because George cannot separate, segregate and thereby secure his family's Islamic identity from the pervasive West Christian civilization in which it exists, conflict is inevitable. Difference leads to disorder. This is not primarily because, as George tells himself, the family live in a Western Christian environment (Salford) rather than a more Pakistani one (Bradford/Bradistan/Pakistan). Rather, it is because George's children, George's wife, and indeed George himself bring difference (the West) into the identity for which George strives (Islam).

All this makes me wonder, is it ever possible to separate, segregate, and secure identity from its fault lines? And, even if it were possible, is it necessary?

By demonstrating that differences can peacefully and respectively co-exist within the Khan family before marriages are forced upon the children and within the younger generation of the Salford community (the Khan and Moorhouse children), *East is East* suggests that Huntington got it wrong. It is not (always) necessary to separate, segregate, and secure identity from difference. In so doing, *the film exposes one of the things that must go without saying in order for Huntington's myth to appear to be true*—Huntington's truth that difference *in and of itself* produces instability. The film also raises the question whether, as Huntington also claims, the move from difference to identity causes instability. While this might indeed be the case *at times*, *East is East* points out that instability and conflict are not always generated from either the mere existence of difference or its transformation to identity. *Instability and conflict can be located firmly within identity, in the desire to be a unified identity and in the impossibility of ever achieving that desire*. This is George's impossible desire, and it is exposed when Tariq confronts him about his wedding.

George: I warning you, Mr! I not bringing you up to give me no respect. Pakistani son always shows respect.

Tariq: Dad, I'm not Pakistani. I was born here. I speak English, not Urdu.

George: Son, you not understand 'cause you not listen to me. I trying to show you good way to live. You not English. English people never accepting you. In Islam, everyone equal see, no black man, or white man. Only Muslim. It special community.

Tariq: I'm not saying it's not, Dad, I just think I've got a right to choose who I get married to.

George: You want bloody English girl? They not good. They go with other men, drink alcohol, no look after.

Tariq [angry]:   Well, if English women are so bad, why did you marry me mam?

George takes a knife to Tariq's throat

Plate 8.5 Tariq/Tony with his girlfriend, Stella.
Courtesy of the Ronald Grant Film Archive © FilmFour.

George: Baster! I tell you no go too far with me. You do what I tell you, understand!
  Hah? Understand?
Tariq [afraid]: Yeah right Dad. I understand. I understand. I'll do what you want.
  I'll get married to a Pakistani. [defiantly] And you know what I'll do then? I'll
  marry a fucking English woman as well. Just like me dad!

By naming the differences *within* his father's identity, Tariq locates the fundamental fault line in the film, *the fault line within his father's identity*. In so doing, the film suggests that it is not possible to separate, segregate, and secure identity from its fault lines because sometimes these fault lines are located *within* identity rather than *between* identities. *It is the fault line within George's identity that is the location and the motivation for the conflict in the film.* It provides George with an identity crisis, instills in him the desire to be a unified identity, and confronts him with his inability to achieve this desire.

George's desire to be a unified identity creates conflict and violence because in failing to be an identity himself, he first attempts to help his children and then demands that his children and his wife become the identities he wants (them) to be. This move, of course, fails. It fails not only because it meets the resistance of his family (in a comic sequence that turns violent at the close of the film, George's authority in the household passes to Abdul when Abdul literally de-hoods Sajid while stopping his father from again beating his mother). It fails because *there is no such thing as a singular, unified identity. Identity is itself conflictual.* Being an identity is about managing and interpreting differences within so-called identities like selves, states, and civilizations as much as it is about managing and interpreting differences *between* them.

This is the crucial point that Huntington's myth "there is a clash of civilizations" misses. Unsurprisingly, it is the same point IR theory misses. For by beginning from the assumption that difference produces instability and identity produces stability, Huntington's myth and traditional IR theory turn blind eyes toward the possibility that identity—and, indeed, the impossible quest to be an identity—*also* produces instability. This is the crucial point that must go without saying in order for Huntington's myth "there is a clash of civilizations" to appear to be true.

Identity, desire, and culture

Why do we wish that identity were coterminous with culture? This is the question posed both by Huntington's myth and by the film *East is East*. In each case, the answer lies in the politics of security.

If identity were coterminous with Huntington's idea of culture—if my empirical existence ("being" me) mapped precisely onto some stagnate set of collective normative values embedded in my history, customs, religion ("being" from my culture), then answering the question, "Who am I?" would be easy. And by knowing who I am, I would also know who I am not. For example, if I answer the question, "Who am I?" with the answer, "I am Islamic," then my answer is also, "and I am not Western or Japanese or Hindu or ...." This is precisely what Huntington's construction of civilizations as cultural identities offers contemporary subjects grappling with questions of identity.

While *East is East* rejects Huntington's construction of civilizational identities by complicating the notion of culture—by both multiplying culture ("being" simultaneously from Western Christian *and* Islamic cultures) and thereby allowing for the birth of new cultural identities ("being" multicultural)—the film still enables contemporary subjects to answer questions of identity with reference to culture. For some people, the answer will still be "I am a singular identity," whereas for others (like the Khan children) the answer will be "I am a multiple identity." But either way, identity is secured with reference to culture because, as we all should know by now, "being" multicultural is the new identity of many individuals in the era of globalization.

All of this is terribly reassuring. For culture and multiculturalism not only provide individuals with identities. They provide individuals with security, not only personally but politically. Why? Because cultural identities that ground individuals are easily collectivized so that they can also ground states and civilizations, whether they are singular or multiple. So, for example, *East is East* explores how a state like post-World War II Britain identified itself by "being" one culture, and how contemporary Britain increasingly identifies itself by "being" multicultural. Because Britain now officially claims a multiple cultural identity as its answer to the question, "Who am I?", Britain has translated its problem of cultural difference into the cultural source of its secure identity. Britain is multicultural. Multiculturalism is the new singular identity to which Britain officially refers.

Huntington's myth "there is a clash of civilizations" also attempts to secure collective identities through claims to cultural identities. His identities are single-culture civilizations that provide the highest level of meaningful identifications not only to individuals but also to states. So, for example, while not every individual in the contemporary multicultural state of Britain would identify as Western, the British multicultural state as a collective identity does identify as Western. In this way, cultural differences among people within states—even when they are celebrated as the cultural foundations of the state—are rendered less meaningful in Huntington's civilizational terms. But, for Huntington, this can only be a good thing, for it seems to solve the problem of cultural difference within states and civilizations, and it seems to locate worrying cultural differences that can make the identities of states insecure, not within states but between civilizations. For example, when British-born Muslims fought against British forces on the side of the Taliban in Afghanistan after September 11, these individuals were read in civilizational terms (as the "disturbing difference" of Islam) rather than in national terms (as the "disturbing difference" in British multiculturalism).

So, equating identity to culture is a contemporary response to the problem of cultural difference which seems to provide individuals, states, and civilizations with internal security and which banishes the insecurity of difference outside these secure identities. Yet while this is the desired solution to the problem of cultural difference, this does not mean it is always a successful solution. Indeed, a disturbing irony of Huntington's attempt to solve the problem of cultural difference for the West/US—thereby securing the realm of international politics in a post-Cold War era—is that it has had precisely the opposite effect. In the wake of September 11, Huntington's civilizational discourse has been appropriated by all sides to justify why the immutable cultural differences embodied by their uncivilized enemy leaves them no alternative but violence. The result is that the world is a far less secure place. This is not to say that the insecurity sparked by the events of September 11 can be pinned on Huntington's thesis; but it is to say that much of the insecurity emanating from "civilizational consciousness" in its aftermath can be. For even though Huntington's thesis got lots of academic attention upon its publication in 1993, it was only after September 11 when media, government, and scholarly commentators publicly debated his thesis that "civilizational consciousness" seeped into popular imaginaries.

With people's global terms of reference so unhinged by September 11, it is not surprising that many of them turned to a thesis that promised to equate identity with culture and thereby resecure their personal, national, and international boundaries. At that particular historical moment, the desire for identity to be coterminous with culture proved to be a very strong desire indeed. But as the trauma of September 11 gives way to critical reflection, there is an increasing recognition by some that the desire to be an identity and the corresponding desire to mark oneself off from difference is unattainable. Whether embodied by the rise of the New Right within Western multicultural states like Britain and the US or by the rise of funda-mentalisms that fracture Huntington's civilizational categories of Islam and Western Christianity, we are reminded that "being" an identity—whether as an individual, a state, or a civilization—is not as easy as Huntington suggests. This is because identity is as contentious, unstable, and conflictual as difference. In other words, both identity (and its impossibility) and difference (and its impossibility) produce stability and instability, order and disorder.

Suggestions for further thinking

Topic 1 Critiques of modernization and development theory

It should be clear even from this very brief discussion of the modernization and development tradition that it reflects not only the liberal ideological beliefs of US political and economic theory but also a specific rendering of what is historically possible. What was historically possible for Third World states attempting to become developed in the early years of the Cold War and remains historically possible for them today is what was historically possible for the US when it was developing. Such a view relies upon what Louise Hartz (1955) calls an exceptionalist view of US political history—one that generalizes the US historical experience to other nations, even though US history bears little resemblance to that of the rest of the world. In the case of modernization and development, the US generalizes its history of "development" to that of the newly independent states even though the US "developed" politically, economically, and socially when capitalism was dawning and not when it had to—like later former colonies—compete in a globalized capitalist marketplace with states who have dominated that marketplace for over one hundred years. These are precisely the sorts of critiques that Marxists and neo-Marxists such as André Gunder Frank, Cardoso and Faletto, and Immanuel Wallerstein have put forward. Yet as we saw in Chapter 7 on Hardt and Negri's *Empire*, in their desire to opposed liberal ideologies and liberal capitalist readings of history, Marxists and neo-Marxists often repeat Huntington's move of constructing collective ontologies out of disparate forces. For Hardt and Negri, these collective ontologies are "Empire" and "the multitude." Another good example is Wallerstein's work which constructs the collective ontologies of core, periphery, and semi-periphery.

Suggested reading

F. Cardoso and E. Faletto (1979) *Dependency and Development in Latin America*. Berkeley: University of California Press.

Andre Gunder Frank (1969) *Capitalism and Underdevelopment in Latin America*. New York: Monthly Review Press.

Louis Hartz (1955) *The Liberal Tradition in America*. New York: Harcourt Brace Jovanovich.

Robert Packenham (1973) *Liberal America and the Third World: Political Development Ideas in Foreign Aid and Social Science*. Princeton, NJ: Princeton University Press.

Immanuel Wallerstein (1974) *The Modern World System*. New York: Academic Press.

Immanuel Wallerstein (1995) *Historical Capitalism with Capitalist Civilisation*. London: Verso, especially pp. 68 and 71–2.

Immanuel Wallerstein (2002) "Revolts Against the System," *New Left Review*, 18: 29–39.

Topic 2 Critiques of identity

With the rise of postmodernism, identity and difference have been the subjects of what Jacques Derrida terms "deconstruction." Yet identity remains a difficult category to displace, as Stuart Hall explains. And so there is no shortage of literature debating the necessities and impossibilities of identity. In the light of Huntington's myth, a good way to focus these debates would be around the questions of post-colonial identity (Homi Bhabha), racial identity (Frantz Fanon), and multicultural identity (Slavo Zizek).

Suggested reading

Homi K. Bhabha (1990) "Interrogating identity: The Post Colonial Prerogative." In D.T. Goldberg (ed.) *Anatomy of Racism*. Minneapolis: University of Minnesota Press, pp. 118–209.

Jacques Derrida (1991) "*Différence*," in P. Kampuf (ed.) *A Derrida Reader: Between the Blinds*. Brighton: Harvester Wheatsheaf, pp. 60–7.

Frantz Fanon (1991) "The negro and psychopathology," *Black Skins, White Mask*. London: Pluto, pp. 141–209.

Stuart Hall (1996) "Introduction: Who needs 'identity'?" in Stuart Hall and Paul du Gay (eds.) *Questions of Cultural Identity*. London: Sage, pp. 1–17.

Slavo Zizek (1997) "Multiculturalism, Or, the Cultural Logic of Multinational Capitalism," *New Left Review* 225: 28–52.

Postscript

Samuel P. Huntington is not only concerned with "the problem of cultural difference" between states and civilizations but with "the problem of cultural difference" within states. In particular, Huntington's most recent obsession is with the cultural differences within the United States, specifically between "black-and-white American natives" (Huntington, 2004: 32) whose core language is English and whose core culture is "Anglo-Protestant" (2004: 32) and predominantly Catholic, non-Anglo Hispanics. As Huntington so alarmingly puts it, "In this new era [now], the single most immediate and most serious challenge to America's traditional identity comes from the immense and continuing immigration from Latin America, especially from Mexico, and the fertility rates of these immigrants compared to black and white American natives" (2004: 32). Not only does Huntington's construction of the United States erase (among others) native Americans and replace them with Anglo-Protestants; it also casts Mexican immigration as the newest threat to US national/cultural security. This is because, from Huntington's point of view, a large number of Mexican immigrants are not only coming to the United States; they are failing to integrate into US culture. And "in the long run," Huntington warns us, "numbers are power, particularly in a multicultural society, a political democracy, and a consumer economy" (2004: 44).

Many have pointed out that Huntington's construction of the threat of Mexican immigration to the US seems to be in stark contrast with what he wrote about the so-called "clash of civilizations." The *Guardian* reporter Dan Glaister goes so far as to wonder if Huntington "even bother[ed] to re-read *The Clash of Civilizations* before embarking on his latest tome." In the earlier book, he concluded, somewhat perplexingly, that "the cultural distance between Mexico and the United States is far less than that between Turkey and Europe," and that "Mexico has attempted to redefine itself from a Latin American to a North American identity" (March 15, 2004). All this leads Glaister to conclude that "Either a lot has changed in Huntington's mind in the intervening eight years, or in searching for new sport he simply chose not to worry too much about the detail" (March 15, 2004).

Yet considered through Huntington's on-going preoccupation with "the problem of cultural difference," how this might threaten the security of the sovereign nation-state (particularly the US), and how culturally complex states complicate and compromise Huntington's desire for state identity to be coterminous with cultural identity, it is not that difficult to square Huntington's myth "there is a clash of civilizations" with his newly emerging myth that "unintegrated Mexican immigrants are the new threat to US culture." This is not only the case because Huntington's clash of civilizations myth is full of hedges about what civilizations are, where their boundaries lie, and how these boundaries and identities shift. More importantly, it is because (as we saw) Huntington's larger project has always been about protecting the US from cultural difference. His clash of civilizations thesis might be regarded as a traditionally cast "international" expression of how to cope with this problem, while his emerging myth about the threat of unintegrated Mexican immigrants into the US is a more "domestically" inflected expression of how to cope with this same problem. When teaching Huntington's work, then, it is important not to jump to the conclusion that his 1993 essay and his 2004 essay are opposed to one another but rather to bring out the ways in which they complement Huntington's larger project and his underlying desire to yet again equate identity with stability and difference with instability.

Chapter 9

Environmentalism

Is human-made climate change
an inconvenient truth?

Fast forward to 2006. While the so-called war on terror rages on, the "war" on human-made climate change heats up. This war has a different kind of urgency than the war on terror. For if the war on terror might pit civilization against civilization (as Samuel Huntington controversially claimed—see Chapter 8), human-made climate change resulting mainly from excessive carbon dioxide emissions threatens every civilization on earth because it threatens the earth's ability to support human life itself. As former US Vice President Al Gore, Jr puts it, "[The Earth] is our only home. And that is what is at stake. Our ability to live on planet Earth—to have a future as a civilization" (Gore, 2006: 298). These are among the claims Gore makes in his 2006 documentary film and accompanying book *An Inconvenient Truth: The Planetary Emergency of Global Warming and What We Can Do About It*.

According to Gore, the urgency of addressing human-made climate change is both strategic and moral. Strategically, Gore claims that "the environment is becoming a matter of national security—an issue that directly and imminently menaces the interests of the state or the welfare of the people" (1989). This environmental-strategic danger means that "a new moral courage to choose higher values in the conduct of human affairs" is required. Now, we are called upon to choose strategic values like "cooperation over conflict" and environmental values like "efficiency and conservation" (1989). Gore tells us that by embracing this strategic and moral urgency,

> [t]he climate crisis . . . offers us the chance to experience what very few generations in history have had the privilege of knowing: a *generational mission*; the exhilaration of a compelling *moral purpose*; a shared and unifying *cause*; the thrill of being forced by circumstances to put aside the pettiness and conflict that so often stifle the restless human need for transcendence; the *opportunity to rise*.
>
> (2006: 10)

All that sounds pretty good. Indeed, it sounds so good that it is actually quite difficult *not* to get swept up by the warm embrace of Gore's global environmental movement. For who wouldn't want to transcend the day-to-day pettiness of global political life and become part of planetary solutions rather than planetary problems? And who wouldn't want to do this in the knowledge that what we were doing was morally enlightened and enlightening—for the planet, for future generations, and for ourselves? It is not surprising, then, that Gore's project is spawning a new generation of eco-warriors fighting to keep "earth in the balance" (Gore, 1992). Nor is it surprising that domestically, Gore's popularity led many Democrats to urge Gore to be their 2008 Presidential candidate and that internationally, Gore's work earned him a share of the 2007 Nobel Peace Prize because it focused "on the processes and decisions that appear to be necessary to protect the world's future climate, and thereby reduce the future threat to the security of mankind" (Norwegian Nobel Peace Committee, quoted in Gibbs and Lyall, 2007).

Given Gore's emphasis on cooperation and morality as a way to achieve human security, it is pretty easy to make the case that Gore is a typical idealist (see Chapter 3). For without explicitly saying so, Gore seems to embrace all of the core principles of idealism. He seems to believe in the goodness of human nature, the possibility of progress through enlightenment/learning, the idea that bad things happen because people either don't have good enough information or they are badly organized or both, that conflict is not inevitable, that collective action can redress injustices and avoid conflict, and that the reorganization of international society is what will contribute most to the solving of global problems (Kegley, 1995: 4). All of these ideas are implied in Gore's writings, film, and political projects on environmentalism and climate change.

Even so, Gore is *not* a typical idealist. For while he may embrace the core principles of idealism, he does so with a difference. For example, Gore seems to accept that international society can moderate conflict. But unlike typical idealists, the conflict Gore is most interested in is not state-to-state or even human-to-human conflict but the conflict between humans and the earth that interferes with the earth's ability to sustain life. For Gore, then, international society should not address itself only to traditional security problems like conflict among peoples and wars among states but must also urgently address itself to the new environmental security problem of tackling the planetary issue of human-made climate change, an issue that figures very differently, if at all, on traditional idealist agendas.

By redefining traditional idealist security issues to include—and indeed to be dominated by—environmental issues, Gore shifts how idealists ought to think about global governance. Yes, there is still an important place for international society, for increasing communication, for learning and progress. But this must be accompanied by a commitment to "greening" the planet, so much so that the "preservation of the earth [becomes] our new organizing principle" (1992: 295). And this means that traditional idealist governance strategies must be reconfigured as non-conventional "green governance" (Dobson and Bell, 2006; Eckersley, 1995, 2004; Luke, 1997).

As Matthew Paterson explains, "environmentalist" or "green" projects and governance strategies like Gore's cross, recombine, and exceed traditional categories of IR theory (Paterson, 1996). To come to grips with Gore and his project, then, one must come to grips not only with idealism but also with environmental/green theory.

Table 9.1 Gore's idealist assumptions

Assumptions typical of idealism	Assumptions atypical of idealism
• Humans are good by nature • Progress is possible • Bad things happen because of bad organization • Conflict is not inevitable • Collective action can redress injustice and avoid conflict • International society can solve global problems	• Human–environmental conflict is more urgent than human–human conflict at this moment in history • International society must address itself to the new environmental security problem of tackling human-made climate change • The preservation of the planet must become our new organizing principle

So what is environmental/green theory and politics?

Like any theoretical or political perspective, there are a variety of environmental/green positions and lots of heated debates among them. Yet they seem to share at least one core premise—that *our received wisdom about the relationship between nature (the natural environment) and culture (the human environment) must be questioned*. Whether we turn to Plato or Old Testament Christians or modern industrialists or Marxists, all these non-environmentalist/greens espouse the view that nature is a resource that the human species (culture) should tame. This is done in a variety of ways, like enclosing/privatizing nature, extracting fossil fuels from nature, and "developing" nature. Whatever the means, the end is always the same— for humans (culture) to dominate nature and bend it to their will so that nature can provide for human needs and wants.

Environmental/green theory begins from the position that such a view of the nature/culture relationship is at best outdated and at worst morally wrong. While this view might have made sense before the world became so densely populated, before human demands for clean land, water, and air were in danger of exceeding the earth's capacity to provide them, and before the earth's ability to naturally recycle poisonous by-products of industrialization became oversaturated, this view is no longer legitimate because it does not make sense of the world in which we currently live. Now we have to worry about all manner of environmental dangers—holes in the ozone layer, shortages of safe water and air, rising temperatures, rising sea levels, the extinction of a vast array of species resulting in the earth's decreased biodiversity, and ultimately the inability of the planet to sustain life.

Environmental/green theorists argue that more than anything else, what causes these dangers is how humans (culture) use nature. Starkly put, the way humans use nature is killing humans, other species, and the planet in general. So to make the world safe for current and future generations, what is required is a change in the human–nature relationship.

Box 9.1 The core premise of environmental/green theory

What is the core premise of environmental/green theory and the foundation for environmental/green political action?

Our received wisdom about the relationship between nature and culture (that humans should dominate nature and extract from it whatever humans want and need) must be questioned.

Why is this the case?

Because the current human/nature relationship is literally killing humans, other species, and the planet as a whole.

What might make an environmentally-positive change in the human–nature relationship possible?

Matthew Paterson argues that such a change can be brought about by combining green theory and IR theory. Specifically, what is called for are three things—a new understanding of ontology (being), a new understanding of global limits, and a new global order. Green theory provides the first two of these three elements; IR theory provides the final of these three elements.

So what do these elements mean, and how might they combine to change the human–nature relationship in ways that are environmentally beneficial and strategically safe?

Ontologically, environmental/green theory claims that we need to move away from an "anthropocentric" (that is, human-centered) understanding of the world to an "ecocentric" (that is, environmentally-centered) understanding of the world. This is necessary because anthropocentrism only values the human species and is therefore only concerned with the survival of the human species. Ecocentrism, in contrast, values ecosystems in and for themselves which results in a valuing of all living things rather than just the human species. As such, ecocentrism generally refuses the traditional division of nature and culture, recognizing that humans are part of nature, not above nature (Bennett and Chaloupka, 1993). Ecocentrism therefore understands that the fate of humans is intrinsically linked to the fate of the natural environment.

For Paterson, this shift in ontology must be accompanied by a new understanding of global environmental limits. The argument here is that planet earth has a finite capacity to sustain humans and that the earth is in danger of exceeding its limited capacity. What pushes the earth to its limits are two things—the exponential growth of human populations that fuels an exponential growth in industrialization and its by-products (resource depletion, pollution) coupled with the near saturation of the earth's capacity to naturally recycle pollution.

Environmental/green theorists are well aware that as early as the eighteenth century predictions that population growth would lead to famine, disease, and social and political unrest have been made yet have not come to pass (Malthus, 1798). Yet they argue that when we add widespread industrialization into this mix of population growth and scarcity, we have to take seriously the limits-to-growth argument, popularized by Meadows and her colleagues in the 1970s (Meadows et al., 1972). While some debate whether or not Meadows and her colleagues were wrong about the details of when the earth would reach its limits (Turner, 2008), Meadows and her colleagues insist that the underlying logic of the limits-to-growth argument is sound and that to ignore it is to miss the opportunity to save the planet and thus save ourselves from extinction.

Saving the planet and ourselves on this planet will, however, require more than just an environmental/green theorization of ontology and a renewed appreciation of the limits to environmental growth. It will also require specific actions on the part of humans—the implementation of an environmental/green politics (Paterson, 2005: 237). And this raises the question, "What governance arrangement might best facilitate the implementation of an environmental/green politics?"

Paterson claims the answer is to be found in turning to IR theory as a guide to creating a new global order. For Paterson, this new global order needs to be one that is far more decentralized than the current states system and gives less power to states (Paterson, 2005: 237). We get an idea of the kind of new global order environmentalists/greens have in mind though their slogan "Think Globally, Act Locally." What this expression conveys is that local action has global effects, and these effects are not necessarily governed by states (Paterson, 2005: 238–50) or, I would add, by an overarching international community.

Overall, Paterson claims that this combination of environmental/green theory and politics with IR theory provides "an *explanation* of the destruction of the rest of nature by human societies, and a *normative* foundation for resisting this destruction and creating sustainable societies" (2005: 236).

Gore's understanding of and responses to the planetary emergency of human-made climate change embrace all three of Paterson's key points about environmental/green theory and politics. Gore accepts that they must rethink their relationship to nature and embrace the fact that humans to do not stand above nature but are a part of it. Gore agrees that the earth's capacity to absorb the by-products of industrialization is limited and that exceeding these limits is what has created the current planetary emergency. And he embraces the environmental/green political agenda to "Think Globally, Act Locally" as a way to address this planetary emergency. The result is a hoped-for reordering of international governance as Gore's specific brand of "green governance," which embodies an idealist-inflected moral commitment to "green the earth" and to make the "preservation of the earth . . . our new organizing principle" (1992: 295) without necessarily having to radically restructure either the states system or international society.

Gore's work has brought the debate about human-made climate change to the attention of individuals and state leaders across the globe. In so doing, it has reignited the debate about whether or not human-made climate change is scientifically true, leading to discussions about whether or not Gore's proposals to rescue the planet must be urgently implemented or whether or not if his diagnosis of environmental problems is alarmist to the extreme and his solutions are therefore too costly and ultimately unnecessary (Horner, 2007).

These sorts of questions about Gore's myth go to the truth or falsity of his myth. But what concerns us here is not whether or not Gore's myth is true but what makes it *appear to be true*. So maybe we can get out of this "true/false" debate by shifting the terms of this debate. One way to do this is to leave aside questions about the scientific truth or falsity of human-made climate change and focus on a different part of Gore's myth—the part about convenience and inconvenience. For even if we assume human-made climate change is true, we still have to ask ourselves if it is *inconvenient*, particularly in the terms in which Gore describes it.

If we choose to interrogate the presumed inconvenience of human-made climate change rather than its truth or falsity, a whole new range of questions emerges. For example, we can ask not just whether or not human-made climate change and Gore's solutions to it are inconvenient, but precisely for whom they might be inconvenient. Could it be that human-made climate change and specifically Gore's solutions to it are actually convenient for some while inconvenient for others?

If that is that case, then what is it that makes Gore's myth "human-made climate change is an inconvenient truth" *appear to be true* for everyone everywhere? Might it have something to do with Gore's combination of environmental/green theory and politics and some additional idealist assumptions that are too often left uninterrogated, assumptions that have less to do with strategic and moral agendas than they do with economic agendas? Might it be that the idealist economic assumption (often called a neoliberal economic assumption, see Chapter 6) that international economic relations are harmonious has spilled over into Gore's understanding of the relationship between culture and nature, humans and the environment? Or, as stated through liberal modernization and development theory (see Chapter 8), might it be that Gore is convinced that "all good things go together," including sustainable economic growth and a healthy environment, as sustainable development theory holds (World Commission on Environment and Development, 1987)?

All of this might be fine if sustainable development were unquestionably sustainable in environmentally healthy ways. But is economic development sustainable? Or does Gore's brand of sustainable economic development jeopardize not only the fate of the earth but the fate of humankind to inhabit the earth?

These questions are raised by the 2008 Pixar animated film *WALL-E*. *WALL-E* takes place in a environmentally post-apocalyptic world in which earth was abandoned by humans because toxins and garbage made the planet uninhabitable. This abandonment of the earth was meant to be temporary, lasting some five years while machines like WALL-E (an acronym for Waste Allocation Load Lifter Earth-Class) cleaned up the garbage and made earth inhabitable again. But some 700 years later, WALL-E is still clearing up the trash, and humans are still living on spaceships awaiting their return to earth. *WALL-E*'s depiction of earth's future supports Gore's idea that human-made climate change is a planetary emergency. But it also tells us something else about Gore's myth. It tells us what must go without saying in order for Gore's myth to appear to be true. It does this by exploring the relationships humans have to economic consumption and economic governance, and it raises the question whether or not "sustainable economic development" can sustain both healthy economic growth and a healthy planet.

What does the myth say?

The 2006 documentary film and accompanying book *An Inconvenient Truth* are Gore's best-known statements about global climate change. But as Gore has pointed out, long before this film came into being, he had been taking his message around the world to anyone who would listen in the form of a one-man travelling slideshow. When Gore's act caught the attention of Hollywood Director David Guggenheim, this little slideshow became the documentary film *An Inconvenient Truth*. Since then, this documentary has done more to popularize Gore's myth "human-made climate change is an inconvenient truth" than the rest of his work put together.

An Inconvenient Truth is a highly intimate film. What is so effective about this intimacy is that it is not just about Al Gore, Jr's relationship to his family, to his country, and to the environment. It is about each individual viewer's moral relationship to the earth. These ideas are established in the film's opening sequence.

The film opens to the sound of a quiet chorus of notes rising, reminiscent of a low buzzing you might hear in a forest or the low hum of traffic. Somewhere in this sound is the suggestion that something is wrong. As we see the first image—a close-up of a leafy green tree—we hear a piano strike a clear note, twice. As the camera pans left from this tree in the foreground to a river in the background, we hear Gore's voiceover, which is punctuated by more single piano notes.

Gore: You look at that river gently flowing by. You notice the leaves rustling with the wind. You hear the birds. You hear the tree frogs. In the distance, you hear a cow. You feel the grass. The mud gives a little bit on the river bank. It's quiet. It's peaceful. And all the sudden, it's a gearshift inside you. And it's like taking a deep breath and going [Gore deeply inhales, then exhales, saying] "Oh, yea, I forgot about this."

Cut to a close-up of Gore's laptop. On the laptop screen is a picture of the earth shot from the moon. As this slide fills the cinema screen, we realize that this is the first image in Gore's slideshow. Cut to shots of different crowds across the globe listening to Gore's presentation. These images are interspersed with shots of Gore travelling from one destination to another. Finally, Gore introduces himself.

Gore: I am Al Gore. I used to be the next President of the United States. [The crowd laughs. Gore continues, deadpan.] I don't find that particularly funny.

As the montage of Gore's travelling show continues, Gore tells us in voiceover, "I've been telling this story for a long time, and I feel as if I've failed to get the message across." Gore's confession of failure is narrated over a series of images that evidence global warming—melting snow, rain-starved soil, polluting factories. Cut to Gore working with footage from Hurricane Katrina.

Gore [voiceover]:   There are good people who are in politics in both parties who hold this at arm's length because if they acknowledge it and recognize it, then the moral imperative to make big changes is inescapable.

We see one final shot of Gore on the road, looking out the window of the backseat of a car as it rolls through a gray city littered with skyscrapers. The title of the film appears on the window. This is the end of the opening sequence.

This opening sequence provides us with all of the core elements of *An Inconvenient Truth*. It establishes our main character Al Gore, Jr as a flawed, folkie hero wandering in the wilderness of post-party political life desperate to beat the overwhelming odds stacked against him in his quest to communicate the moral urgency of his mission—that human-made climate change is a planetary emergency and that it is a problem we can solve. It establishes the film's tone as a mix of gravity and levity by intercutting heavy facts with well-placed jokes. And it offers us a glimpse of the mesmerizing graphics that our hero will mobilize to achieve his mission.

The rest of the film cuts between some of Gore's most personal experiences—the near death of his son Albert, the death of his only sibling Nancy—and some of the most "inconvenient truths" about the earth's climate crisis, all the while exploring how these personal tragedies inspired Gore to take on the environmental crisis as a moral issue. Along the way, Gore briefly discusses the environmental crisis as a strategic and economic issue as well. For example, as Gore uses graphics to demonstrate the global flooding that would occur if Greenland's glaciers melted, he shows one such slide of New York City.

Gore: After the horrible events of September 11, we said never again. But this is what would happen to Manhattan [slide shows flood waters rising]. . . . The area where the World Trade Center memorial is to be located would be under water. Is it possible that we should prepare against other threats besides terrorists? Maybe we should be concerned about other problems as well.

Turning to economics, Gore mocks an image that has been used to suggest that economic and environmental issues are in conflict—a cartoon-like drawing of weighing scales with gold bars presenting economic wealth on one side and the whole planet representing environmental concerns on the other. The images suggest that we have to choose between making money or protecting the environment.

Gore: I think this is a false choice for two reasons. Number one, if we don't have a planet, . . . [laughter of crowd, affirming to Gore that he doesn't need to finish this sentence]. The other reason is that if we do the right thing, then we're gonna create a lot of wealth and we're gonna create a lot of jobs because doing the right thing moves us forward.

Gore never explains what "the right thing" is, what it means to "move us forward" or how "doing the right thing moves us forward." Rather than burdening its viewers with the ways Gore solves difficult political dilemmas about economics and the environment, the film instead just keeps hammering home Gore's moral message based upon scientific fact.

Gore: Ultimately, this is really not a political issue so much as a moral issue. If we allow [temperatures to rise because of CO_2 emissions], it is deeply unethical.

This "we" is then translated into individual US American "me's" who need to effect this solution.

Gore: Each one of us is a cause of global warming, but each of us can make choices to change that, with the things we buy, the electricity we use, the cars we drive. We can make choices to bring our individual carbon emissions to zero. The solutions are in our hands. We just have to have the determination to make them happen. Are we going to be left behind as the rest of the world moves forward?

The film ends with a look back at the opening river sequence.

Gore: Future generations may well have occasion to ask themselves—what were our parents thinking? Why didn't they wake up when they had a chance? We have to hear that question from them now.

Fade to black.

Cue Melissa Ethridge singing her Oscar-winning song, "I need to wake up," as tips for how individuals can solve the environmental crisis are interspersed with the final credits.

Part of what made *An Inconvenient Truth* so popular was *what it said and how it said it*. What the film said is not only that "human-made climate change is an inconvenient truth." It also stressed that because global warming is largely a human-made problem, it can be solved by human action. How it said this, of course, was by using the documentary film form. And this was an incredibly smart move. For unlike environmental disaster dramas like *The Day After Tomorrow*, for example, which viewers could easily dismiss as over-the-top, this film was about a morally-motivated, Harvard-educated former US Vice President (and almost President) doing what he was already doing—telling the truth as he saw it about human-made climate change. Yes, the film recalled some moments in Gore's life to dramatic effect, but for the most part this was a talking-head documentary, with Gore as about the most credible talking head one could find on this subject. And so documentary—which in film studies is defined as a "creative treatment of actuality" (Grierson quoted in Rabiger, 1998: 3)—was the perfect form to call upon to circulate Gore's message. It makes the message appear to be honest, intellectual, and interesting all at the same time.

Having said this, Gore's documentary is at its best as a "creative treatment of actuality" with respect to *what the film does not say and how it does not say it*. What the film does not say are any of the more controversial ideas about human-made climate change and its convenience or inconvenience which are found in Gore's other writings on global warming. And how the film does not say these things is by editing them out of Gore's presentation in *An Inconvenient Truth* so that viewers are never burdened by details or policy recommendations or any troubling contradictions in Gore's argument that cannot be smoothed over by a joke, a cartoon or a cool graphic. Yet there is so much more to Gore's position on global warming that is a less "creative treatment of the truth." And because *An Inconvenient Truth* is a gloss of Gore's earlier ideas without contributing a single new idea to Gore's opus on global warming, it is important to take a look back at his earlier work to appreciate just how clever it was *not* to mention this stuff in too much detail in the film.

Box 9.2 What *An Inconvenient Truth* says and how it says it

What the film says:
Human-made climate change is an inconvenient truth that can be solved by humans because it is a human-made problem.

How the film says it:
By using the "factual" documentary film form

> **Box 9.3 What *An Inconvenient Truth* does *not* say and how it *does not* say it**
>
> What the film *does not* say:
> Any controversial details, policy recommendations or troubling contradictions in Gore's argument
>
> How the film *does not* say it:
> By glossing these aspects of Gore's argument that appear in his earlier work on the environment

Aside from *An Inconvenient Truth*, Gore's most important works on global climate change are his influential *Washington Post* editorial entitled "Earth's Fate is the Number One National Security Issue" and his 1992 book *Earth in the Balance: Forging a New Common Purpose*.

Gore's 1989 editorial "Earth's Fate is the Number One National Security Issue" was written a few months after the Berlin Wall came down, which marked the symbolic end to the Cold War and which opened up a space for new strategic thinking about global politics. Gore seized this moment to suggest a new security agenda. Criticizing President George Bush, Sr for his lack of vision about the future of global security, Gore argued that just because the Soviet Bloc no longer threatened the US as it had in the past, this did not mean that US security was assured. For, as the title of Gore's essay puts it, environmental issues are now the US's number one security issue. Chiding Bush, Sr for his neglect of environmental issues, Gore states

> This indifference must end. As a nation and a government, we must see that America's future is inextricably tied to the fate of the globe. In effect, the environment is becoming a matter of national security—an issue that directly and imminently menaces the interests of the state and the welfare of the people.
>
> (1989)

Gore explains that he does not mean to overstate this "national-security analogy," noting that military threats have been and continue to be real. "And yet, there is strong evidence the new enemy [of environmental crisis] is at least as real as the old" (1989). He makes a strong argument for using the language of national security to argue his case. As he puts it,

> When nations perceive that they are threatened at the strategic level, they may be induced to think of drastic responses, involving sharp discontinuities from everyday approaches to policy. In military terms, this is the point when the United States begins to think of invoking nuclear weapons. The global environment crisis may demand responses that are comparatively radical.
>
> (1989)

Gore spends the rest of his editorial outlining what this radical response should be. But before he does this, he draws a clear distinction between typical "radical" proposals to the environmental crisis and his own. Specifically, Gore makes it clear that he does not agree with "radical" analyses that tell us that "the notion of environmental sustainable development at present may be an oxymoron," that "we face a choice between economic growth in the near term and massive environmental disorder as the subsequent penalty," and that we should give in to "simplistic demands that development, or technology itself, must be stopped for the problem to be solved" (1989). Quite the contrary. Yes, Gore concedes that "The tension between the imperatives of growth and the imperative of environmental management represents a supreme test for modern industrial civilization and an extreme demand upon technology" (1989). But that does not lead Gore to conclude that economic growth should be sacrificed in the name of saving the environment. Rather, Gore argues that this problem "will call for the environmental equivalent of the Strategic Defense Initiative [i.e., President Ronald Regan's 'Star Wars' Missile Defense Initiative]: a Strategic Environment Initiative" (1989).

Rather than sacrifice economic development to environmental management, Gore's Strategic Environment Initiative (SEI) seeks to apply innovative and increasingly efficient new technologies to every major sector of the economy as a way to make economic development and environmental protection simultaneously achievable goals (1989). Gore outlines three planks in his SEI platform. The first is an "Energy SEI" that "should focus on producing energy for development without compromising the environment" by encouraging conservation and developing new solar, biomass and nuclear power sources. The second is a "second green revolution, to address the needs of the Third World's poor" by developing new technologies of agricultural production and reorganizing the international financing of Third World development. The third is a "Transportation SEI" that improves mileage standards in US vehicles, looks to develop alternative fuels, and in the longer term restructures the US transportation system to emphasize public transportation over personal vehicles (1989).

Overall, Gore argues that

> we must transform ourselves. . . . The solutions we seek will be found in a new faith in the future of life on earth after our own, a faith in the future which justifies sacrifices in the present, a new moral courage to choose higher values in the conduct of human affairs, and a new reverence for absolute principles that can serve as guiding stars for the future course of our species and our place within creation.
>
> (1989)

Strategically, morally, and economically, then, Gore makes a strong case for US policymakers to prioritize the global environmental crisis just as much as they would any other strategic issue. Gore makes this case *strategically* by elevating the environmental crisis to the status of America's new post-Cold War enemy, *morally* by elevating his SEI strategic response to the environmental crisis to a set of absolute principles that requires moral courage to follow, and *economically* by promising that his SEI will achieve environmental protection without sacrificing economic growth.

Gore's 1992 book *Earth in the Balance* carries on with this agenda. But instead of directing his message primarily to politicians and policymakers (as a *Washington Post* editorial does), Gore begins to direct his message to a broader US public. In so doing, Gore begins by "forging a new common purpose" on the environment. Gore does this by striking a personal tone in this book, foreshadowing things we will see in *An Inconvenient Truth* about what growing up on a farm in Tennessee taught him about caring for the environment, what his son Albert's near death taught him about the value of life, and what we owe to future generations. As in *An Inconvenient Truth*, these personal stories are mobilized to encourage each of us to "take a greater personal responsibility for this deteriorating global environment" (1992: 12). How we can do this is by taking "a hard look at the habits of mind and action that reflect— and have led to—this grave crisis" (1992: 12).

By arguing that it is the little, everyday things that individuals do that have created this planetary emergency, Gore widens responsibility for solving the environmental crisis from just states and state leaders to individuals. Gore does this because he recognizes that "forging a new common purpose" about the environment will require winning the hearts and minds of individuals as much as (or even more than) those of states and state leaders. For if Gore can mobilize the US public to "go green," then the US public can put pressure on the US government to introduce and implement environmental/green policies. For such a mobilization to be effective, though, it cannot be posed in the combative, strategic language of Gore's 1989 editorial. For by 1992, global cooperation via "globalization" (see Chapter 6) defined the terms of national and international debate. And so in *Earth in the Balance*, Gore's assessment of the environmental crisis as a "new enemy" that must be tamed by a Strategic Environmental Initiative fades to the background, making way for Gore's more cooperative proposal of a Global Marshall Plan.

Like Gore's Strategic Environmental Initiative which recasts President Regan's Strategic Defense Initiative in environmental terms, Gore's Global Marshall Plan recasts the US-led post-World War II Marshall Plan in environmental terms. The original Marshall Plan was a US-led initiative to revitalize economically devastated Europe by restructuring European national economies so that economic development and free trade would flourish throughout the region. Gore argues that "something like the Marshall Plan—a Global Marshall Plan, if you will—is now urgently needed" (1992: 297). He continues:

> The scope and complexity of this plan will far exceed those of the original; what's required now is a plan that combines large-scale, long-term, carefully targeted financial aid to developing nations, massive efforts to design and then transfer to poor nations the new technologies needed for sustained economic progress, a worldwide program to stabilize world populations, and binding commitments by the industrial nations to accelerate their own transition to an environmentally responsible pattern of life.
>
> (1992: 297)

While Gore is absolutely clear that he wants to make "the preservation of the earth ... our new organizing principle" (1992: 295), it isn't immediately clear how reworking an economic plan like the Marshall Plan into a Global Marshall Plan would in any way help to achieve this goal. But this becomes clearer when we remember the history of the original Marshall Plan. For it wasn't just about the US benevolently helping Europe to recover economically after World War II. The US led this European economic recovery because it believed this was the best way to keep Europe from falling into Soviet control and turning to communism (recall the goals of modernization and development theory, Chapter 8). So the original Marshall Plan used economic strategies to achieve military and ideological goals. Similarly, Gore hopes to use a Global Marshall Plan with its environmental strategy to achieve a wide range of goals. For what Gore argues is that a US-led Global Marshall Plan would not just bring economic development to the Third World. In so doing, it would also make democracy and capitalism the foundations for "sustainable societies" in the Third World—politically, economically, and environmentally.

Gore outlines six strategic goals that his Global Marshall Plan hopes to achieve:

1 the stabilizing of the world's population;
2 the rapid creation and development of environmentally appropriate technologies;
3 a comprehensive and ubiquitous change in the economic "rules of the game" by which we measure the impact of our decisions on the environment;
4 the negotiation and approval of a new generation of international agreements;
5 the establishment of a cooperative plan for educating the world's citizens about our global environment; and
6 the establishment, especially in the developing world—of social and political conditions most conducive to the emergence of sustainable societies.

(1992: 305–7)

As you can see, many of these goals are identical to those Gore first proposed in his 1989 editorial. Indeed, as Gore makes clear in his book, his second goal about "the rapid creation and development of environmentally appropriate technologies" is actually his original Strategic Economic Initiative. What we have in *Earth in the Balance*, then, is everything we already had in Gore's 1989 editorial. The only real difference between the editorial and this book is that the book both fleshes out Gore's ideas in more detail and broadens responsibility for solving environmental problems from states and state leaders to individuals as well. As such, it is the perfect precursor to *An Inconvenient Truth* which emphasizes what individuals (and particularly what individual US citizens) can do to curb human-made climate change. Effectively, then, *An Inconvenient Truth* was designed to finally "forge a new common purpose" on the environment by implementing Strategic Goal Number Five of Gore's Global Marshall Plan—"the establishment of a cooperative plan for educating the world's citizens about our global environment" (1992: 306), starting primarily with the US public.

The similarities between Gore's three major works on human-made climate change are striking. But what is also striking is how *An Inconvenient Truth* omits all of Gore's sometimes less interesting and sometimes more controversial claims—

not because Gore has changed his position on these issues but because they function in *An Inconvenient Truth* as assumptions upon which his myth "human-made climate change is an inconvenient truth" functions. None of the detailed arguments that burden us in either Gore's 1989 editorial or in *Earth in the Balance* reappear in this work. Nowhere are we asked to think about how to mobilize economic development so that democracy and capitalism can become the basis of sustainable economic development. Nowhere are we hit over the head with policy recommendations for either an SEI or a Global Marshall Plan. And nowhere are we reminded that submitting to Gore's brand of "Green Governance" is a way of achieving the US national interest. Instead, all we have to do is focus on is the "inconvenient truth" of human-made global warming and grab hold of the idea that we can solve this problem if we act now.

Taken together, Gore's film and writings on the environmental crisis make a pretty good case for Gore's myth "human-made climate change is an inconvenient truth." They do so by slickly presenting scientific evidence to support his claim that human-made climate change has created a planetary problem and by methodically laying out plans to solve this problem—through a Strategic Environmental Initiative, a Global Marshall Plan, and by reductions in individual CO_2 emissions. So all of this supports the "truth" of Gore's claim that human-made climate change exists.

Even if we bracket these issues and look instead at the second part of Gore's myth—about how human-made climate change is "an inconvenient truth"—we again find strong evidence for this in Gore's work. For it is a pretty persuasive case for inconvenience that there will be no human winners if climate change happens on the catastrophic scale Gore suggests it could because the earth will not be able to sustain any human life. This makes human-made climate change inconvenient for everyone. It also explains why Gore makes the case that it is necessary for rich industrial states and individuals in these states to take the lead to reverse the potentially catastrophic effects of human-made climate change by helping the "Third World" to become more stable politically by adopting democracy, and more stable economically through a technology-led "second green revolution," a revolution that will spark not only economic development but also (Gore tells us) agricultural efficiencies, population decreases, and overall environmentally sustainable societies. This is what industrialized states can do. In the meantime, the citizens of these states can erase their carbon footprints altogether by bringing their own CO_2 emissions down to zero and mobilizing public opinion to ensure that their states "go green." Gore's plan for green governance, then, offers clear directives to states and to citizens about precisely how they ought to behave in order to solve the climate crisis.

In these ways, Gore's underlying idealist assumptions about cooperation around a common moral purpose that might even decrease conflict and enhance peace and stability all seem to be achievable. They don't require a world government, nor do they necessarily require a new international society. Rather, all that is required are states and citizens (especially the US state and its citizens) with the political will to assume global leadership on environmental issues so that we can all then solve this planetary crisis together. And all of this can be accomplished *without* sacrificing economic growth for environmental protection.

It is this last point that is the underlying "feel-good factor" of Gore's analysis of the global environmental crisis—that having a healthy planet is not at odds with having healthy sustained economic development. If this is the case, though, then doesn't this call into question the "inconvenience" part of Gore's myth? For isn't it terribly *convenient* especially for the US state and its citizens that all good economic and environmental things go together? For while Gore might be asking the US state and US citizens to "go green" and to help lead others across the world into doing the same, this may not inconvenience the US much at all. For while the US may have to fork out more money in aid and US citizens may have to drive hybrid-powered vehicles, for example, the US state does not have to forfeit its global power which is based largely upon its economic power and US citizens do not have to forfeit their modern conveniences. Indeed, thanks to ever-improving technologies, efficiencies will just keep increasing and life it seems will keep getting easier. The driving force behind our future political, economic, and environmental "good life" is economic growth. So long as US consumers continue to increase their consumption (albeit by making incrementally "greener" choices), then there will be no contradiction between sustainable economic development and a healthy sustainable environment. Or will there?

The film *WALL-E* takes a different stand than does Gore on the relationship between economics and environmental protection. It does this not by focusing so much on states and citizens (because in the environmentally post-apocalyptic world of *WALL-E*, there no longer seem to be any states or citizens). Rather, it does so by looking at an actor very much neglected in Gore's economic and environmental analysis—the global corporation. In so doing, *WALL-E* suggests to us what must go without saying in order for Gore's myth "human-made climate change is an inconvenient truth" to appear to be true.

WALL-E

The 2008 animated Pixar film *WALL-E* is a film about the future that takes as its central theme a nostalgia for the past. Set some 800 years in the future, what *WALL-E* is nostalgic for is the present we are currently living. For this is a time when humans lived on the earth and engaged in genuine loving relationships. The film's title character WALL-E (short for Waste Allocation Life Loader Earth-Class) is a small, mobile robot who is particularly nostalgic for love, a concept this binocular-eyed, tractor-treaded trash compactor learned about from endlessly watching the 1969 film *Hello, Dolly!* Two songs from *Hello, Dolly!* structure WALL-E's world, as well as the film *WALL-E*—"Put on Your Sunday Clothes" and "It Only Takes a Moment."

The film's opening sequence begins with the lyrics of "Put on Your Sunday Clothes," which in *Hello, Dolly!* is a song about New York City that shop clerk Cornelius sings to his fellow clerk, Barnaby.

Cornelius: Out there. There's a world outside of Yonkers. Way out there beyond this hick town, Barnaby. There's a slick town, Barnaby.

As this song plays, animated scenes of outer space appear. We see stars, moons, galaxies. As the song's second stanza plays, the camera pans down from space to a shot of the earth. The camera passes through a dense ring of trash orbiting the earth

Plate 9.1 WALL-E, a mobile trash compacting robot, at home in his Buy N Large container. Courtesy of the Ronald Grant Film Archive © Walt Disney/Pixar Animation.

(old satellites, space stations, telescopes). Once the camera enters the earth's atmosphere, we see the East Coast of the United States. The camera zooms in on New York City.

Cornelius: Out there. Full of shine and full of sparkle. Close your eyes and see it glisten, Barnaby. Listen, Barnaby . . .

In a long-shot, we see the giant skyscrapers that epitomize New York City. But as the camera shoots these in close-up, we realize that these skyscrapers are crumbling and abandoned. And what shines and sparkles in this New York City are even taller skyscraper-like piles of trash. We hear the wind echo through this mass of empty buildings and dense rubbish piles. The camera shifts position, giving us an overhead shot of a small robot—WALL-E—maneuvering across dirt pathways through the debris. The music continues.

Cornelius: Put on your Sunday clothes, There's lots of world out there. . . .

But now the music has a metallic twang to it. Instead of being played as a clear, unsituated opening track, this music is coming from WALL-E's built-in playback device. The camera follows WALL-E as he selects treasure from trash, crushes rubbish in his "belly," and assembles his belly-made blocks of junk into enormous stacks that look like the abandoned buildings of the New York City skyline. All the while he is accompanied by his pet cockroach, the only sign of life on earth.

As the sun begins to fade, WALL-E heads home across the waste-scape that is now New York City—enormous deserted stores, parking lots, gas stations, and banks. All of these are branded with the same company label—Buy N Large, a kind of Walmart on steroids due to the size and reach of this corporation. Buy N Large is not just a global corporation; it extends beyond planet earth and into other galaxies. For not only does the company have lunar ambitions, as illustrated by its sign on the moon reading "Buy N Large Outlet Coming Soon." The company has intergalactic ambitions. We learn of these from a commercial broadcast on a motion-activated billboard WALL-E passes.

Plate 9.2 WALL-E with his indestructible pet cockroach.
Courtesy of the Ronald Grant Film Archive © Walt Disney/Pixar Animation.

Commercial (VO): Too much trash in your face? We'll clean it up while you're in space. BnL StarLiners leaving each day. We'll clean up the mess while you're away.

Cut to holographic images of humans on board spaceships that resemble current-day ocean cruise liners while the voiceover expounds upon the pleasures of Starcruising.

Cut to Shelby Forthright, the CEO of Buy N Large: Because at BnL, space is the final FUN-tier!

This commercial explains why we don't see any people in WALL-E's world, for humans who could afford a BnL StarCruise abandoned the earth and its moon because of the excesses of trash and pollution, while the rest of the human species and every other species (apart from cockroaches) presumably died out. Another billboard tells us that a battalion of WALL-E robots stayed behind, operating under their programmed directive of "working to dig you [humans] out." As WALL-E wanders through the rubble, we see the remains of other WALL-Es that have long since ceased functioning. The WALL-E we meet in this opening sequence is the last working robot on earth. But WALL-E isn't all work and no play. Over the past 700 years, he has developed a personality which makes him curious about the earth, and nostalgic for what he understands to be human relationships. These traits were developed through his contact with the treasures and trash left on earth and with his *Hello, Dolly!* videotape.

Humming "Put on your Sunday Clothes," WALL-E enters his home (a Buy N Large container), puts on a videotape of *Hello, Dolly!*, and adds treasures to his collection—a hubcap, a spoon/fork, a cigarette lighter. On most items the Buy N Large label is still visible. In the background, the video plays "It Only Takes a Moment," a love song between Cornelius and his love interest Mrs Molloy.

Cornelius: And that is all that love's about.
Mrs Molloy: And we'll recall as time runs out.
Both: That it only took a moment to be loved your whole life long.

As they sing, Cornelius and Mrs Molloy join hands. An emotional WALL-E imitates this gesture by linking his "hands" together. He then finishes organizing his stuff, closes his container to protect himself from one of earth's many sudden violent storms, and settles onto a shelf to await the next day's sunlight that will recharge his energy supply. The screen fades to black.

This is the end of the opening sequence.

As in the opening sequence of *An Inconvenient Truth*, the opening sequence of *WALL-E* introduces the core elements of the film. It establishes our main character WALL-E as a lonely, nostalgic, curious and persistent robot who is wandering in the wilderness of environmentally post-apocalyptic earth relentlessly working against overwhelming odds to achieve his environmental mission—cleaning up the mess humans have left behind. It establishes the film's tone as a mix of gravity and levity by intercutting shots of earth's bleak environment with the humorous antics of this little robot trying to make sense of his world. And it offers us a glimpse of how the plot will unfold thanks to WALL-E's reaction to the music from *Hello, Dolly!* This little robot whose glitch was to develop a personality is destined to leave behind his daily routine and set off across the universe in search of love, which he will find with another robot EVE (short for Extra-terrestrial Vegetation Evaluator). Or, as one of the taglines of the film puts it, "After 700 years of doing what he was built for, he'll discover what he's meant for" (http://www.imdb.com/title/tt0910970/taglines).

In a lot of ways, WALL-E seems to be an automated Al Gore, Jr—another guy on a mission who seems to have developed a personality after an apocalypse (this time political), who has since devoted himself to his against-the-odds environmental mission, and who after decades of performing the public service he was built for (following in the footsteps of his politician father) discovers what he's meant for. Also like WALL-E, Gore is out to promote "love," but unlike WALL-E this love is less

Plate 9.3 EVE, short for Extra-terrestrial Vegetation Evaluator.
Courtesy of the Ronald Grant Film Archive © Walt Disney/Pixar Animation.

a love for himself than it is a love by all human beings for earth's natural environment. Gore casts this love relationship in the same nostalgic terms as does WALL-E. Gore isn't inspired by the lost love relationships depicted in an old 1969 film, but he is inspired by the river that runs through his childhood and that river's representation of the natural environment as it is now but is in jeopardy of not being in the future if the human–nature relationship is not urgently reevaluated. And so just as *WALL-E* begins and ends with songs from *Hello, Dolly!*, *An Inconvenient Truth* begins and ends with shots of this Tennessee river and Gore's monologue about how we humans have taken the existence of a nurturing nature for granted and how we need to stop doing that before it disappears forever and life on earth becomes unsustainable.

By the time we enter the world of *WALL-E*, though, this balanced relationship between humans and their environment seems to have disappeared forever.

Plate 9.4 WALL-E on his way to work in the trash-scape that was New York City.
Courtesy of the Ronald Grant Film Archive © Walt Disney/Pixar Animation.

This is part of *how the film makes sense of the world*—by suggesting that the inconvenient truth of human-made climate change created an environmental catastrophe so severe that the earth could no longer support life. It is because of this that rich humans who could afford a Buy N Large Starcruise were evacuated from the earth to live on spaceships while machines like WALL-E remained on earth to try to clean up the mess. This, the film tells us, has been the normal state of affairs for the past 700 years.

Another element in how *the film makes sense of the world* is in its claim that what has been lost with the earth's ability to sustain human life has also been the ability for humans to sustain meaningful relationships, either with the earth itself or with one another. That humans have no meaningful relationship with the earth any more is evidenced in the film not just by the absence of humans living on earth but by how the space-dwelling humans think about earth. Or, to put a finer point on it, how they *don't* think about the earth. For example, to the Captain of the spaceship Axiom (the place where WALL-E travels in pursuit of EVE and encounters the humans who left earth), earth is little more than a round ball that he can fly his toy spaceship around. Earth only begins to become meaningful for him when he has the ship's computer analyze some debris that rubbed off of WALL-E. The computer identifies this debris as "earth," which leads the Captain to ask a series of questions about earth and what goes on there. This leader of the hovering human race has so little knowledge of the earth that when the computer tells him facts about earthly food and farming, he concludes that pizza comes from pizza plants.

It's not surprising that space-dwelling humans have little awareness of earth, for they have little awareness of anything beyond their daily diet of Buy N Large-fed messages and meals. Space-bound for some 700 years, human bodies have lost so much bone density and have become so big with excess fat that humans no longer walk from place to place. Instead, they move about on floating electronic hover-chairs, sipping liquidized Buy N Large lunches from supersized cups, chatting with "friends" who appear on holographic screens mounted inches from their faces, and responding to ubiquitous Buy N Large advertisements suggesting what they should eat, wear and do next. Daily chores are performed for them by a range of roving robots, each of which follows their specific BnL-programmed directive—PR-T gives humans makeovers and flattery, MO cleans up any "foreign contaminants," and AUTO pilots the spaceship. It is these command relationships with robots that constitute the bulk of daily human engagements.

Box 9.4 How does the film *WALL-E* make sense of the world?

- By suggesting that the inconvenient truth of human-made climate change created an environmental catastrophe so severe that the earth could no longer support life; and
- By claiming that what has been lost with the earth's ability to sustain human life is the ability for humans to sustain meaningful relationships, either with the earth or with one another

Space-bound humans have become so individualized, technologized, and corporatized that they are oblivious to their immediate surroundings. The descendants of the hyper-consumers who abandoned earth once they'd shopped it 'til *it* dropped, they embody the logical outcome of humankind's estrangement from the earth, of humankind's loss of love for nature. For as the name of their Buy N Large spacecraft home "Axiom" suggests, for these hovering humans consuming is the self-evident truth that structures their lives. And this axiom leaves no room for an awareness of anything else, much less a nostalgia for an over-shopped earth. Like the robots who care for them, humans, too, seem to be programmed with one specific directive—consume.

What is typical in the world of WALL-E, then, is for humans to have abandoned inconvenient earth to machines like WALL-E and opted to live instead in hyper-convenient corporatized space where human consumption can carry on uninterrupted. This was an easy transition for twenty-eighth-century humans to make, because outer space was merely an extension of their "natural" environment—the administrative space of the Buy N Large corporation. As such, it matters not one iota to these twenty-eighth-century hovering humans whether they are on earth or the earth's moon or in a BnL Starcruiser, so long as they can carry out their BnL directive to consume.

This day-to-day routine is interrupted by WALL-E. The action begins on earth, where WALL-E presents EVE (whose directive is to seek out vegetation on earth) with a plant he found in an old refrigerator. When EVE cocoons the plant inside her, all of her functions, apart from her retrieval beacon that tells the Axiom she has successfully accomplished her directive, shut down. When a spaceship returns to collect EVE, WALL-E follows EVE to the Axiom. After a series of adventures, EVE eventually delivers the plant to the ship's Captain, who reads up on what he is supposed to do in such an event. What he learns is that the plant is evidence that life is again sustainable on earth and that he is to initiate Operation Recolonize, which will return humans to earth. But when the Captain attempts to implement this initiative, he is stopped by AUTO (the ship's autopilot). AUTO reveals to the Captain that a top secret directive given by the BnL CEO directly to AUTO has overridden the Captain's orders.

BnL CEO: Bad news. Operation Cleanup failed. Rising toxicity levels made life on earth unsustainable. Rather than try to fix this problem, it's just easier to stay in space.

He then directs AUTO to assume full autopilot, meaning that the Captain has no authority to return the spaceship to earth. But by now the Captain has become

---

Box 9.5 What is typical in the world of WALL-E?

What is typical is for humans to have abandoned inconvenient earth to machines like WALL-E and opted to live instead in hyper-convenient corporatized space where human consumption can carry on uninterrupted.

---

enchanted with earth. The computer images he saw on the ship's computer excited him. The plant EVE presented to him activated his sense of responsibility for the care of life on earth. And his review of video images taken by WALL-E of the earth as it is now convinced him that all the earth needs is for humans to look after it for it to flourish. And so the Captain eventually succeeds in standing up to AUTO (figuratively and literally), defying the BnL top secret directive, and returning the StarCruiser to earth.

The Captain's actions illustrate *what is deviant in the world of WALL-E*—for humans to return to inconvenient earth to try to live there again. This is deviant because it requires humans to give up convenient corporate life by defying the top secret BnL directive for them to stay in space where they can follow their individual directives to consume. In so doing, what becomes possible is for humans to restore their relationships with one another. In other words, it allows humans to restore their humanity. And it is these fully-human humans who begin to take responsibility for themselves and, crucially, for the earth.

The film ends with the Captain placing the plant EVE gave him into the New York City soil of earth while explaining to the children what he is doing.

Captain: This is called farming. You kids are gonna grow all kinds of plants—vegetable plants, pizza plants. Awe, it's good to be home!

In the closing credits sequence, a series of hieroglyphic-like images created by the formerly space-bound humans tell us that this human–robot interaction has resulted in two tales of happily-ever-after. One, of course, is about the love shared by WALL-E and EVE. The other is about the love humans have finally shown for their natural environment, which results in an environmental rebirth of the planet. This is symbolized by that original, fragile little plant having grown strong roots and sprouted into a flourishing tree. To erase any doubt as to the success of the human rehabitation of the earth, the lyrics to Peter Gabriel's song "Down to Earth" are sung over the closing credits.

Peter Gabriel: Do you feel you've been tricked by the future you picked? Well, come on down. . . . We're coming down to the ground. There's no better place to go. We've got snow on the mountains. We've got rivers down below.

Of course, this is a terribly unrealistic ending for a film about an earthly environmental apocalypse. The toxicity, the garbage, the sudden violent storms on earth, the lack of human understanding about the earth and about humans' place on earth all suggest that these humans would likely die quick deaths if they stayed

---

Box 9.6 What is deviant in the world of WALL-E?

What is deviant is for humans to overthrow the directive of the Buy N Large corporation and return to inconvenient earth to try to live there again.

on earth. What is more likely is that humans would return to space again and resume their "normal" lives. And if by some miracle humans did somehow manage to live on earth again, they would most likely just reproduce their corporatized relationship to the earth thanks to their ignorance of "nature" (including their own biology) and their dependence on corporate service (like the production of industrialized food symbolized in the cultivation of "pizza plants"). But this is an animated film with a "general audience" rating, so this sort of ending is not unexpected.

Yet regardless of how unrealistic the ending is, this film is instructive for us as we consider *what must go without saying in order for Gore's myth "human-made climate change is an inconvenient truth" to appear to be true*. For however much the film seems to realize Gore's goal of having humans reconsider their relationship to their natural environment and make "the preservation of the earth . . . our central organizing principle" (albeit through very different practices of preservation rooted in different nostalgias; 1992: 285), the film does a lot of things that Gore takes great pains *not* to do. In particular, the film introduces a central character who is almost absent in Gore's work on the environment. This is the Buy N Large corporation, which stands in for US-based multi-national corporations. And what the film tells us is that for better or worse, human life took the form it did because of how the Buy N Large corporation directed that life. For as a global corporation, Buy N Large ended up becoming a global governance structure, with its CEO acting as a sort of planetary President governing through a series of sometimes explicit and other times subliminal directives. Robots were directed to care for humans. Humans were directed to consume. And although this is never explicitly stated, it is pretty clear that the Buy N Large corporation itself was directed to do what corporations the world over are directed to do—make a profit. All human activity, then, is derivative of the corporate profit motive. And so to change human activity, it is vital to either change how corporations function or to overthrow them by ignoring their directives.

It is only when the Captain finds the power to overthrow the BnL corporation that humans are positioned to refigure their relationships with nature. Without this, the convenient life of human consumption would carry on endlessly.

Crucially, when we look at Gore's myth "human-made climate change is an inconvenient truth" and the national and individual solutions to this planetary crisis that Gore proposes, there is never any suggestion that such a rebellion against how corporations subtly and not so subtly direct us is required. Quite to the contrary, because of Gore's deep-seated beliefs in liberal economic principles such as the

---

Box 9.7 What must go without saying in order for Gore's myth to appear to be true?

That human-made climate change is not necessarily inconvenient for (particularly US-based) global corporations because Gore's solutions to the problem of global warming do not require corporations to sacrifice economic growth to some presumed "environmental sustainability."

harmony of international economic relations and his deeply-held belief that "all good things go together" including economic growth and environmental sustainability, corporations are never asked to rethink their directives to make a profit and consumers are never asked to rethink their directive to shop. Yes, both are asked to make more environmentally friendly choices (1992: 342–3). For consumers, this means buying environmentally-friendly products. And for corporations, this means developing new technologies that will result in more environmentally-friendly products, taking a public concern for the environment into account as they make production choices, and abiding by national and international laws designed to protect the environment.

Is this enough? Can the margin of environmental protection Gore seeks to achieve through such a convenient conversion to environmentalism be realized without a much more thorough restructuring of international economic relations that includes a drastic reconsideration of the corporate directive to make a profit at a cost to the environment? The answers to these questions depend on whether or not one adheres to neoliberal economic principles (see Chapter 6) and where one stands in relation to debates about how much faith one can reasonably place in technology (Lacy, 2005). But regardless of how you might position yourself, one thing is clear—there is nothing very inconvenient about Gore's solution to the planetary emergency of human-made climate change, either for US-based global corporations that continue to make a profit, for the US state that claims its global power based upon this economic power, or for US citizens who now have a whole new range of "environmental" consumer options to select from as they carry on with their corporate, national, and now environmental directive to consume.

It's not easy being Gore's shade of green

Gore's environmentalism—like the Axiom spaceship in *WALL-E*—relies upon a couple of self-evident truths—that the planet must be saved from environmental disaster and that to do this the universally-accepted principle of corporate profit built upon individual consumption need not be seriously interrogated. As we have seen, Gore's axioms come from Gore's unique mixture of environmental/green theory and idealist/liberal economic theory.

In light of this strange mix of theory and political problem-solving, it is worth asking one last question: "Just how green is Gore?"

If we return to our earlier discussion of environmental/green theory and politics, we will recall that Matthew Paterson identified a core belief in the need to question the human/culture relationship as what all environmentalists/greens agree on. And Paterson went on to claim that the best way to do this was to change how we think about ontology (from "anthropocentric" to "ecocentric"), accept that there are very real consequences to exceeding global environmental limits, and reorganize the global order so that it is more environmentally friendly (e.g., "Think Globally, Act Locally"; Paterson, 2005).

As I suggested earlier, it seems that Gore accepts all of these environmental/ green principles and modes of action. Yet as our re-reading of Gore's myth through the film *WALL-E* points out, there may be limits to Gore's environmentalism, particularly when it comes to what Gore expects of (particularly US-based) global corporations.

Yes, Gore believes that it is necessary to question the human–culture relationship, and he does this in every one of his environmental works by explicitly arguing that humans are part of nature rather than somehow separate and above nature. And so Gore urges particularly states and their citizens to act with this new knowledge in mind. This does not mean that Gore lets global corporations off the hook here. *But Gore does not expect global corporations to rethink their relationship to nature to the point that it might interfere with economic growth born out of the corporate directive to make profit.*

This understanding of the corporation–nature relationship might well influence our understanding of Gore as "ecocentric." For because of his protection of business interests and economic growth, the "eco" in Gore's "ecocentrism" may stand as much if not more for "economics" as it does for "ecology" (see Luke, 1997, 1998, 2008). Moving on to Paterson's next point, it might mean that economic growth is where Gore draws his environmental limit, for he steadfastly objects to any claims that economic growth and sustainability of a healthy planet are ever at odds. This reading is consistent with Gore's proposals to solve the planetary emergency on global warming by making "the preservation of the earth . . . our new organizing principle" (1992: 295). For, as we've seen, the preservation of the earth must always be accompanied not just by a preservation of economic activity but by increased economic growth.

None of this is to say that Gore is wrong to suggest that we ought to address human-made climate change by, in part, lowering our CO_2 emissions as a way to reduce global warming and trying to restore earth to its balance, nor is it to detract from Gore's achievement of persuading millions more people to take global climate change seriously. Rather, all of this is to say that if the burden for achieving environmentally-friendly changes falls to states and individuals, with both persuaded by Gore that the greatest contribution corporations need to make to these efforts is providing new technologies, then we may come nowhere near solving this presumed problem. For example, not only are most of the new technologies Gore wants corporations to provide not yet viable; they could well have unintended, environmentally devastating side-effects (an example in the way in which the turn to bio-fuels is creating its own climate crisis, not to mention global food crisis). Such technological solutions could well turn out to be too little too late if not the wrong "solutions" altogether, when an urgent rethinking of the relationship between economic growth and environmental sustainability could have a far greater, more immediate impact.

In all these respects, Gore may not be as green as he at first appeared to be. Instead, Gore's myth about human-made climate change and his solutions to it might, as Timothy W. Luke puts it, at best "green-wrap corporate technocracy with renewed institutional legitimacy that 'greenwashes' an unsustainable economic status quo in the refreshing, but not cleansing, waters of sustainable development" (Luke, 2008: 1811). In so doing, environmentalism gives way to more highly held economic principles.

All of this seems to suggest that for Gore, environmentalism is neoliberal economics by other means. As such, this is the "inconvenient truth" behind Gore's myth and Gore's solutions *that must go without saying in order for Gore's myth to appear to be true.*

Suggestion for further thinking

Topic 1 Environmentalism and IR

How should International Relations approach environmental issues? Is the environment a security issue (Dalby, 2007; Deudney, 1990; Lacy, 2005), an economic issue (Luke, 2008; Dalby and Paterson, 2009), and/or a moral/ethical issue (Jamieson, 2008; Bennett and Chalupka, 1993)? How do our cultural representations of the environment encourage us to think of the global environmental issues one way or another (Evans, 2006)? Would we gain new insights into these issues if we were to tell a story about nature in the absence of humans (Weisman, 2007)? The readings below explore these questions from a variety of perspectives.

Suggested readings

Jane Bennett and William Chalupka (1993) *In the Nature of Things: Language, Politics and the Environment.* Minneapolis: University of Minnesota Press.

Simon Dalby (2007) "Ecology, Security, and Change in the Anthropocene," *Brown Journal of World Affairs* 8(2): 155–64.

Simon Dalby and Matthew Paterson (2009) "Over a Barrel: Cultural Political Economy and Oil Imperialism," in François Debrix and Mark Lacy (eds) *The Geopolitics of American Insecurity: Terror, Power, and Foreign Policy.* London: Routledge, pp. 181–96.

Daniel Deudney (1990) "The Case Against Linking Environmental Degradation and National Security," *Millennium* 19(3): 461–7.

Kate Evans (2006) *Funny Weather.* Brighton: Myriad Editions.

Dale Jamieson (2008) *Ethics and the Environment.* Cambridge: Cambridge University Press.

Mark Lacy (2005) *Security and Climate Change: International Relations and the Limits of Realism.* London: Routledge.

Timothy W. Luke (2008) "The Politics of True Convenience or Inconvenient Truth: Struggles Over How to Sustain Capitalism, Democracy, and Ecology in the 21st century," *Environment and Planning A* 40: 1811–24.

Alan Weisman (2007) *The World Without Us.* New York: Thomas Dunne Books.

Topic 2 Green governmentality

How environmental concerns affect issues of national and global governance is an issue of "green governance." This can be understood from the perspective of Michel Foucault's notion of "governmentality" (Foucault, 1979/1986; also see Luke, 1997), which is about how individuals might become so self-disciplined in environmental/green strategies that their new habits of green living not only become normal for them, but these habits change how our everyday political/environmental relationships are organized so that we are "green enough" (as in Gore's shade of green) but not so green that our environmental activities threaten to disrupt neoliberal capitalism (Weber, 2009). Alternatively, green governance might concern more formal changes to structures of governance, be these national systems of governance such as democracy or how sovereign states interact internationally (Dobson and Bell, 2006; Eckersley, 2004).

Suggested reading

Andrew Dobson and Derek Bell (2006) *Environmental Citizenship*. Cambridge, MA: MIT Press.

Robyn Eckersley (2004) *The Green State: Rethinking Democracy and Sovereignty*. Cambridge, MA: MIT Press.

Michel Foucault (1979/1986) "Governmentality," *Ideology and Consciousness* 6: 5–21.

Tim Luke (1997) *Ecocritique: Contesting the Politics of Nature, Economy, and Culture*. Minneapolis: University of Minnesota Press.

Cynthia Weber (2009) *Will Potter: "I am an American"*, 4 minute film posted on the web at http://www.greenisthenewred.com/blog/i-am-an-american.

Conclusion

What does it all mean?

So far, we have concerned ourselves with how meanings are produced, mythologized, circulated, and contested in, through, and as culture, ideology, and IR theory. We've done this by thinking broadly about culture and ideology and then using what we have learned about these concepts to consider what makes some of the stories IR theory tells about the world appear to be true. How we have done this is by focusing on what I have called IR myths, apparent truths upon which IR traditions rely in order to appear to be true. And we have considered the relationships among IR theory, IR traditions, and IR myths by consulting not only classic statements in the IR literature but popular ideas about international politics and everyday life found in popular films.

This is what we have done. But why have we done it? What is at stake in this exercise of rethinking IR theory through culture, ideology, mythology, and popular film? What does it all mean?

I will address these questions by raising two more: how does IR theory make sense of the world?; and what does IR theory say is typical and deviant in that world? Addressing these questions will allow me to consider how our IR myths work not only individually but together. And this will lead us to a discussion of the politics of IR theory, of "the popular," and of storytelling generally.

How IR theory makes sense of the world

Up to this point, we have analyzed how IR theory makes sense of the world by asking questions about the stories told through individual IR myths. But what if we take our questions about sense-making and storytelling and apply them to IR theory as a whole? Then we will get an idea of how our individual IR myths work together—not only as a set of individual stories about international politics but as a general framework for storytelling.

To do this, let's return to those two questions that have guided us through our individual myths and re-cast them for IR theory generally:

1   How does IR theory make sense of the world?
2   What does IR theory say is typical and deviant in that world?

Mainstream IR theory (represented by realism, idealism, and Wendtian constructivism) makes sense of the world by focusing on specific actors, contexts, and interactions. As our first three myths tell us, the actors that matter in international politics are sovereign nation-states. According to realist, idealist, and constructivist myths, sovereign nation-states may just exist (as they seem to for realists and idealists) or their identities and interests may be the effects of practices (as constructivists claim). But in mainstream IR theory, both claims amount to the same thing. States are the fundamental actors in international politics, and all analysis of important events must begin and end with states.

The context in which states interact for mainstream IR theorists is not "international politics" broadly defined but the tightly theorized realm of international anarchy. All mainstream IR theorists agree on the importance of international anarchy for understanding international politics. Debates and disagreements about the nature of anarchy (what it is "really" like) and the effects of anarchy (what anarchy makes states do) only serve to underscore the importance which mainstream IR theorists attach to anarchy.

Finally, mainstream IR theorists concern themselves with sovereign nation-states in a situation of international anarchy because they are worried about a specific set of international interactions. These international interactions are found in what is often called the world of "high politics," a world that focuses on diplomatic practices, on wars among sovereign nation-states, and increasingly on international economic issues like globalization. Other international interactions pale in comparison to the "serious" questions of war and peace and the "serious" activities undertaken by statespeople to confront and possibly resolve these issues (see Table 10.1).

As we read through the concerns and considerations of mainstream IR theory, we quickly notice that Jones's, Fukuyama's, Huntington's and Gore's myths also meet all of these criteria. While this might at first strike us as surprising, it shouldn't. Let us consider each of these authors in turn.

Jones is in some ways the least straightforward mainstream mythologizer, for his myth "gender is a variable" seems to honor and expand the place of gender studies in IR theory. Yet, as we saw in Chapter 5, the effect of Jones's myth is to protect the classical tradition of IR theory from feminist challenges. In so doing, it enables mainstream IR theory to carry on making myths about sovereign nation-states, anarchy, and diplomatic practice.

In Fukuyama's case, his myth "it is the end of history" not only describes the "triumph" of liberal capitalism in an era of so-called globalization. It also seeks to explain questions of war and peace. So it divides the anarchical world of international politics in two—liberal sovereign nation-states in post-history and not-yet-liberal sovereign nation-states in history. And then it claims wars will occur between liberal and not-yet liberal states as well as among not-yet-liberal states, until the ideal of liberalism manifests itself in all states. So, even though he got there differently, Fukuyama fits in with mainstream IR concerns.

Similarily, so too does Huntington. Like Fukuyama, Huntington relies not on realism or idealism or some supposed bridge between them to describe contemporary conflict. He instead goes back to the tenets of modernization and development theory. But remember that modernization and development theory's roots are in fighting the Cold War. Security has always been a hidden agenda of this tradition. All Huntington's work has done and continues to do is accentuate the security agenda of modernization and development theory. And so sovereign nation-states, anarchy, and states at war in anarchy are of as much concern to Huntington as they are to Waltz, Kegley, and Wendt.

Table 10.1 How does IR theory make sense of the world?

Actors	Sovereign nation-states
Context	International anarchy
Interactions	Practices of states and statespeople to confront and possibly resolve questions of war and peace

Even Al Gore's myth "human-made climate change is an inconvenient truth" fits easily within traditional IR Theory concerns. For while it appears that Gore's concerns about the clash between humans and the environment ("culture" and "nature") transcend the petty policies of everyday international politics, in fact Gore's claims rest upon traditional idealist strategic understandings of cooperation and conflict among states and individuals in an anarchic international order and upon idealist economic understandings that "all good things go together," like economic growth and environmental sustainability.

Of the theorists we considered, it is only Hardt and Negri who examine war and peace in a non-traditional way. Hardt and Negri make three non-traditional claims. First, sovereign nation-states matter less than the logic of Empire. Second, Empire is not just the new world order; it is the new world orderer. So anarchy myths are beside the point. And, third, this means that explanations of war and peace among sovereign nation-states in a situation of international anarchy are trivial compared with explanations of the logic of Empire and the multitude's resistances to it.

What this discussion suggests is that one would be hard pressed to find an IR theorist who does not take seriously questions of war and peace or of conflict more generally. But it also suggests that it is *not* hard to find IR theorists who contest the terms in which these questions are asked. One of the reasons for this is that, as mainstream IR theorists tell their stories about international politics and construct a template through which all "serious" stories about IR theory must be told (must focus on states, anarchy, and diplomatic practice), they are (as we have seen in our individual IR myths) proscribing what is typical and deviant in the world of international politics and in the culture of IR theory. While mainstream IR theorists are happy to discuss what is typical and deviant in their world of international politics, they are less comfortable with interrogating the mainstream (dominant) culture of IR theory.

So, for example, following from how IR theorists make sense of the world (through states, anarchy, and diplomatic practice), IR theorists come up with some compelling "truths" about the world of international politics. What is typical and deviant in this world in some ways depends upon which tradition of IR theory one subscribes to (realism, idealism, constructivism). For realists, the harsh realities of international life mean we will never overcome conflict among sovereign nation-states because we will never escape international anarchy (Chapter 2). Or, in Huntington's terms, we will never solve the problem of security under anarchy in relation to development among clashing civilizations (Chapter 8). For idealists, we might escape conflict either by moving out of international anarchy into an international hierarchy led by a world government, or we may escape conflict by mitigating state behavior through an international society (Chapter 3). Or, in Fukuyama's terms, we will escape the conflicts of anarchy when all sovereign nation-states become liberal, post-historical states (Chapter 6). For constructivists, international outcomes are unclear. They will be conflictual (as realists claim) or cooperative (as idealists claim) depending upon what states make of anarchy (Chapter 4).

Yet while mainstream IR theorists cannot agree on what is typical and deviant within their general framework of states, anarchy, and diplomatic practice, critics of mainstream IR theory have no trouble showing what their general theoretical framework for analysis makes typical and deviant of IR theory. Not only does mainstream IR theory unduly confine analysis of international politics to questions about states, anarchy, and diplomatic/policy practices. In so doing, it is also typically ethnocentric, racist, classist, and sexist.

The North-American-centrism of mainstream IR theory begins with the nationalities of its authors, all of whom are North American, and this tells us something about which authors matter in the discipline of international relations (they are also all male, middle or upper class, and all but one is white). But, of course, an author's own subject position does not doom him or her to write from that position alone. Yet we find ethnocentric and other biases reproduced in our individual IR myths. Kegley's myth "there is an international society" is among the examples of ethnocentrism, for in this myth Kegley seems to mistake post-Cold War US hegemony for an international society (Chapter 3). More boldly, Al Gore's idealist-infected environmental myth is grounded upon arguments that justify environmental behavior for US Americans because these behaviors are in the US strategic and economic national interest (Chapter 9). Fukuyama's myth is another example. The liberalism that he so staunchly defends and supports the spread of globally is an Anglo-American-centric ideology, the power politics of which is never discussed (Chapter 6). And, of course, however much Huntington claims to give agency to "the rest" of the world, his "clash of civilizations" myth reads "the rest" primarily as a problem for "the West."

Race is another concept that seems to drop out of traditional IR theory. It seems to be assumed that the world of IR theory and international politics, like the world of most of the authors of our IR myths, is a white world. And white is taken as a non-race, as beyond race (Dyer, 1997). This may explain why few of our myths explicitly address race. Samuel Huntington and Francis Fukuyama (our one non-white theorist) both bring race into play in their theories, but they do so in ways that preserve the centrality of white cultures at the expense of non-white ones (Ling, 2000; Said, 2001).

Class is another of those concepts which sits uncomfortably in relation to mainstream IR theory. This is not surprising for two reasons. First, all of our authors writing in defense of mainstream IR theory are North American (and all but one is US). Second, and relatedly, class has never been a concept that has been terribly well interrogated in the US. Most US citizens of whatever economic or social group would call themselves "middle class." Because of this, class often drops out of everyday and academic analyses. It is no exception in our mainstream IR myths. Nowhere is there any consideration of either economic or social classes (or even categories) within states, nor is there an analysis of classes *of* states (see Wallerstein, 1974, 1980, 1989). Worse still, myths like Fukuyama's myth "it is the end of history" with its positive spin on globalization obscure class relations within and among sovereign nation-states, making any analysis of them all the more difficult (Chapter 6). If class is not considered in IR theory, then analysis of the power relations that keep some people, groups, and states "upper class" in international politics (like being "great powers" or a hegemon) and other states in a "lower class" of international politics (like "third world" or "post-colonial" states) will not find its way into core IR myths. It is only Hardt and Negri's myth of Empire, written from a non-mainstream, neoMarxist perspective, that gives any serious consideration to class.

Finally, mainstream IR theory is gendered, and its gender is primarily masculine. Jones's lament aside (Chapter 5), IR theory has traditionally taken masculinity engendered bodies and activities to be its objects of analysis, whether those gendered bodies/activities are (borrowing the title from Waltz's book) men, states, or war. Whether looking to realism or idealism, the theories of "human" nature that IR theorists draw upon as building blocks of their theories about individuals, states, and their interactions are theories about the "nature" of man (Chapter 2). As a result, not only are individuals gendered in IR theory. So too do we find "gendered states" (Peterson, 1992) and gendered activities like war (masculine) and peace (feminine) (Elshtain, 1987). And, as a reading of Jones's myth through *Fatal Attraction* highlights, when relationships among gendered bodies are considered by mainstream IR theorists, they seem to be exclusively heterosexual (Weber, 1999).

Taken together, mainstream IR theory makes sense of the world by focusing on states, anarchy, and diplomatic practice in ways that draw upon a particularly biased way of thinking about place, race, class, and sex. All of this is typical of mainstream IR theory. And if this is what is typical of mainstream IR theory, then it is easy to see how theories of international politics that defy and/or question the terms in which IR theory tells its stories about the world are labeled deviant. How Jones does this to feminist IR theory is the most elaborated example in this text (Chapter 5). Other examples are how constructivism constructs poststructuralism as deviant (Chapter 4) and how liberal theories of globalization construct historical materialism as deviant (Chapter 6) (see Table 10.2).

This is not to suggest that feminism, poststructuralism, and historical materialism are free of any bias. These alternative perspectives on international politics depend upon their own mythologized understandings of the world, and their myths often employ the same or similar types of exclusions that mainstream IR theory does. For example, as we saw in Chapter 7, Hardt and Negri's myth "Empire is the new world order" must exclude by selectively remembering what postmodern theorists say about ontology/agency and resistance in order to appear to be true. The point, however, is that these alternative perspectives make some of the same "mistakes" as traditional IR theory in different ways—ways which challenge the postulates for storytelling found in mainstream IR theory. It is for this reason—and not because they are themselves "true stories"—that these alternative takes on international politics are "deviant" from the perspective of traditional IR theory.

Table 10.2 What is typical and deviant for IR theory?

Typical	Deviant
• North-American-centric • Racist • Classist • Masculinist	To defy or question the terms in which IR theory tells stories about international politics

Making sense of IR theory

If this is how IR theory makes sense of the world—both the world of international politics and the world of IR theory—then how do we make sense of IR theory? What does all of this tell us about how IR theory relates to culture, ideology, mythology, and popular media like film? And, most crucially, where is the politics in all of this?

The argument put forward in this book is that IR theory is a site of cultural practice. It is a place where stories that make sense of our world are spun, where signifying practices about international politics take place, where meanings about international life are produced, reproduced, and exchanged. We have seen all of this illustrated in our five IR myths. Each of them makes sense of the world by telling a particular story about international politics. When we read these myths together (as we did in the last section), we find that IR theory is a site of cultural practice not only because it provides us with "an ensemble of stories" we tell about international politics (Geertz, 1975: 448). What is more important is that *IR theory is a site of cultural practice because it provides a framework for storytelling itself.* Culturally, IR theory tells us not only what makes sense about the world of international politics out there, but also which stories in the realm of international theory we should take seriously in classrooms, at conferences, and in policy meetings.

What this means is that how IR theory makes sense of the world through the stories it tells about international politics (either via specific myths like "international anarchy is the permissive cause of war" or through broader traditions like realism) is already indebted to the template for storytelling that these IR myths and IR theories depend upon in order to appear to be meaningful, serious, and important. This has unsettling implications for mainstream IR theory. For what it means is that we cannot understand international politics by adopting an IR tradition as our guide or by memorizing IR's sacred myths. This is because IR traditions and myths are both products of and productive of IR theory as a cultural site where "giving and taking of meaning" (Hall, 1997: 2) about international politics and about IR theory itself occurs. In other words, IR theory as a model for storytelling has already restricted what international politics can mean as it is narrated by IR traditions and IR myths.

When we investigate IR theory as a site of culture, we find ideological practices at work. Reading our IR myths together as we did in the last section, we quickly spotted several named ideologies at work—ethnocentrism, racism, classism, and (hetero)sexism. These are the sorts of ideologies for which we have long been trained to look. But another purpose of this text has been to demonstrate how ideologies work in less familiar ways that are more difficult to identify. They work, for example, through not only what we can name and say (conscious ideologies) but also through what we cannot name and what goes without saying (unconscious ideologies; Barthes, 1972: 11). And, arguably, it is unconscious ideologies that are the most powerful. Since they are so difficult to identify, they are all the more difficult to examine critically.

When they crop up in IR theory, I call these unconscious or unnamed ideologies IR myths. They are *apparent truths*, usually expressed as a slogan, that an IR theory or tradition relies upon in order to appear to be true. They seem to be so true, so right on, so correct about the world of international politics that, to those adhering to the tradition that employs them, IR myths describe just the way things are. For a realist, international anarchy *is* the permissive cause of war. For an idealist, there *is* an international society. For a Wendtian constructivist, anarchy *is* what states make of it. And so on. But, as I have tried to point out, international politics is a lot more complicated than this. So how do IR traditions still get away with relying upon so many ideological positions as if they were not ideological positions but factually described the world as it is? They get away with it because, as I have suggested, these ideological positions are mythologized. They are transformed from what is seen to be "cultural" and constructed into what is taken to be natural and therefore goes without saying. IR myths become habitual ways of thinking about the world of international politics.

We traced how the myth function in IR theory works by examining our individual IR myths. Ideologies are mythologized in IR theory by making sure that what must go without saying in order for a myth to appear to be true is either deferred or displaced. Deferral means that the knowledge about the myth as a myth is delayed so much that we never receive it. Displacement means that the knowledge about a myth as a myth is placed beyond the bounds of our consideration. Some myths defer knowledge (we must never know that liberalism's empty core contradicts our desire for the good life or that fear is what makes us believe either in international anarchy as the permissive cause of war or in international society as that which will unify us in cooperation). Other myths work through displacement ("authors" must be placed behind productive practices so that authors appear to be the producers of these practices, and gender must be placed within a variable so that feminist concerns can be placed outside the bounds of the discipline of IR). And, more often than not, deferral and displacement work together, even if one of them dominates.

This is what we see happening in the individual stories we read about IR theory. But what about IR theory as a whole? Is there a myth function to IR theory itself, greater than the sum of its individual IR myths? And, if so, how does it work? What does it defer or displace?

Just as individual IR myths tend to work at the level of stories, IR theory more generally works at the level of framing those stories. As a site of cultural practices, IR theory provides not just the stories about international politics but the framework which makes these stories meaningful, serious, and important. And it is this grid, this support, this basis for storytelling that goes without saying in IR theory itself— that it is reasonable, rational, and objective to narrate stories about IR theory which focus almost exclusively on sovereign nation-states in anarchy and the "high political" practices to which their interactions give rise. This is the "Truth" of IR theory that makes other IR "truths" possible. And, like any truth, this one may not be as true as it *appears* to be. For, as we have already seen, this premise for storytelling is indebted to numerous ideological positions, some of which are named and others of which are more difficult to name. So, somewhere along the line, *IR theory itself underwent (and is always really undergoing) a mythologizing function so that its framework for analysis appears to be natural, neutral and common sense rather than cultural, ideological, and in need of critical analysis.*

What does this mean, then, that IR theory itself defers or displaces? Simple. It defers and displaces any knowledge that its stories and most importantly its

Table 10.3 IR theory's myth function

What IR theory defers	How IR theory defers it
IR theory defers the myth function itself	How it defers the myth function is by (dis)placing criticism of IR theory beyond the bounds of IR theory. Critique *of* IR theory does not count as serious IR theory itself

framework for telling stories is mythologized. *IR theory defers and displaces the myth function itself.* How does it do this? *IR theory does this by placing critical examinations of IR theory beyond the bounds of meaningful, serious, and important IR theory.* This should not surprise us. For indeed, if IR theory did not do this, it could not function. Its myth function—both in terms of the specific stories it tells and in terms of its template for telling these stories—might be exposed. While exposing the myth function in IR theory would not put an end to it (for we never escape culture and ideology), it may temporarily disrupt it. And if IR theory's myth function is disrupted, then this might open up new possibilities for uncharted stories about international politics to be told. This would be a terrible threat to traditional IR theory.

The politics of the popular

If exploring the myth function in IR theory is such a serious undertaking, then why have I carried it out by reading IR theory through a medium that lacks the status of serious—popular film? Hopefully, reading IR theory through popular film is more interesting and entertaining than it otherwise would be. And, for some, that might be reason enough for using films. But there are more important and indeed extremely serious reasons for using popular films (or other popular media that tell stories).

One reason for rethinking IR theory through popular film is that films bring the story aspects of IR theory into relief. We are accustomed to viewing films as narratives about specific worlds. We are less accustomed to viewing IR theory in this way. But, by pairing IR traditions and IR myths with a popular film, the drama, story points, flow, links, lapses, and effects of action are all easier to see.

Another reason for pairing IR theories with popular films is that popular films present all this drama and trauma to us in contained spatial and temporal locations. They offer up worlds to us that are familiar enough for us to relate to (like 1980s' New York City in *Fatal Attraction* or 1990s' Los Angeles in *Wag the Dog*) without actually being those places. This is another reason why we can relate to popular films and relate them back to IR theory.

So, selecting popular films as a medium through which to revisit IR theory makes sense in part because popular films enable us to access what IR theory says, how it plots its story, and how all this together gives us a particular vision of the world. In effect, then, using popular film to help us think about IR theory seems to work because of some of the similarities between how films tell stories and how IR theory tells stories.

Even when we read IR theory through popular film, however, we assume that the kinds of stories told by IR theory and those told by popular film differ in important ways. The stories IR theory tells are supposedly "true" stories. In contrast, popular films offer us stories that we know to be fictional. This is why the stories told in IR theory are taken seriously, whereas those in popular film are so often regarded as frivolous. We assume that popular films offer us escapes from reality, whereas IR theory confronts us with the hard facts about the world. And so, like mainstream IR theorists, we generally place IR theory in the realm of "high culture" and "high politics" while we place popular film in the realm of "low culture" and "low politics." It might be fun to see how the realities of international life might be dramatized in popular films, but, as mainstream IR theorists warn us, we should guard against taking these dramatizations too seriously. They are not part of the "cut and thrust" of international politics or of IR theory.

Or are they?

Each of the IR myths we have looked at is paired with a popular film. In some cases this is because the film plays out the plot of an IR theory (as in the cases of *Lord of the Flies* and *Independence Day*). But while parallel plots might be one reason for the pairing of films and myths in some cases, *in every case films and myths are paired because they produce and circulate the same myth*. The myth we find about anarchy in Waltz's books *Man, the State, and War* and *Theory of International Politics* is the same myth we find in the film *Lord of the Flies*. The myth we find about the author function in Wendt's essay "Anarchy is What States Make of it" is the same myth we find in the film *Wag the Dog*. The myth we find in Fukuyama's essay "The End of History?" is the same myth we find in the film *The Truman Show*. And on and on.

If the same myths are at play in shallow popular films as we find in serious IR theory, then what does this mean for each of these mythologized sites and the relationship between them? Are films more serious than we at first thought? Is IR theory more trivial than we dared to imagine? Does this pairing of the "popular" and the "serious" transform them both? If so, where do we now locate "high culture" and "high politics" and "low culture" and "low politics"?

Pairing "serious" IR theory with "superficial" popular films suggests that IR theory may not be located in the realm of "truth" and "reality" any more than popular films are. Maybe IR theory is just a bunch of stories that, like popular films, mixes and mythologizes fact and fiction. And since the stories and myths we find in IR theory are often the same ones we find in popular films, then this pairing of IR theory and film shows that the meanings IR theory uses to make sense of the world are not only produced and circulated in traditional academic "high cultural" realms but in popular "low cultural" locations as well. If the work of propagating and circulating IR myths occurs in popular films as well as in IR theories, then neglecting this realm of "low politics" in our attempts to come to grips with how the world works would be a mistake. We must interrogate IR theory as a site of cultural practice *wherever* it occurs—in classic IR texts, in classrooms, and in more popular sites of culture like film, literature, art, and television.

Maybe popular films do a lot more political work than we at first credited them with doing. Not only do they illustrate (and sometimes overtly critique) the stories found in IR myths by circulating similar (or different) myths. Popular films tell us

---

Box 10.1 Why pair IR theory with popular films?

1 Films bring IR theory's story points into relief.
2 Films offer us contained, nearly parallel worlds in which to critically rethink IR theory.
3 IR myths and popular films produce and circulate similar myths. Therefore, we must analyze the popular in order to understand IR myths and international politics.
4 Pairing popular films with serious IR theory exposes IR theory as a mythologized mix of fact and fiction.
5 Popular films dramatize the myth function of IR theory and how what must go without saying is deferred and displaced.

"too much" about IR theory. They also tell us how IR myths function. They do this by showing us what must go without saying in order for a myth to appear to be true. And, most importantly, *popular films dramatize for us how what must go without saying is kept in the place of non-knowledge through strategies of deferral and displacement.* That's a heck of a lot of work for a frivolous medium to do!

But if popular films do a lot of serious political work by de-mythologizing and re-politicizing IR myths (Barthes, 1972), then why are investigations of popular films so often relegated to the nether regions of the negligible by IR theorists—to "mere" cultural studies or film theory which they take to be superficial and therefore unimportant? One answer might be that IR theorists simply do not yet appreciate how the popular functions politically in relation to international politics and international theory. Because they don't appreciate it, they don't take it seriously. For this reason, these sorts of IR theorists simply ignore popular cultural phenomena.

A more cynical answer might be that IR theorists do recognize how the popular functions politically in relation to international politics and international theory. They sense how the popular might function resistively and disruptively in relation to cherished IR traditions and the IR myths that make them appear to be true. And they recognize that taking the popular seriously might challenge the very framework through which IR theory tells its stories about international politics. For this reason, these sorts of IR theorists might work to defer a widespread appreciation of what the popular might do to IR theory, and they might work to re-place the popular in the realm of the frivolous, before the popular displaces IR theory from the realm of the serious.

And, of course, there is a third reason why IR theorists might not take the political power of the popular seriously. They might be so taken in by their own mythologized ways of viewing the relationship between the political and the popular that they can no longer imagine this relationship differently. This is why, for these theorists, the popular belongs in a different realm than the political.

Whether by neglect, by design, or by displacement, the politics of the popular is among the most undervalued and therefore underanalyzed aspects of international politics. And this is a grave oversight for both mainstream and critical IR theorists. For the popular poses a significant challenge to IR's cherished cultural practices.

Where does all of this leave us?

So, where does all of this leave us? It is to be hoped that it leaves us knowing "too much" about IR theory and IR myths—not because of what they say but because of what they do culturally *and* politically. Indeed, thinking about IR theory as a site of cultural practice through formal, academic cultural practices such as writing IR theories and myths and through less formal cultural practices like popular films has demonstrated that *all cultural sites are powerful arenas in which political struggles take place*. And, maybe what is most important, is that this way of rethinking IR theory has helped us to rethink the relationship between culture and politics. *Culture is not opposed to politics. Culture is political, and politics is cultural.*

What this means is that the cultural stories all of us tell—whether in film, in IR theory, or in everyday life—are political. Knowing how stories function—what makes them appear to be true—gives us the means to both critique and create politically powerful stories.

Bibliography

Almond, Gabriel A. and G. Bingham Powell, Jr (1978) *Comparative Politics: Systems, processes, and policy*, 2nd edition. Boston: Little, Brown and Co.

Althusser, Louis (1969) *For Marx*. London: Allen Lane.

Antze, Paul and Michael Lambek (eds) (1996) *Tense Past: Cultural Essays in Trauma and Memory*. New York: Routledge.

Ashley, Richard K. (1984) "The Poverty of Neorealism," *International Organization* 38(2): 225–86.

Ashley, Richard K. (1989) "Living on Borderlines: Man, Poststructuralism and War," in James Der Derian and Michael Shapiro (eds) *International/Intertextual Politics: Postmodern Readings of World Politics*. Lexington, MA: Lexington Books.

Ball, Terrance and Richard Dagger (1995) *Political Ideologies and the Democratic Ideal*, 2nd edition. New York: HarperCollins.

Barkawi, Tarak and Mark Laffey (2002) "Retrieving the Imperial: *Empire* and International Relations", *Millennium* 31(1): 109–27.

Barthes, Roland (1972) *Mythologies*, trans. Annette Lavers. New York: Noonday Press.

Barthes, Roland (1974) *S/Z: An Essay*, trans. Richard Miller. New York: Hill and Wang.

Baudrillard, Jean (1987) *Seduction*, trans Brian Singer. New York: St Martin's Press.

Baylis, John and Steve Smith (eds) (1997) *The Globalization of World Politics*. Oxford: Oxford University Press.

Beitz, Charles (1999) *Political Theory and International Relations*, revised edition. Princeton, NJ: Princeton University Press.

Bennett, Jane and William Chaloupka (1993) *In the Nature of Things: Language, Politics, and the Environment*. Minneapolis: Minnesota University Press.

Bennett, Jane and Michael J. Shapiro (2002) *The Politics of Moralizing*. New York: Routledge.

Bhabha, Homi K. (1990) "Interrogating Identity: The Post Colonial Prerogative," in D.T. Goldberg (ed.) *Anatomy of Racism*. Minneapolis: University of Minnesota Press, pp. 118–209.

Biersteker, Thomas and Cynthia Weber (eds) (1996) *State Sovereignty as Social Construct*. Cambridge: Cambridge University Press.

Blaney, David L. and Naeem Inayatullah (2002) "Neo-Modernizations? IR and the Inner Life of Modernizations Theory," *European Journal of International Relations* 8(4): 103–37.

Bleiker, Roland (1997) "Forget IR Theory," *Alternatives* 22(1): 57–85.

Bull, Hedley (1987) *The Anarchical Society.* London: Macmillan.

Bush, George W. (2001a) "Address to a Joint Session of Congress and the American People", United States Capitol, Washington, DC, September 20, http://www.whitehouse.gov/news/releases/2001/09/20010920-a.html.

Bush, George W. (2001b) "'Islam is Peace' Says President," Remarks by the President at Islamic Center of Washington, DC, http://www.whitehouse.gov/news/releases/2001/09/20010917-11.html.

Buzan, Barry, Charles Jones, and Richard Little (1993) *The Logic of Anarchy: Neorealism to Structural Realism.* New York: Columbia University Press.

Callinicos, Alex (2002) "The Actuality of Imperialism," *Millennium* 31(2): 319–26.

Campbell, David (1999) *Writing Security,* revised edition. Minneapolis: University of Minnestoa Press.

Cardoso, F. and E. Faletto (1979) *Dependency and Development in Latin America.* Berkeley: University of California Press.

Carroll, Berenice (1972) "Peace Research: The Cult of Power," *Journal of Conflict Resolution* 16(4): 585–616.

Carver, Terrell (1996) *Gender is Not a Synonym for Women.* Boulder, CO: Lynne Rienner.

Carver, Terrell, Molly Cochran and Judith Squires (1998) "Gendering Jones: Feminisms, IRs, Masculinities," *Review of International Studies* 24(2): 283–97.

Conlon, James (1996) "The Place of Passion: Reflections on *Fatal Attraction,*" in Barry Keith Grant (ed.) *The Dread of Difference: Gender and the Horror Film.* Austin: University of Texas Press, pp. 401–11.

Connell, Robert W. (1995) *Masculinities.* Cambridge: Cambridge University Press.

Dalby, Simon and Matthew Paterson (2009) "Over a Barrell: Cultural Political Economy and Oil Imperialism," in François Debrix and Mark Lacy (eds) *The Geopolitics of American Insecurity: Terror, Power, and Foreign Policy.* London: Routledge, pp. 181–96.

Dalby, Simon (2007) "Ecology, Security, and Change in the Anthropocene," *Brown Journal of World Affairs* 8(2): 155–64.

Debrix, François (1999) *Reinvisioning Peacekeeping: The United Nations and the Mobilization of Ideology.* Minneapolis: University of Minnesota Press.

Debrix, François (2003) "Tabloid Realism and the Space of American Security Culture," *Geopolitics* 8(3): 151–90.

Debrix, François and Cynthia Weber (eds) (2003) *Rituals of Mediation: International Politics and Social Meanings.* Minneapolis: University of Minnesota Press.

De Certeau, Michel (1988) *The Practice of Everyday Life,* trans. Steven F. Rendall. Berkeley: University of California Press.

Deleuze, G. and F. Guattari, (1987) *A Thousand Plateaus: Capitalism and Schizophrenia,* trans. B. Massumi. Minneapolis: University of Minnesota Press.

Derrida, Jacques (1991) "*Différance,*" in P. Kampuf (ed.) *A Derrida Reader: Between the Blinds.* Brighton: Harvester Wheatsheaf, pp. 60–7.

Deudney, Daniel (1990) "The Case Against Linking Environmental Degradation and National Security," *Millennium* 19(3): 461–67.

Dobson, Andrew and Derek Bell (2006) *Environmental Citizenship.* Cambridge, MA: MIT Press.

Doty, Roxanne (1996) *Imperial Encounters: The Politics of Representation in North–South Relations.* Minneapolis: University of Minnesota Press.

Dyer, Richard (1985) "Taking Popular Television Seriously," in David Lusted and Phillip Drummond (eds) *TV and Schooling.* London: British Film Institute, pp. 41–6.

Dyer, Richard (1997) *White.* London: Routledge.

Eckersley, Robyn (1995) *Markets, the State and the Environment: Towards Integration.* Sidney: Macmillan.

Eckersley, Robyn (2004) *The Green State: Rethinking Democracy and Sovereignty.* Cambridge, MA: MIT Press.

Edkins, Jenny (1999) *Poststructuralism and International Relations: Bringing the Political Back In.* Boulder, CO: Lynne Rienner.

Edkins, Jenny (2003) *Trauma and the Memory of Politics.* Cambridge: Cambridge University Press.

Elshtain, Jean Bethke (1987) *Women and War.* New York: Basic Books.

Enloe, Cynthia (1989) *Bananas, Beaches and Bases: Making Feminist Sense of International Politics.* Berkeley: University of California Press.

Ermarth, Elizabeth Deeds (1992) *Sequel to History: Postmodernism and the Crisis of Representational Time.* Princeton, NJ: Princeton University Press.

Evans, Kate (2006) *Funny Weather.* Brighton: Myriad Editions.

Fanon, Frantz (1991) "The Negro and Psychopathology," *Black Sins, White Mask.* London: Pluto, pp. 141–209.

Foucault, Michel (1979/1986) "Governmentality," *Ideology and Consciousness* 6: 5–21.

Foucault, Michel (1980) *Power/Knowledge*, trans. C. Gordon, L. Marshall, J. Mepham, and K. Soper. Hemel Hampstead: Harvester Wheatsheaf.

Foucault, Michel (1984) "What is an Author?," in Paul Rabinow (ed.) *The Foucault Reader.* New York: Pantheon, pp. 101–20.

Foucault, Michel (1990) *The History of Sexuality, Volume 1: An Introduction*, trans. Robert Hurley. Harmondsworth, UK: Penguin.

Fukuyama, Francis (1989) "The End of History?" *The National Interest* 16(Summer): 2–18.

Fukuyama, Francis (1992) *The End of History and the Last Man.* London: Hamish Hamilton.

Geertz, Clifford (1975) *The Interpretation of Cultures.* London: Hutchinson.

George, Jim (1994) *Discourses of Global Politics: A Critical (Re)Introduction to International Relations.* Boulder, CO: Lynne Rienner.

Gibbs, Walter, and S. Sarah Lyall (2007) "Gore Shares Peace Prize for Climate Change Work," *New York Times*, October 13, http://www.nytimes.com/2007/10/13/world/13nobel.html

Gilpin, Robert (1983) *War and Change in World Politics.* Cambridge: Cambridge University Press.

Gore, Albert, Jr (1989) "Earth's Fate is the Number One National Issue," *The Washington Post*, May 14, http://www.washingtonpost.com/wp-dyn/content/article/2007/10/12/AR2007101200827.html

Gore, Albert, Jr (1992) *Earth in the Balance: Forging a New Common Purpose.* London: Earthscan.

Gore, Albert, Jr (2006) *An Inconvenient Truth: The Planetary Emergency of Global Warming and What We Can Do About It.* New York: Rodale Books.

Grant, Rebecca and Kathleen Newland (eds) (1991) *Gender and International Relations.* Milton Keynes: Open University Press.

Gunder Frank, André (1969) *Capitalism and Underdevelopment in Latin America.* New York: Monthly Review Press.

Hall, Stuart (1996) "Introduction: Who needs 'identity'?" in Stuart Hall and Paul du Gay (eds) *Questions of Cultural Identity.* London: Sage, pp. 1–17.

Hall, Stuart (ed.) (1997) *Representations: Cultural Representations and Signifying Practices.* Milton Keynes: Open University Press.

Hardt, Michael and Antonio Negri (2000) *Empire.* Cambridge, MA: Harvard University Press.

Hartz, Louis (1955) *The Liberal Tradition in America.* New York: Harcourt Brace Jovanovich.

Hay, Colin and David Marsh (eds) (2000) *Demystifying Globalization*. Boulder, CO: St Martin's Press.

Herod, Andrew, Gearoid Ó Tuathail, and Susan M. Roberts (eds) (1998) *An Unruly World?: Globalization, Governance, and Geography*. London: Routledge.

Hirst, Paul and Grahame Thompson (1996) *Globalization in Question*. Cambridge: Polity Press.

Hoberman, J. (2001) "Persistence of Memory," March 12, http://www.villagevoice.com/issues/0111/hoberman.php

Horner, Christopher C. (2007) *The Politically Incorrect Guide to Global Warming (and Environmentalism)*. Washington, DC: Regnery.

Huntington, Samuel P. (1968) *Political Order in Changing Societies*. New Haven, CT: Yale University Press.

Huntington, Samuel P. (1993) "The Clash of Civilizations?," *Foreign Affairs* 72 (Summer): 22–49.

Huntington, Samuel P. (2004) "The Hispanic Challenge," *Foregin Policy* (March/April): 30–45.

Independent Focus (2000) Interview of Director Christopher Nolan by Elvis Mitchell. Special Feature of *Memento* DVD, Remember Productions.

Jackson, Robert (1990) *Quasi-States: Sovereignty, International Relations and the Third World*. Cambridge: Cambridge University Press.

Jameson, Fredric and Masao Miyoshi (eds) (1998) *The Cultures of Globalization*. Chapel Hill, NC: Duke University Press.

Jamieson, Dale (2008) *Ethics and the Environment*. Cambridge: Cambridge University Press.

Jones, Adam (1996) "Does 'Gender' Make the World go Round?: Feminist Critiques of International Relations," *Review of International Studies* 22 (4): 405–29.

Jones, Adam (1998) "Engendering Debate," *Review of International Studies* 24 (2): 299–303.

Kegley, Charles W., Jr (1993) "The Neoidealist Moment in International Studies?: Realist Myths and the New Internatonal Realities," *International Studies Quarterly* 37 (June): 131–46.

Kegley, Charles W., Jr (ed.) (1995) "The Neoliberal Challenge to Realist Theories of World Politics: An Introduction," in Charles W. Kegley, Jr *Controversies in International Relations Theory: Realism and the Neoliberal Challenge*. New York: St Martin's Press.

Keohane, Robert O. (1984) *After Hegemony*. Princeton, NJ: Princeton University Press.

Keohane, Robert O. (ed.) (1986) *Neorealism and its Critics*. New York: Columbia University Press.

Keohane, Robert O. (1988) "International Institutions: Two Approaches", *International Studies Quarterly* 32: 379–96.

Keohane, Robert O. (1989) "International Relations Theory: Contributions of a Feminist Standpoint", *Millennium* 18 (2): 245–53.

Kofman, Eleonore and Gillian Youngs (eds) (2003) *Globalization: Theory and Practice*, 2nd edition. London: Continuum.

Krasner, Stephen D. (ed.) (1983) *International Regimes*. Ithaca, NY: Cornell University Press.

Kublakova, V., Nicholaas Greenwood Onuf, and Paul Kowert (eds) (1998) *International Relations in a Constructed World*. New York: M.E. Sharpe.

Lacy, Mark (2005) *Security and Climate Change: International Relations and the Limits of Realism*. London: Routledge.

Lapid, Yosef and Freidrich Kratochwil (eds) (1996) *The Return of Culture and Identity in IR Theory*. Boulder, CO: Lynne Rienner.

Leyshon, Andrew (1997) "True Stories?: Global Dreams, Global Nightmares, and Writing Globalization," in Rodger Lee and Jane Wills (eds) *Geographies of Economies*. London: Arnold Press, pp. 133–46.

Ling, Lily (2000) "Hypermasculinity on the Rise, Again: A Response to Fukuyama on Women and World Politics," *International Feminist Journal of Politics* 2(2): 277–86.

Luke, Timothy W. (1997) *Ecocritique: Contesting the Politics of Nature, Economy, and Culture.* Minneapolis: Minnesota University Press.

Luke, Timothy W. (1998) "The (Un)Wise (Ab)Use of Nature: Environmentalism as Globalized Consumerism?," *Alternatives* 23: 175–212.

Luke, Timothy W. (2008) "The Politics of True Convenience or Inconvenient Truth: Struggles Over How to Sustain Capitalism, Democracy, and Ecology in the 21st Century," *Environment and Planning A*, 40: 1811–24.

MacKinnon, Catherine (1989) *Toward a Feminist Theory of the State.* Cambridge, MA: Harvard University Press.

Malthus, Thomas (1798/2004) *An Essay on the Principle of Population.* Whitefish, MT: Kessinger Publishing.

Marchand, Marianne (2000) "Gendered Representations of the 'Global': Reading/Writing Globalization," in Richard Stubbs and Geoffrey R.D. Underhill (eds) *Political Economy and the Changing Global Order*, 2nd edition. Oxford: Oxford University Press, pp. 218–28.

Meadows, Donnella H., Dennis Meadows, Jorgen Randers, and William W. Behrens (1972) *Limits to Growth.* New York: Universal Books.

Micklethwait, John and Adrian Wooldridge (2000) *The Future Perfect: The Challenges and Hidden Promises of Globalization.* New York: Times Press.

Mirzoeff, Nicholas (1999) *Visual Culture.* London: Routledge.

Modelski, George (1987) *Long Cycles in World Politics.* Seattle, WA: University of Washington Press.

Monaco, James (2000) *How to Read a Film.* Oxford: Oxford University Press.

Murphy, Craig (1996) "Seeing Women, Recognizing Gender, Recasting International Relations," *International Organization* 50(3): 513–38.

Nardin, Terry and David Mapel (eds) (1993) *Traditions of International Ethics*, revised edition. Cambridge: Cambridge University Press.

Onuf, Nicholas Greenwood (1989) *World of Our Making.* Columbia: University of South Carolina Press.

Onuf, Nicholas Greenwood (1999) "Worlds of Our Making: The Strange Career of Constructivism in IR," in Donald J. Puchala (ed.) *Visions of IR.* Columbia: University of South Carolina Press.

O'Sullivan, Tim et al. (1994) *Key Concepts in Communication and Cultural Studies.* London: Routledge.

Ó Tauthail, G. (1998) "Political Geography III: Dealing with Deterritorialization?," *Progress in Human Geography* 22: 81–93.

Packenham, Robert (1973) *Liberal America and the Third World: Political Development Ideas in Foreign Aid and Social Science.* Princeton, NJ: Princeton University Press.

Paterson, Matthew (1996) *Global Warming and Global Politics.* London: Routledge.

Paterson, Matthew (2005) "Green Politics," in Scott Burchill *et al.* (eds) *Theories of International Relations*, 3rd edition. Basingstoke: Palgrave Macmillan.

Peterson, V. Spike (ed.) (1992) *Gendered States: Feminist (Re)Visions of International Relations Theory.* Boulder, CO: Lynne Rienner.

Pettman, Ralph (1998) "Sex, Power, and the Grail of Positive Collaboration," in Marysia Zalewski and Jane Parpart (eds) *The "Man" Question in International Relations.* Boulder, CO: Westview, pp. 169–84.

Rabiger, Michael (1998) *Directing the Documentary*, 3rd edition. Oxford: Focal Press.

Rubins, James (2001) Comments made on BBC2 *Newsnight*, September 11, wysiwyg: //11//http: //news.bbc.co.uk/hi/eng/ents/newsnight/newsid_1533000/1544810.stm

Ruggie, John G. (1998) *Constructing the World Polity*. London: Routledge.

Said, Edward W. (2001) "The Clash of Ignorance," *The Nation*, October 22, http: //www.the nation.com/docPrint.mhtml?I=20011022&s=said

Saper, Craig J. (1997) *Artificial Mythologies: A Guide to Cultural Intervention*. Minneapolis: University of Minnesota Press.

Seitz, Matt Zoller (2001) *Memento*. New York Press online, http: //www.nypress.com/ content.cfm?content_id=3841&now=03/14/2001&content-section=4

Shapiro, Michael J. (1997) *Violent Cartographies: Mapping Cultures of War*. Minneapolis: University of Minnesota Press.

Shapiro, Michael J. (1999) *Cinematic Political Thought: Narrating Race, Nation and Gender*. New York: New York University Press.

Shaw, Martin (2002) "Post-Imperial and Quasi-Imperial: State and Empire in the Global Era," *Millennium* 31(2): 327–36.

Storey, John (1997) *An Introduction to Cultural Theory and Popular Culture*, 2nd edition. London: Prentice Hall.

Strange, Susan (1996) *The Retreat of the State*. Cambridge: Cambridge University Press.

Sylvester, Christine (1994) *Feminist Theory and International Relations in a Postmodern Era*. Cambridge: Cambridge University Press.

Tickner, J. Ann (1992) *Gender in International Relations: Feminist Perspectives on Achieving Global Security*. New York: Columbia University Press.

Turner, Graham M. (2008) "A Comparison of the Limits to Growth with 30 Years of Reality," *Global Environmental Change* doi: 10.1016/j.gloenveha.2008.05.001.

Walker, R.B.J. (1993) *Inside/Outside: International Relations as Political Theory*. Cambridge: Cambridge University Press.

Walker, R.B.J. (2002) "On the Immanence/Imminence of Empire," *Millennium* 31(2): 337–45.

Wallerstein, Immanuel (1974, 1980, 1989) *The Modern World-System*, 3 vols. San Diego: Academic Press.

Wallerstein, Immanuel (1995) *Historical Capitalism with Capitalist Civilisation*. London: Verso.

Wallerstein, Immanuel (2002) "Revolts Against the System," *New Left Review* 18: 29–39.

Walt, Stephen M. (1998) "International Relations: One World, Many Theories," *Foreign Policy* Spring: 29–46.

Waltz, Kenneth (1959) *Man, the State and War*. New York: Columbia University Press. (First published 1954.)

Waltz, Kenneth (1979) *Theory of International Politics*. Reading, MA: Addison-Wesley.

Waltzer, Michael (2000) *Just and Unjust Wars: A Moral Argument with Historical Illustrations*, 3rd edition. New York: Basic Books.

Weber, Cynthia (1994) "Good Girls, Little Girls, and Bad Girls: Male Paranoia in Robert Keohane's Critique of Feminist International Relations," *Millennium* 23(2): 337–49.

Weber, Cynthia (1998) "Reading Martin Wight's 'Why Is There No International Theory?' as History," *Alternatives* 23: 451–69.

Weber, Cynthia (1999) *Faking It: US hegemony in a "Post-Phallic" Era*. Minneapolis: University of Minnestoa Press.

Weber, Cynthia (2002) "Flying Planes Can Be Dangerous", *Millennium* 31(1): 129–47.

Weber, Cynthia (2009) *Will Potter: "I am an American"*, 4 minute film posted on the web at http://www.greenisthenewred.com/blog/i-am-an-american.

Weiner, Myron and Samuel P. Huntington (eds) (1987) *Understanding Political Development*. Boston: Little, Brown.

Weisman, Alan (2007) *The World Without Us*. New York: Thomas Dunne Books.

Weldes, Jutta (1999) "Going Cultural: *Star Trek*, State Action, and Popular Culture," *Millennium* 28(1): 117–34.

Weldes, Jutta (ed.) (2003) *To Seek Out New Worlds: Exploring Links Between Science Fiction and World Politics*. London: Palgrave Macmillan.

Wendt, Alexander (1992) "Anarchy is What States Make of it: The Social Construction of Power Politics," *International Organization* 46: 391–425. Reprinted in James Der Derian (ed.) (1995) *International Theory: Critical Investigations*. New York: New York University Press, pp. 129–77.

Wendt, Alexander (1994) "Collective Identity Formation and the International State", *American Political Science Review* 88(2): 384–96.

Wendt, Alexander (1999) *Social Theory of International Politics*. Cambridge: Cambridge University Press.

Williams, Raymond (1983) *Keywords*. London: Fontana.

World Commission on Environment and Development (1987) *Our Common Future*. Oxford: Oxford University Press.

Zalewski, Marysia (1993) "Feminist Standpoint Theory meets International Relations Theory," *Fletcher Forum* (Summer): 13–32.

Zalewski, Marysia (1995) "Well, What is the Feminist Perspective on Bosnia?," *International Affairs* 71(2): 339–56.

Zalewski, Marysia (1999) "Where is Woman in International Relations?: 'To Return as a Woman and Be Heard'," *Millennium* 27: 847–67.

Zalewski, Marysia and Jane Parpart (eds) (1998) *The "Man" Question in International Relations*. Boulder, CO: Westview.

Zehfuss, Maja (2003) "Forget September 11," *Third World Quarterly* 24(3): 513–28.

Zizek, Slavo (1997) "Multiculturalism, Or, the Cultural Logic of Multinational Capitalism," *New Left Review* 225: 28–52.

Index